APPROACHES
TO
SEMIOTICS

edited by

THOMAS A. SEBEOK

Research Center for the Language Sciences
Indiana University

33

Speech as Instruction

Semiotic Aspects of Human Conflict

by

Harley C. Shands

Mouton · The Hague · Paris

ISBN 90-279-7725-9

Printed in The Netherlands

TABLE OF CONTENTS

INTRODUCTION

The papers presented below include some previously published and others written for various purposes that have not yet appeared in print. All of them present various aspects of my primary interest in the field of psychiatry, with some widening of application as the basic notions appear to have relevance for more general problems of social living. The central preoccupation, perhaps an idée fixe, is that of how much the principal human 'instrument', language, interpenetrates every aspect of human life.

Human life differs comprehensively from the life of all other animals in two ways: first, every human group lives in a highly complex structure we call 'culture', and, second, each such culture is idiosyncratic in many ways although participating (in 'deep structures') with every other culture. Language mediates both the complexity and the difference, making possible the kind of organization that constitutes a 'city' in the generic sense. Human beings live in some form of polis as citizens (denizens of a city) and all human affairs must be considered at base political. Whenever a human group is constituted (and the minimum is a group of two) there immediately enter political problems that have to be regulated or ordered according to some set of consensually accepted rules. The basic set of rules, requiring comprehensive allegiance and submission, is that of language. Those who do not (cannot ?) accept the requirement that they 'submit' or 'bow' to the demands of language are those whom we call mad -
- hence, the close association of language and psychiatry.

Language and Information

Two areas that have increasingly seemed to interpenetrate in my own interests have curiously been left far apart by most of the specialists in the specific areas. It would seem axiomatic that a principal concern of language is with the transmission of information - but information theory has for the most part totally ignored the particular peculiarities of language. Probably the most significant item in this ignoring is the way in which information theory rests upon a highly significant linguistic simplification, in the use of a 'language' consisting of a single 'phoneme' and its absence - i.e., one and zero - in which the messages that can be transmitted are formulated purely in terms of sequence without any of the connotational richness of ordinary language.

It is here perhaps that one can see the primary problem of the psychiatrist-psychoanalyst-psychotherapist in a culture in which the highest goal is that of reaching scientific validity. Science uses - or is the correlate of - a particular form of language in which numbers have traditionally been given first place. Along this line of development, the reduction of numbers to one and zero in the development of a binary system is a triumph of reductionism and simplification - and thus of enhancing the clarity of communication. In this effort, numeration (and binary numeration all the more) greatly increases the possibility of universalization of communication - while at the same time, the possibility of emotional meaningfulness is correspondingly reduced. The more easily a message is communicated to a larger number of people, the less the personal meaningfulness of that message; perhaps this is the lesson of the television, and that of the best-seller.

The more idiosyncratic, the more specific any message, the more of a demand does the transmission of that message put upon its recipient. In communication engineering, it is accepted as axiomatic that both termini in a communication system deal with the same stored 'ensemble' of messages, arranged in a rank-order hierarchy. Such an assumption totally ignores the importance of learning - and systems in which the neophyte is ignorant whereas the preceptor is learned. If two 'termini' have such different 'ensembles', how then is any 'information' to be transmitted? My answer, implied in the title of this book, is that structure has to be put in through a relation in which the neophyte submits to 'indoctrination' - he 'takes what the doctor orders' to turn the word into a pun. Learning is always a political process in which the core of the method is some form of 'brain washing' or 'thought control' - generally, the more effective the less apparent.

As implied in the terms 'indoctrinate', 'inform', and 'instruct', the learning process is a process of internalization. What is often ignored - perhaps most significantly in the ancient preoccupation with the notion of a 'reflective' intelligence - is that internalization necessarily implies deformation, both in the sense that what is internalized can only be related to a sample of what is 'out-there', and in the sense that the preparation for processing necessarily fragments the perceivable and rearranges the fragments.

What we 'know' is only a collection of what the psychoanalysts, with vast inaccuracy, call 'internal objects'. The point simply is that whatever is 'inside' cannot be at the same time an 'object' - because there is no way, metaphorically speaking, of getting the whole object through the narrow input channels. What is 'inside' is what Piaget calls an 'object-concept' corresponding in some ways to the class to which a given 'object' belongs. But the whole notion of an 'object' is a primary example of nounization, that most essential and most fundamentally inappropriate of linguistic tricks.

One demonstration that is mostly overlooked although daily exemplified is that no 'object' can be said to 'exist' until and unless it can be expected or predicted. The notion of an 'object-concept' is apparently timeless in its application - but it can readily be seen that such a 'concept' is necessarily historical in its development and predictive in its operation. When 'reinforcement' of such predictive patterns is missing for a long period of time, the concept becomes obsolete. The demonstration is that, at base, the distinction between 'synchronic' and 'diachronic' contexts is illusory.

When we understand how much any kind of knowing has to be current in this sense (while at the same time, like Janus, looking both before and behind), we understand better how it is that novelty is incompatible with knowing. Then it becomes apparent that all forms of knowing are related, inasmuch as they have to do with the partially novel, or the incompletely predictable, to uncertainty and thus with what we call 'emotion'. By derivation, emotion is motion-out, in the course of encounter as different from anticipation. The quality of the emotion is specifically related to the content of the experience - but the fact of emotion has to do with discrepancies in prediction and expectation.

By creating large classes in systems of expectation, human beings manage to reduce the intensity of novelty by being able to identify the new as 'one of those', in categories already known. The two methods basic to all forms of categorization - which is to say all forms of naming - are those having to do with similarities, likenesses or identities on the one hand, and with neighborhoods or contexts or contiguities on the other. When we meet people, we try to establish these relations by asking, "Are you related to the X's of the same name I already know?" or "Whom do you know that I might have had some contact with?" Whenever a new item can be categorized as 'like X' or 'next to X', then its relation to an already known X 'vouches for it', removing at least some of the otherwise unbearable novelty. In technical linguistic usage, these two methods are basic to the figures of speech we call metaphor and metonymy, and operations with these tropes are discussed at some length below.

To repeat, what is to be put in has to be related to what is already there. What is already there is not a random collection but a system, composed of many subsystems so diverse as often to seem unrelated - but when one investigates more deeply, the simple fact of a mutual internal status is proof positive of some kind of systematic relation. In relation to what is already there, the subsequent shape, or form, or pattern encountered has a revisionary or supplementary function. Principal among all the possible encounterables in human affairs are utterances of others - and it is my conviction that every sentence uttered by any human being has as a principal function the instructing of another or others. The part, 'struct-', is derived from the notion of structure, and the universe in which we find ourselves is one in which the basic theoretical notion is that anything that can exist or be thought is a dual unit in which the significant relation is that of instructing to instructed, following the example given by Saussure who tells us that the double unit of language is the relation of the signifying to the signified.

The 'universe' cannot in any sense be a simple matter of 'one turn', as its derivation suggests. The ancient philosophical idealization of an ultimate monism must, it seems to me, be abandoned in favor of a term that is, as many appropriately human terms are, internally contradictory. The term I suggest is a dualistic monism,

to convey the importance of the communication-system as the basic
unit. When we examine some of our anciently accepted units, the
suggestion becomes less radical, since Plato offered as an explanation of sex the idea that male and female were once a single unit,
separated in such a way that the descendent halves seek always to
reunite themselves, and, as Gooddy emphasizes, the animal body
can be considered as a system of mirror-image halves fused in the
midline.

To say that every utterance is an instruction is not to say that each
is obeyed. The destiny of an instruction is covered in saying that any
instruction may be obeyed, rejected, or ignored - with all of the
variants to be included in each category. To a very considerable extent, the history of any person's experience is that of discovering
ways of increasing the number of potential respondents susceptible
to 'my' instruction, and one of the major methods of doing this is
through learning how 'I' may submit to the instruction of the 'other'
such that 'I' develop a reciprocal capacity for instructing him or her.
The most significant means of gaining control over another human
being is through placing oneself at his disposal, a lesson implicit in
the importance of the mother to the child, and of the 'therapist' to
the 'patient' in the curious artificial human relation we call 'psychotherapy'.

In very general terms, we can see the course of human cultural
evolution as a progressive exploration of the implications of increasing sophistication in methods of communication in linguistic-symbolic
terms. When human beings talk about the ideal of freedom, they
mostly mean the possibility of making decisions among sets of alternative procedures or behaviors. In seeking increasing 'freedom', each
increment of variation from tradition increases the number of decisions to be made, and thus, according to the quantification of information in terms of the amount necessary to decide between equally
probable alternatives (i.e., one 'bit'), an increasing load is placed
upon the capacity of the data-processing system. The more freedom
for variation, the greater the load, and the more likely the system
to break down under stressful conditions. Conversely, when appropriate educational assistance is available, decision-making is enormously simplified by the development of categorical strategies that
automatically cover novel situations. The most effective such strategy
is scientific method.

When we consider the benefits of 'civilization', we often ignore the
observable: the anti-benefit, the 'entropy' balancing the 'negative
entropy' so apparent in the system as idealized, is that of a progressive difficulty in making decisions, in processing information, in allo-
cating resources in the face of conflicting theoretical and ideal possibilities. For example, shall we eradicate poverty or send astronauts
to the moon? shall we promote the sanctity of human life or shall we
allow widespread abortion in the interest of containing the population?
shall we protect and support the aged and the infirm, or shall we re-
sort, as many human groups have, to infanticide and geriatricide?
The number of unanswerable questions increases apace, and every
'advance' represents some kind of coordinate 'retreat'. Some of the

implications of 'progress' are considered below in the paper "The Challenge of Innovation".

The Specifically Human Strategy

The principal strategy we see abstractly as most useful for the 'conquest of nature' is that of scientific method. Science provides an institutional context in which the new is systematically confronted as a matter of choice. This choice succeeds a traditional fear of or 'resistance to' change, and as we go along, we find that the value of novelty in a contemporaneously developed situation is remarkably great to the consensus. Through the development of abstract thinking, scientific logic and reasoning, and then through the instrumentation of many of the methods of abstract reasoning in calculators and computers, the process continues apace.

I would contrast this method, especially in a psychiatric context, with the traditional human method that all of us take for granted. I propose that what we call 'emotional states' are primarily to be understood as data-processing methods, strategies of the most basic sort. These methods differ from those of analytic reasoning in that they become 'intuitive', operating 'unconsciously' as the base from which decisions are usually made - except when they are altered and inhibited by formal training in 'rational thought'. The process is most interesting in the degree to which after long and intensive training rational thought itself becomes intuitive, so that sophisticated human beings think rationally as 'second nature' to a remarkable degree.

Emotional data-processing occurs mostly as a whole, without separability of parts - without analysability, that is to say. Retrospectively, many highly creative unconscious syntheses through which extraordinary achievements appear can be recreated - as Lowes did in analyzing the sources from which Coleridge synthesized Kubla Khan. Much modern speculation in neurophysiology suggests that intuitive, emotional data-processing takes place in the 'silent' or 'minor' hemisphere - and that these names simply indicate the ignorance with which human beings have traditionally approached brain function. The suggestion emerges that as an initial comment, it may be useful to discuss briefly the usefulness of emotional data-processing as a basic human technology.

Emotion and Expression

The ease with which human beings are misled by their own forms of speech is nowhere more evident than in the classic error involved in the phrase, the 'expression' of 'emotion', a phrase used in the title of Darwin's early treatise (1859) on emotion in man and animals. The phrase suggests that for every expression there must be a corresponding emotion. But this leaves open the question of how the emotion is to be discovered in the absence of an expression.

Freud's answer is that emotions may have an 'unconscious' existence; in this case the emotion is located in a vague area, 'The Un-conscious'. If one asks a follower of Freud how he proposes to dem-onstrate this relation, he characteristically will cite an instance in which he as a therapist discovered an 'unconscious' emotion, then through a process of interpretation, encouraged the patient to ex-press it. When such an interpretation results in the expression of the emotion, the therapist assumes usually with a good deal of self-congratulation that the suspected emotion was indeed there.

But where? In many instances, after the occurrence of sexual intercourse in a fertile pair of animals, it is possible to predict that an offspring will in due course appear. Reasoning in the pattern mentioned above, we could make the interpretation that "You have an unconscious baby" to the prospective mother, then feel quite con-firmed in the opinion when the baby does in due course 'become conscious', or at least, get 'expressed'.

Using a different kind of metaphor, what we see is that the psycho-therapist may well make useful predictions by sensing early evidence of probable later events, as one may predict that he will encounter a fire if he pursues the cue provided by a faint trace of smoke in the distance. But this is a very different operation from that of the 'unconscious emotion'. The use of abstraction in human affairs lets us, by establishing categories, become more and more sensitive to cues which are significant parts of a later-emerging whole. Cues suggest latent, potential, or possible eventualities which depend upon a subsequent course of investigation or of development. We would be laughed out of the profession were we to say that the dis-covery of a trace of sugar in the urine indicates 'unconscious dia-betes', but the subsequent course of investigation may or may not confirm a suspicion of diabetes, in a manner quite parallel to the way in which interpretation and 'working through' may or may not confirm the prediction that some emotional state will develop in overt form.

In animals, we often observe patterns of excitation allowing us to make predictive, interpretative statements. In a cat, an arched back, erected hairs over the body, and a snarling expression of the mouth allow us to feel fairly safe in predicting that under certain conditions, the state observed will develop into a fight. We can say loosely that the cat is 'angry', but the anthropomorphic implication can be avoided if we say instead that the cat looks threatening or has assumed a fighting posture.

If a male animal mounts a female and proceeds to carry out pelvic thrusts, we can assume·with some accuracy that the male is involved in potentially reproductive activity. Some of the complications of study in this field become apparent when we find in many animals that males mount males and females females; here we have to begin to separate 'reproductive' and 'sexual'. But even further, we find that in some reported observations, this homosexual mounting has the implication of a statement about dominance, in that the mounting animal usually demonstrates in other ways that he (or she) is domi-nant over the other. What 'emotion' then is 'expressed'?

In the above instance, mounting, a 'sexual' response, appears to take its place at times in series in which the goal is dominance rather than reproduction. In another frequent variation in animals, we find that 'emotional' display appears to have principally a communicative function. If we observe a threatening posture in one of a pair of animals and predict that the animal will soon be involved in a fight, we may find ourselves very badly mistaken. In many such situations, a threatening posture on the part of the protagonist is followed by the assumption of a submissive posture on the part of the antagonist. Such submission appears to be "a soft answer (which) turneth away wrath". This repetitively available observation indicates that a description cannot be separated from its developmental context, and more specifically that animal behavior is often most significantly social behavior relating to other animals.

When we describe emotional states in animals, and frequently in human beings as well, we are making interpretations, and the observed situations are often susceptible to more than a single interpretation. 'Anger' is not a thing, it is an interpretation, as we learn when we try to argue with a paranoid person interpreting a variety of actions he observes as threatening to him and assuming the world to be angry with him. We try to intervene with the paranoid patient to keep his interpretation from being manifested in what he considers to be retaliatory action. In both the attempt to stop him, and his attempt to eliminate danger, we see attempts to gain 'control'. Control in emotional states involves predictive interpretation and action related to the state observed, as in either a) preparing to fight, or b) assuming a conciliatory air in response to a state interpreted as threatening. Human beings as scientists have the further option of reacting to emotional behavior in others or in animals from whom one is protected by observing them and categorizing the data observed.

'Emotions' do not occur in either-or separate form, as for instance either 'expressed' or 'unexpressed', 'conscious' or 'unconscious', but rather in a developmental series the final outcome of which depends upon 1) behavioral mechanisms built into the structure of the organism on the basis of genetic instructions, 2) the anatomical structure and the physiological state of the organism (sexual responses are unlikely to occur in a castrate or in a patient with pituitary cachexia), 3) the training of the organism in various ways, and 4) the immediately current situation, including most prominently the other participants. In the phrase of Homer Smith, the eventual form of the expression or lack of expression depends upon "heredity, environment, and circumstance".

When we work with adult human beings, the situation is somewhat different from that with animals because there are additional sources of information. The information which cannot be elicited from animals is primarily introspective. A human being can report states which may not be outwardly obvious, and in addition, by the use of subtle or sometimes even subliminal cues, it is possible for one human being to make judgments about others through interpreting his own feelings. An outwardly apparently composed human being may report that he 'feels' angry, or anxious, or sexually interested, in some context. In general, the more sophisticated and more competent the human being, the more he can control himself while being aware of the inner feeling. Speaking again loosely, we often say that children 'show their feelings' while adults may keep them concealed. This common method of speaking suggests that if certain types of behavior are exhibited, it must therefore indicate that certain feelings are involved. Occasionally, it is possible to find convincing evidence that this may be far from true. In a case personally followed, a rather psychopathic young man asserted that he had never been angry in his life. When asked how then he explained his not infrequent involvement in fights, he explained that the other person got in his way and had to be removed, but not with anger. After many months of intensive psychotherapeutic work, carried out under the threat of serious sanction if he did not 'succeed', he found himself on one occasion confronting his girl friend and a competitor talking earnestly to each other. Formerly, he would simply have attacked his rival. In this instance, having learned some self-control, he merely made it quite plain to the two that he was there and aware of their tête-à-tête. As he did so, he had for the first time a vivid fantasy of attacking the rival and a curious novel feeling which he realized 'must be anger'! The suggestion is strong that from a common base there may emerge 1) attack, or 2) a fantasy and a feeling. In another such alternative, gasoline may 1) explode or 2) run an automobile or a stove. The question is not that of simple expression, but that of the transformation undergone by certain potentialities on their way to a different state. In another instance, a group investigated the occurrence of fatigue in hypnotized and non-hypnotized subjects repetitively lifting a weight. When the non-hypnotized subjects became unable to continue, they reported feeling tired, but when the hypnotized subjects, relatively later, finally became unable to continue, they reported (under hypnotic influence still) that the arm wouldn't work.

Both these reports suggest that the common association of behavior with feeling we observe in ourselves (assuming we are relatively standard in this characteristic) is not necessary in all cases. Reporters at the not infrequent trials of mass murderers often report that the murderer 'shows no feeling'; it seems entirely possible that an important predisposition to the committing of such mass slaughter is an inability to feel human in the way we ordinarily expect normal adults to feel human.

With reference to the patient mentioned above, many psychiatrists would dismiss the objection made by saying that the patient was 'really' angry, he just "didn't know it'. But if we say this, we completely deny the patient's own statement that he later became able to differentiate anger and non-anger, and that attack in his ancient pattern is associated with non-anger. Does the lion feel 'angry' with his victim? I would think not, any more than the diner feels 'angry' with his steak as he destroys it, or than the businesslike slaughterer in the abattoir. If we undertake to make judgments on the basis of the introspective descriptions of the self given by patients, we must at least allow them equal value in the ultimate judgment reached. Surely the therapist cannot be entirely correct when he tells the patient that what he thinks about himself is untrue. The significant distinction often ignored by the psychotherapist is that between the interpretation of behavior (e.g., attack behavior) and feeling (e.g., anger). In the instance cited, there is evidence that the feeling is <u>alternate</u> to the action; if we look for another similar but more well-known sequence, we find the repetitive testimony of many that the anxiety of stage-fright disappears when the performance begins, suggesting here again that <u>feeling</u> often means <u>inhibited</u> or <u>predicted</u> action.

Psychotherapists learn that situations in therapy can often be changed very quickly by either an interpretation or a predictive comment. It is possible to reassure a patient one thinks potentially anxious, or to suggest to the patient that he go ahead and allow the implicit state predicted (or suggested) by the therapist to become explicit. If one guesses ahead that the situation may become difficult, he can adopt either of at least a pair of strategies. He can say or demonstrate, "I am not going to hurt you", assuming from his awareness of the situation that further development will precipitate some kind of unmanageable response: the wolf, lying on his back and baring his throat, makes the same kind of predictive interpretation in his behavior. On the other hand, the psychotherapist wishing to help a patient learn a new pattern of display may say, "Go ahead and try being angry, it's all right in the context of this professional situation", very much in analogy to the ski instructor who says to the frightened student, "Go ahead and try a snow-plow". When the patient succeeds in finding a new method of exhibiting an appropriate response, he may report that the feeling he did not know he was in the process of having is disappearing as it appears; this indicates that the conflict with the therapist is being replaced by confidence in the demonstration of the accuracy of the therapist's prediction. It is obvious that the traditional relatively concrete ways of describing this event are in fact parsimonious, although inaccurate.

The Form of the Book

The subject matter presented below is divided into several sections with a loose or general topic as a central theme. In the first section, the instructive implications of human communication are explored at some length. In the second, a group of specifically clinical problems is considered with special reference to the psychoanalytic or psychotherapeutic praxis from which the material is drawn. In the third section, the use of notions from information theory is presented, with an affirmation of my conviction that this system, when appropriately disengaged from the merely mechanical, serves to illuminate many specifically human problems, as for instance in the similarity of 'emotional' data-processing to the forms known as 'analogical'. In the fourth section, some of the psychosocial implications of semiotic theory, with special relevance to the psychiatric profession, are presented. The fifth section concerns some rather specific ways in which semiotic understanding changes traditional ways of thinking about 'mentation' and 'reality'.

In an appendix that forms the sixth section of this book, I have gathered three papers that date back to the earliest period of my interest in language in psychiatry. These papers have not previously been published, although some of the material from each has appeared later in altered form. The rationalization for presenting these papers at this late date is simply an increasing confidence that 'clinical semiotics' is a useful new name for psychiatry, and that as interest grows - as I think it must - it may be useful to have earlier formulations easily available to compare and contrast with later versions. In a word, this appendix is a form of autobiography.

PART ONE

THE REGULATORY FUNCTION OF SPEECH

I

SPEECH AS INSTRUCTION

Prescriptive Description

We say that speech reveals a universe to us, allowing us to share that
universe with others, assuming the universe to be unitary. In so
doing, we overlook the possibility that the universe 'perceived' is a
function of the description heard. We ignore the mediation of speech,
and it is routine to assume that what speech reveals to us is what is
there - as implied by the word, reveal, i.e., 'unveil'. The metaphor
suggests that speech 'raises a curtain' as in the theatre, showing us
what was already there, waiting to be discovered.

As one is forced by comparative inquiry to turn his attention more
to the technology of knowing, he is increasingly forced to come to
grips with the inescapable fact that every observation, every description is necessarily mediated, and that the mediation introduces 'artifacts' - and indeed, the identifying characteristics of any culture are
preeminently its artifacts.

The possibly radical conclusion, emerging from a protracted study
of the diverse universes discoverable among psychiatric patients, is
that any universe in which any group of human beings lives is a vast,
comprehensive artifact, to the mutual validation of which redundant
and ritual behaviors everywhere evident are devoted. As we come to
'know' speech carefully, retrospectively, and reflexively, it becomes
more and more apparent that neutral descriptions quite miss the point.
Speech - and even more, its derivatives: written language and tech-
nologically sophisticated computelevision - prescribes, defines, constructs, or produces what we 'see'. The metaphor of the stage can
be re-used, with a difference, if we recognize that speech is a highly
significant participant in the 'realization' of a universe, understanding
'realization' here in the French sense indicating a theatrical production.

It is through prescription that the 'universe' emerges into 'reality'
- as best understood when one re-reads (for the hundredth time, in
my case) the extraordinarily dramatic story of Helen Keller's introduction to conscious life at the moment when it dawned on her (perhaps as a memory of a prior state that had disappeared from disuse)
that the finger-movements of her teacher were significant, and that
these sequences of tactile impressions could be integrated into verbal
signs that named the familiar furniture of her previously 'unconscious'
life. Miss Keller tells us how the implicit instruction in this realization was obeyed as she ran from one to another of these familiar
things to 'ask' by offering her hand for the different combinations of

finger movements that 'meant' this one. Speech 'says' to the awakened, "<u>This</u> has a name, and therefore <u>everything</u> has a name".

We live in a culture long dominated by the ideal of value-free, objective, science. The basic ideological assumption of such a social system is that, with appropriate training in method, it will be possible to get a clear, unbiased description of the 'external world', a world consisting of objects, out there, that 'signal' to us through symbols that transmit perfectly. Any suggestion that these symbols are themselves highly active and necessarily biassed transformers (Whorf, 1941) rather than transparent transmitters challenges the whole tradition of objective, value-free science. I suggest that if we want a metaphor for speech, it is much more nearly that of Lewis Carroll, describing the use of flamingoes as croquet mallets and hedgehogs as croquet balls, with all of their 'own' intervention in the game being played (1), than that of the limpid, stable, all-reflecting mirror that tradition tells us 'reflective thinking' with abstract description' can be.

Naming and Creating

Western civilization is called 'Judaeo-Christian' for very good reasons. The Jewish heritage - a tradition that its offspring, Christianity, turned on as Zeus turned on Chronos, Oedipus on Laius - is even more powerful in implicit than in explicit fashion (in 'unconscious' operation, one might say). Witness the derivation of 'alphabet' from 'alpha, beta ...' and prior to that from the 'aleph, beth ..' of the Semitic language. If, as many think, all scientific knowledge emanates from the patterning (cause-effect) imposed by the form of alphabetic coding in its linear context, the rise of the West to world domination is traceable directly to this original patterning. In its transformation in Greek developments of logic and rationality, alphabetic-linear data-processing was stripped of the rich emotionality and irrationality that still characterizes the orthodox in Jewish circles, especially the 'joyously devout' Hassidim. No more interesting contrast can be cited than the emotionality of this tradition confronting the aesthetic-ascetic intellectuality of an Einstein or a Gell-Mann.

The Bible tells us that God's act in creating the world was a verbal act; He said "Let there be light, and there was light". (2)

The Name of God is so sacred that in orthodox circles, special circumlocutions are employed to avoid its use - and when the Name of God was written on his forehead, the legendary Golem came to life.

In fairy tales and legends, much is made of the importance of keeping a name secret, in a tradition that derives from some of the tenets of sympathetic magic, where any person has to be careful in disposing of finger-nails, excreta, hair, and the like - since each item of the <u>disjecta membra</u> retains a significant trace of the identity that gives to the sorcerer holding the part a measure of control over the whole. A name is such a significant part, albeit arti-

21

ficial - and there are many legends in which naming equals controlling. Rapunzel won her freedom by learning the name of Rumpel-
stilskin, and Elsa lost her Lohengrin (as Psyche nearly lost her
Cupid) because of the curiosity with which she pursued the goal of
discovering the name of her lover.

Such ideas appear not uncommonly in the madhouse, as attested
by comments made by a severely disturbed young man following a
suicide attempt. Describing his fear of being controlled, he said,
"I have this degree of fear - it comes through in very silly things,
such as I lost a shirt in the ward, somebody borrowed it or took it.
There's a fear that that shirt will incriminate me. I have a tremendous fear of being incriminated by evidence, I will not write things
for an example. I rarely sign my name, my wife signs almost all of
our checks. And I will not write things down, I will have somebody
else write it. And there's the fear of - I will literally wipe my fingerprints off things, off doors, I will wear gloves rather than touch
doors". (3) The transformation of modern scientific method is apparent in the fact that police (like the sorcerers of old) often do gain
control of offenders by identifying them through disjecta membra -
fingerprints, bloodstains, tire tracks, bullets taken from wounds,
identifiable belongings, and the like.

Power and Control

Because listening to another's words requires putting the self at the
disposal of the other for whatever period is required for comprehension, the matter of speaking a language is always an exercise in
controlling, and in being controlled by another. As societies seek
stability over the generations, they begin to formalize speech into
statute (note the stationary connotation, quite the opposite of the
evanescence of any spoken sentence, and then note that 'sentence'
is used both to describe a series of words and to designate a punishment for a criminal offense). Statutes depersonalize power, enhancing the acceptability of the system for all of its members - and
as civilization progresses, we see an increasing emphasis upon recruiting conscious consensus as the basis of power.

Because of the inherent instructive-directive implications of any
conversation (a 'turning together', suggesting that speech is a mutual
dance with 'steps' as formal as those of the minuet), the notion of a
'detached statement' is as absurd as the idea that science is free of
value judgments. Hume says, in an early comment about science, that
any statement not containing rigorous logical argumentation should
be 'cast into the flames' - is that a value judgment? The power structure of speech is submerged, made unconscious and inapparent, by
the training of any group to ignore the medium in favor of the 'object'. A simple example may serve to point up this idea. If I want
a light to go on, I must move the switch that controls that light - but
this means, at a deeper level of significance, that if I want that light
on, I have to submit to the instructions symbolically presented to me
by the switch. I usually feel 'master' of the light via the switch - but

the 'fact' is more specifically apparent when I realize that I am controlled by that switch fully as much as the light is. To attain a relation of illumination, I am forced to 'obey the rules' of the light-switch game - and so it is with all of the complicated apparatus of modern civilization. The more complex the apparatus, the more do I have to submit to inherent instructions.

Liberation and Oppression

For the past two hundred years the most effective political slogans have called for freedom. "Give me liberty or give me death"! rings down the corridors of time in the United States (in spite of the fact that its speaker was a slave-owner and has remained the hero of white supremacists!). "Liberty, equality and fraternity" was the ideological core of the French Revolution. The destruction of imperialism and of colonialism is the theme of political movements in the twentieth century: "Keep the world safe for democracy!" The Supreme Court's civil rights decision in 1954 opened the way for a torrent of liberation on the part of homosexuals and welfare recipients as well as women. Everyone wants to be free, and political radicals tell us that we are just beginning to understand the phenomenology of oppression and repression.

My understanding of the human condition, in this context, is so antithetical as to amaze even myself. It has seemed to me, more and more as I have studied language in the context of 'mental illness' - metaphor that is itself oppressive and repressive - that the primary characteristic of the human condition is that of being in the service of the principal characteristic of the human condition, speech.

The power of one human being over another or others is a function of the spoken word by means of which one person (with the support of an effective consensus) influences another, overtly or covertly, in a range from frontal assault to seduction. When human beings become sophisticated in the technology of writing, so that speech becomes speech-and-language, the implication of power becomes expanded, and with successive incrementations in sophistication, greater and greater. In our epoch, the emergence of two conjoint technologies in television and in computer science has made a quantum jump in the possibility of control over others and the 'environment'. But all these technologies that we regard as liberating are, in the most impressive sense, oppressive and constricting. We pride ourselves on our 'mastery' of those technologies that 'enslave' us!

No serious student of speech and language can avoid the realization that the transmission of verbal method is, in the most significant sense, coercive (Piaget, 1970). No human being can ever communicate with another in the specifically human way except in speech - and there is no way in which two respondents can avoid mutual subservience to a code and a context independent of either speaker. There is no way in which one can command a computer without 'speaking a language', i.e., writing a program in a language that 'makes sense' to the computer. We understand computers as mech-

anical slaves - but as we grow more accustomed to modern life, controlled as it is by credit cards and computerized accounting, we are
more and more slaves to our slaves, the computers!

Symbolic Method and Distance Reception

Human beings live with each other in universes that are structured
by speech, and re-structured serially by the derivatives of speech.
The human primary competitive advantage is a specialized development in the distance receptors, with their central connections and
data-processing apparatus (Sherrington, 1906).

The distance-receptor of mammals as a group is primarily that
of olfaction - but smelling reveals a universe limited to the near-
distance. Sound and vision allow a progressive expansion of the
universe by allowing communication over much larger distances -
and, as technology becomes progressively improved, distance
through time is expanded enormously through the invention of modes
of transmitting and storing significant patterns of sound and sight,
and of reaching out into the far distance to sample sounds and sights
that are otherwise unheard or unseen. When we compare radio and
television, we find a relation similar in many ways to that of sound
and vision, Spoken and Written. The sampling possibility of the
latter in each case is a derivative of methods in the former, but
greatly expanded by the change in techniques.

One significance of the difference between spoken and written is
that only after the widespread use of Written in learned circles do
we begin to find references to 'mind', a 'thing' comparable to the
'objects' that begin to exist when static description ensures that
permanence will be achieved through storage. When we examine some
of the uses of 'mind', we find ourselves bemused by their implications.

When we say that a man has 'lost his mind', what can that mean?
In ordinary parlance, the comment is equivalent to that man's having
a 'disease of the mind'. Surely it would have to be here and not 'lost'
if some diagnostic inquiry is to be begun and some 'objective' investigation undertaken. When we examine those 'objective' methods,
we find that all of them have in common that they are administered
or exhibited in speech and that what makes them 'objective' is that,
with certain statistical maneuvers, numbers can be assigned to the
results (e.g., an 'intelligence quotient'). But numbering is but a
different, more restricted form of linguistic description. It is easy
to get the impression repetitively that mankind is determined to deny
the central significance of speech! The ways in which speech is overlooked would be called, by a psychoanalyst-linguist, a 'defense-mech-
anism' of 'denial'.

Computelevision uses mechanical and metallic forms in mediating
reception over great distances, and with the use of magnetic tapes,
the storage of data over time in the 'memories' of computers becomes fantastically expanded. When we pay careful attention to the
ways in which we have learned to 'instruct' computers through 1)

designing 'hardware' so that many general instructions are 'built into' the structure (as 'instincts'?), and then 2) designing 'software' so as to control and direct the 'potentia' built in, we find a striking set of analogues to the human design that 'biologically' fits human beings to talk, and the educational processes that 'lead out' these potentialities into amazingly different end-products, depending upon the person, the language system, the culture, the family background, the ideology of the period, and so on and on. Computer models thus show the complementarity of hereditary and environmental influences by giving us the metaphor of hardware, i.e., structures in the metal, and software, linguistic-symbolic instructions in a program. In the evolution of culture, it is apparent that the command of speech is the precise advantage that the parent has over the child ('infant' is, by derivation, non-speaker), and learning speech is the main reason for an unbroken experience in childhood. When human beings learn how to write, scribes tend to take possession of the power structure subtly but progressively - and those who idealize that ultimate distribution of power throughout a social system place their fondest hopes on the inculcation of literacy throughout the society, so that all have equal access to the power of the storage of ideas.

The problem that then emerges is that of a new distribution of power, depending upon the differential command of literate-technological modes of dealing with experience and recruiting consensus. The contemporary complication we see is that the progressive idealization of liberation appears to have reached such an extent that obedience to any set of standards is prejudiced, and the notion of a 'normal' group is abandoned in favor of the normalization of any group. The presence of innumerable competing groups gives increasing evidence of a crisis of leadership - as noted in the state of post-war France in which there were perhaps twenty competing parties, and any government had to depend upon an uneasy and temporary alliance of a majority, not of the people, but of the many parties.

Objectification Through Literacy

Writing converts spoken communication into an 'object' - and science as a whole depends upon a technology that transforms 'information' through written or graphic storage - by photography or by graphic representation in charts, etc., as well as in discursive script. It is easily possible to gain the impression that the written becomes timeless, and it is no accident that 1) Moses 'internalized' an abstract deity by asserting that 'He' was somehow identical with the table of the law, and 2) Plato, the first and most powerful scribe-amanuensis, celebrated the beauty and truth of the immobile as over against the untrustworthy evidence given by life and movement.

From such methods there comes immense power, not only the power of technology as we move mountains and invade outer space, but more importantly the power over what we hypostatize as 'men's minds'. It is only through a fallacious application of misplaced con-

creteness that the metaphor, the 'object', <u>mind</u> can appear. The
whole course of Western ghought has been prescribed by the use of
the notion of 'a mind' - a notion that curiously, fantastically, bypasses any consideration of the processes of communication and
relation that it reifies. 'Mind' is never observable, any more than
is the devil or God Almighty or the luminiferous ether. Nevertheless,
in Western civilization, we have been in bondage to the notion of
'mind' for thousands of years - and even most modern experts (cf.
Chomsky) continue to use the substantialistic reification.

With the advent of computelevision, we have been able to see new
sets of (mental or mentational) relations and to begin to use a new
set of metaphors and metonyms. We persist, however, in refusing
to notice that every name can only be some kind of transform from
something we already know, and that no <u>naming</u> process- and therefore, according to Dewey and Bentley, no <u>knowing</u> process - can be
other than derivative form the linguistic forms we happen to use.
When we name the most advanced probes into space, we revert to
Greek and Roman mythology to speak of 'Apollo' missions - a most
interesting demonstration of 'conservation' and the basic conservatism of speech.

Psychotherapy

A major interest for the whole of my career has been the curious,
paradoxical, frustrating, irritating, fascinating praxis we call, in-
appropriately, <u>psychotherapy</u>. Other terms are 'counselling' and the
seeking of 'insight' or 'illumination'. The psychotherapist uses only
speech - but his patients or clients or counsellees tend to be drawn
from the most sophisticated ranks of contemporary society, from
scientists, intellectuals, businessmen, the religious. What generally
characterizes such persons is their extreme expertness in literate
modes of communication. Why then should it be the case that the
practice of psychotherapy takes place purely in speech?

When one examines the distribution of psychotherapists (one might
say, using metaphors from medicine, the <u>prevalence</u> of psychotherapy and the <u>incidence</u> of psychotherapists) one arrives at a fascinating 'epidemiological' conclusion. This practice flourishes differentially in the West, mostly in industrial 'developed' nations, in
urban settings, in Protestant countries, especially those in which
the industrial revolution is oldest (cf. Shands, 1968). But psychotherapy is in many ways a Jewish invention, for a long time mostly
controlled and advanced by Jewish practitioners - how so? The relation is illuminated by the reference to the Protestant preoccupation
with the Old Testament, and with the abstract deity of the Jews rather
than the pantheon of idols recreated in every Catholic Church, and
especially in the idolatory of the Mother, the Virgin.

I take this to mean that as Western intellectuals, in following the
ancient Jewish preoccupation with thought in the abstract, have encountered personal distress, they have 'intuitively' sought help from
their predecessors along the same path. It is a recurrent practice

of Westerners to seek salvation through resorting to Jewish poten-
tials - the while rejecting and denying the significance of the Jewish
heritage. Max Weber suggests that it is the technological application
of the religious core of Protestantism that leads us to capitalism and
all its alienating practices, so what is more reasonable than that we
should seek salvation again in listening to the prescription of the new
Messiah? This time an overtly secular one, a man who defines the
role of the psychotherapist as that of a secular spiritual guide (Freud,
1927).

In these papers, it is the central theme that all Western social-
ization patterns are imbued with the heritage of the very different
Jewish and Greek modes of abstraction with, not uncommonly, a
conflict between. What differentiates the practice of psychotherapy
from other supposedly 'scientific' pursuits is its basically and in-
escapably human character. No matter how much the pressure toward
abstract abstractness, 'meta-abstractness' one might say, in science,
the practice of psychotherapy remains a human relation. Paradoxically, as I have noted before, it is the specifically human characteristic to affirm in denying - as when we say that Christian Science
or psychotherapy is 'really science' when all of the structural components differ so strikingly from the abstract pattern of 'natural
science'.

Speech as Regulator

Again, to return to the beginning, I take this to be a consequence of
the instructive character of human speech, of the manner in which
all of us remain susceptible to accepting statements that Black is
White when those statements are made in the appropriate human context. To say this in succinct form, I can quote from a modern master
in a civilization that is both Western and not-Western, in the very
different world of the USSR. The neuropsychologist, A. R. Luria,
tells us:

> There is no doubt whatever that all the highest functional forma-
> tions with which psychology is concerned - the accomplishing of
> conscious, purposive action, systematic active thought, voluntary
> memory - all these are in greater or less degree linked with the
> regulating function of speech. [emphasis added] In all these cases
> external (or more often internal) speech locks in an existing sys-
> tem of connections, which in normal behavior become dominant,
> and which define the course of all subsequent actions of the person,
> acquiring sometimes - as, for instance, was the case with Gior-
> dano Bruno - a strength which considerably exceeds the strength
> of vital instincts (1958: 28).

Naive Realism and Linguistic Relativity

To the 'intuitive' apperception of the human being, the world is ob-

viously <u>out there</u>, in front, existing quite independently of you or me.
The task prescribed in this stance is to investigate the out-there and,
in the first sacred prescription of Western thought, to dominate it,
bringing it under human control. It is therefore, for those of us who
have 'changed our minds' about the basic situation, a rude shock to
come to the conclusion that the existence of the 'external' world, in
all its nounized objectivity, is a function of those instruments with
which we had thought to 'approach' it. The problem becomes more
acute when we realize that two major ideologies that have enormously
influénced the Western world in the past hundred years both take
origin from nineteenth century materialism. The work of Freud and
Marx, no matter how incompatible their systems have been thought
by some to be, yet share the basic assumption that 'reality' is
'matter in motion'.

The notion of an 'external world' filled with 'objects' is the core
of nineteenth century materialism. In the twentieth century, as physicists use more and more sophisticated instruments and concepts,
they have repetitively realized that it is <u>mediation</u>, the interposition
'between' the 'observer' and the 'object' that in the most important
sense creates <u>both</u> observer and object. The modern physicist-
-philosopher Eugene Wigner, tells us in summarizing his conviction
about 'reality':

> The principal argument against materialism is not that ... it is
> incompatible with quantum theory. The principal argument is that
> thought processes and consciousness are the primary concepts,
> that our knowledge of the external world is the content of our con-
> sciousness and that the consciousness, therefore, cannot be de-
> nied. On the contrary, logically, the external world could be de-
> nied - although it is not very practical to do so. In the words of
> Neils Bohr, "The word consciousness, applied to ourselves as
> well as to others, is indispensable when dealing with the human
> situation. " In view of all this, one may well wonder how materi-
> alism, the doctrine that "life could be explained by sophisticated
> combinations of physical and chemical laws, " could so long be
> accepted by the majority of scientists (1967: 176-177).

In human experience, those who become sophisticated in the use of
speech (and especially in the first derivative as they train themselves to become 'exact men') rapidly lose the awareness of mediation, much as the expert listener to a piece of music loses the
awareness of the piano or violin as he 'listens through'. Moses can
be said to have created Jehovah by formulating his laws - and, if
we examine human speech in many of its major functions, we find
it to be omnipresent, omniscient, and omnipotent in the human world.
It is an error, in this view, ever to detach speech-and-language
from the notion of God. Saint John the Divine states the identity, "In
the beginning was the Word, and the Word was with God, and the
word was God".

The fact that speech directs, transforms, regulates, instructs
(in-structures), prescribes tends to be the last thing (note the

metaphor) that human beings discover - since a communicational medium is not and cannot be a thing, and since the ideology of our communicational system is that only things exist. Speech conceals itself as it reveals a 'universe'. Human experience grows, like a tree in a forest, from the outside, adding layers onto what has already developed. For this reason it is impossible to study studying, since in the process of study we reify, objectify, and thus destroy as we create. By 'selecting a frame of reference' we select a universe. The fact that any one person has only a microscopic contribution to make in constructing the universe also tends to obscure how much 'reality' is not only a construction but a consensual concealing of that fact. The implicit consent of the governed is operative for millennia before the relation becomes describable.

These days, the current of change has become so swift that one can see, in a single lifetime, many of the crucial events related to changed ideologies and to changed modes of communicational technology. Such trends, when here, can be traced to sources - but they are impossible to predict and always appear as surprises. Who could have predicted the long hair of young men, the radical abbreviation of skirts, the loosening of traditional forms of inhibition of sexual activity and drug use, the wholesale acceptance of homosexuality and abortion? But in each such change, although all of us have been involved in a shifting consensus, the details of the changes are concealed while the results are obvious.

Power Behind a Throne

To demonstrate some of the peculiarities of metaphoric and metonynic transformation, it may be useful to speak of speech metaphorically as a 'gray eminence', as that term was used to refer to Cardinal Mazarin, who ruled France through a position contiguous to the king, i. e., 'behind' the throne. 'Your Eminence', the usual form of honorary address to a cardinal (cf. 'Your Highness') leads by nounization to the particularization, 'an' eminence. The uniform of the cardinal is scarlet, so a 'gray eminence' is a disguised or concealed cardinal, exerting his power mysteriously - the term is internally contradictory as befits its applicability to the many paradoxes of speech (4). It is only after the invention of writing that speech can be transformed into an 'object', language. Malinowski points out that to the preliterate savage, speech is as much a part of action as is paddling a canoe. Written emerges from Spoken in a process somewhat like that in which the implicit electrical activity becomes manifested in photographic transformation in the techniques of electroencephalography or electrocardiography used to demonstrate, publish and store patterns otherwise totally embedded in a context-of-action.

Human beings collectively conceal revealingly in myths mysteriously developing and culturally transmitted since preliterate times. Myths have to be compelling to avoid being forgotten, and the process by which certain myths were selected and millions rejected must have a significant relation to other processes of biological and cultural evolution. With specific relation to the usefulness of reflection, we find in the myth of Perseus's relation to Medusa, the mortal one of the three dread Gorgon sisters, a case in point. The Gorgons had the potentiality of turning all viewers into stone - 'freezing' them, as it were, into a state of permanent immobility. Perseus 'turned the tables' by operating on Medusa with the help of a mirror. By beheading Medusa and mounting her head as a trophy on his shield, Perseus neutralized her threat for himself and turned it against others. In a somewhat parallel fashion, man has attempted with much success to conquer language by the reflective technology of writing. Once one submits to the special requirement of literate technology, he can to some extent become its master.

Using symbolic forms to construct a universe is much like using any special kind of building material to build a house. The house as built is a function of the nature of the material, and the builder or architect has to know, intimately, the potentialities of his medium if his house is to be successful. The rule is always that submission is the route to mastery - a rule as old as human culture.

The central technique of language is naming - and a name has a metaphorical resemblance to a handle (a signifiant) attached to a concept (a signifié) in Saussure's term. An old myth says that the infant, Eros, could not grow until the birth of his younger brother, Passion - and a somewhat similar kind of mutual interdependence characterized the word and the concept - never, as crudely taught, the 'object'. Jakobson points out that all naming is prescribed by the use of figures of speech. The end points of this scale are occupied by the relations of similarity and contiguity, with the corresponding figures of speech, metaphor and metonym. We say that some new and previously unknown thing is like something we know already, reducing the amount of novelty and (by the rule that information is the inverse of probability) reducing the amount of information presented by the unknown. At the other end of the scale, we reduce novelty by using a word next to, close to, or part of something already known. Saussure's use of parole (word) to refer to Spoken, and of langue (tongue) to refer to Written, are both metonymic usages.

With reference to the complex relations involved, the tropes used above can be reconsidered. 'Eminence' is a synonym for prominence or height, used to indicate the 'height' reached as a 'prince of the church' - height, that is, in a metaphorical sense since 'height' refers to a 'table of organization'. As used in the mode of address, "Your Highness" or "Your Eminence", the term is a metonym. Height connotes 'being visible', or 'being on a pedestal' - again a metonymic usage requiring previous understanding that honorific statues are usually placed on a pedestal. 'Gray', on the other hand, connotes being invisible, as in "all cats are gray at night". Thus the term, 'gray eminence' is a special example of the internal opposition structurally typical of many language patterns, a term weaving together the warp of similarity and the woof of contiguity, generalized from a particular case to indicate a whole category (much as a 'Lucy Stoner' is a woman who insists on keeping her own name - or

a Mrs. Malaprop, from mal à propos, is one who uses speech clumsi-
ly).
The playfulness of speech underlies all that is lightest and most en-
tertaining about the human condition - while this same playfulness,
with instability, threatens major enterprises and planful activity in
its 'frivolity'. Gaining control of symbolic statement is the principal
purpose of the logician and the mathematician. The scientist submits
himself to the rigid demands of the resulting dialect, scientific, in
an extended training through which the disciple prepares himself for
a place of authority in the given 'field' or 'discipline'.

Free Association

The principal technique of 'insight' psychotherapy is called 'free
association' - a method apparently invented or discovered by Francis
Galton as a method of amusing himself (Shands, 1960). This method
was then re-discovered or adapted by Freud as a technical 'tool' or
'instrument'. This invention of Galton's is like the Chinese invention
of gunpowder used for religious celebration before being eventually
developed by Western rational technology into atomic explosions.
    The hidden agenda of speech use is nowhere better shown than in
the peculiar implications of free association. The 'therapist' (a usage
to be discussed more at length below) encourages the 'patient' to say
just what comes to mind. If we remember the proverb "In vino veri-
tas" we find a similarity - the drunk and the ideal patient reveal the
truth. Similarly, it is not uncommon to hear a report, "I was so
angry I said whatever came to mind!", again an indication that only
in intense states of temporary deviation from 'normality' does this
kind of freedom of expression occur. There appears to be a reciprocity, so that free association occurs spontaneously in intense
states of feeling, but on a planned basis, free association leads to intense states of feeling. The procedure induces, in the 'suitable'
patient, a paradoxical state of dependence upon the therapist. This
state is technically termed a result of 'transference', though it is
never otherwise experienced in just this form - so that it is more of
an 'original' than a 'copy'.
    As the patient comes to work out the method so that he can in fact
say what occurs to him even relatively freely, he finds that, paradoxically, the therapist who listens becomes progressively more
powerful in influencing the patient's behavior. This is to say, quite
specifically, that the method of gaining control of another is that of
submitting oneself to the service of that other. The therapist, as
attendant-servant, establishes an ascendancy over the patient that is
often extraordinary. The usual theoretical explanation, that this is
a 'transference' from early similar states of relatedness to parents
induced in a process of 'regression', pays no attention to the similarity of the intense state engendered to states of 'ecstatic' intensity
in religious conversion, nor to the specific differences of the 'suitable' from the 'unsuitable' patient.
'Free association' is a technique not possible to the poorly educated
person, and thus it is specifically oriented to members of the middle-

-class. The significant relation is one of discipline, here a mostly unconscious discipline absorbed in the course of learning to read and especially of learning to read for pleasure. Reading for pleasure involves a 'willing suspension', not only of disbelief, but of competing activities in favor of 'keeping one's nose in a book'. By and large, such an attitude has to be inculcated by modelling the self upon a preceptor early in life - usually, obviously, a parent or parents, in a setting limiting the ordinary childish tendency to continuous, 'mindless', activity. 'Teaching a child to read' is only in relatively small part a matter of formal indoctrination - it is primarily a matter of transmitting an attitude of curiosity in the context of an insatiable interest in knowing.

'Free association' is a technique that depends upon a developed ability to 'wander', to explore the 'contents of my mind'. This capacity, assumed to be 'spontaneous', by many therapists and patients alike, is in fact one dependent upon a great deal of prior training. Basically, the capacity has to do with 'day dreaming', but the childhood forms of fantasy are greatly changed before 'free association' becomes possible. Piaget points out that in his subjects, the capacity to form hypotheses and to wander in imagination is developed only at adolescence - and there is some fairly persuasive evidence that this development in adolescence in middle-class students depends upon a prior training in early family surroundings. What one sees again is that developing one's imagination involves a selective submission to the influence of writers who both open up the universe and also prescribe what is to be found there.

Reading as an Addiction

The connotation of 'insatiable interest' is addiction, and there are many ways in which the 'book worm' qualifies as an addict. As an 'abstract addiction', reading and the collection of books parallel at a different level the concrete addictions that are characteristically features of lower-class status. In both instances, the effect of submission to the conditions of the 'foreign substance' or the 'foreign patterns' of reading is that of 'liberation' from the ordinary context of human life. The reading-addict often becomes a writing-addict, since for many purposes the generation of one's own liberating patterns is an even more fascinating operation.

Like other addictions, reading - at least for a long time - tends to feed upon itself, in a 'positive feed back' method. Helen Keller was first aware of names and joy at the same time as her universe suddenly became 'conscious'. Most human beings are hopelessly far removed from this primal joy by the passage of time, but it is still possible for some to remember the revelation of learning to cope with reading matter. As in other addicting situations, there is as well a tendency for the joys of reading to 'wear out' as one comes to recognize eventually, with Solomon, that "there is nothing new under the sun" and that "much study is a weariness of the flesh".

The technology of knowledge shows an abstraction of attitude from

a series of interesting events to a generalized attitude of curiosity.
It is this attitude that Goldstein showed to be most affected in brain-
damaged patients, and it is conversely the attitude engendered in the
orientation preparing a child for professional and scientific occu-
pations. The development of an abstract attitude is a matter of taking
a part - in this case, a 'set' - out of a particular context and gener-
alizing it. The same method of pars pro toto, an example of synec-
doche, underlies the use of any word to refer to a whole system (e. g. ,
the church, the state, the school).

It has been said that in the bimillennial existence of the Chinese
Empire, the protracted training of candidates for the civil service
was a training in the extraordinary intricacies of the written language
of the country. This language, using ideographs rather than letters,
presented to the learner a very large number of forms that had to be
learned along with the many allusions and historical pecularities of
each. Knowing how to write Chinese, and passing an examination in
writing, was an automatic 'ticket' of entry into the ruling class.

In the modern industrial-technical society, the same kind of automatic admissibility is achieved through the development of the kind
of generalized attitude that goes along with the performance of 'executive' functions. The abstractness of this kind of attitude is well shown
by the way in which generals retire to become chairmen of the board
of industrial corporation, and scientists primarily known for research
move smoothly into positions of chairmen of departments.

An 'abstract attitude' is manifested by the wish, not only to know
what someting is, but how it works, in whatever context. The curious
person is generally curious, as interested in a random observation
as in some matter of direct interest to his family or business. He
wants to know the rules of Go as well as the rules of baseball, what
the kinship patterns of the Cherokee are as well as those of his own
culture, how Hero's steam engine worked and why it did not achieve
technical implementation in his own time. In the language of language,
the interests of such a curious person are meta-interests. The
student in this mode wants to know not merely the phenomena, but an
explanation of the phenomena in abstract terms - usually in terms of
rules and regulations that classify, clarify and rationalize.

Again, there is a 'hidden agenda' - since, to utilize, to master,
to organize, one has to know how - what are the rules of organization?
what are the permissible variations? what are the absolute limits?
how far can one go in 'bending the system' without breaking anything?
In the specific application of the abstract attitude in the practice of
psychotherapy or psychoanalysis, the process is one of a continuous
interpretative, i. e. , metalinguistic, commentary upon observed behavior. The interpretation is formulated to give a patient a reflective,
retrospective report of hidden relations in his stream of free association (cf. Wm. James's 'stream of consciousness'). The technique
habituates the patient to the 'thrill' of knowing in this intimate fashion.
Once 'hooked' in the pattern, he tends to continue the practice while
reversing the roles - hence the 'didactic analysis' or the 'personal
psychoanalysis' or 'psychotherapy' as training for the practice of the
profession.

Metaphor and 'Mental Illness'

To demonstrate the power of speech, one of the most significant
examples is that of the metaphor, 'mental illness'. The power of
this metaphor is well seen in the billions of dollars spent every year
in the United States on the 'treatment' of this kind of 'sickness' and
the promotion of 'mental health'. This kind of yearly investment
develops a 'vested' interest in those who work in the system, and an
examination of the appropriateness of the metaphor becomes an attack
upon an establishment. Weizenbaum (1972) comments in a similar
relation, that the operating systems of certain large computers are
known to be unsatisfactory - but changes cannot be made because
too many people have become dependent upon these systems in many
different contexts.

An interesting demonstration of the problem is to be found in the
current reduction in the size of state hospitals with a determined effort to return most of the inmates to 'the community'. This effort has
been pushed by the current financial crisis of governments - but what
it shows is that definition is the major point at issue. 'Sick' people
need to be in hospitals, but when the definition changes, deviant people
can, with some help, be expected to remain members of the community. Very little conscious attention is paid to the obvious fact that
all psychiatric and psychological examinations take place primarily in
interviews in which the unspoken program is that the examiner uses
himself as a model and appraises the patient's capacity by comparing
deficits found with the 'normal' function exhibited by the interviewer.
This fact emphasizes that speech requires, as a basic relation, two
similarly-trained respondents taking alternative roles as speaker and
hearer in protracted complex transaction.

Crazy people cannot play this game as the interviewer expects. In
one dramatic example, the 'autistic' child often shows no tendency to
talk spontaneously or to respond, and we conclude that he is 'sick'.
But if a 'wild child' is found who knows no language, we are likely to
assume that he suffers from a lack of education. It would seem more
reasonable to think of both kinds of children as suffering from educational disadvantagement - in a manner similar to, but more extensive then, the disadvantages of 'ghetto' inhabitants.

If, as sometimes happens, an autistic child becomes able, after a
long and intricate process of relatedness, to talk, we say that he has
been well 'treated' - but, in the case of Miss Keller, was her teacher
a 'therapist'? Bartlett (1932) gives a capsule case history of a child
who lost his capacity to speak in the course of a surgical operation,
regaining it later through the efforts of a devoted teacher. When we
say 'therapy' in such a context, we are demonstrating again how effectively a consensually accepted metaphor tends to shape the thinking of generations of human beings - since we remember that it is
only in the recent past that the disease metaphor has been used.
Psychiatry is a term that first appeared, according to the Shorter
Oxford English Dictionary, in 1856.

It is of major interest to note how the two modes of thought implicit
in linguistic function play into this process. The goal of science is to

formulate relations in a <u>synchronic</u> fashion, preferably in a mathematical equation. Such an equation presents a static picture of the universe in which the left hand side balances the right hand side. But such a form allows no place at all for change or learning. The theory of communication-engineering begins with the notion that there are two already existing ensembles of messages at the termini of the channel - no account whatever is taken of how those message ensembles were set up. In principle, in information theory, learning then becomes impossible - just as Zeno's arrow cannot reach the target.

In an interesting parallelism, the notion of two identical ensembles of messages resembles the situation of the scientist who <u>starts with</u> a hypothesis. In both cases, the question is begged as to <u>how did</u> those ensembles become similar? or <u>how did</u> the hypothesis emerge? In linguistic terminology, what we see is that both these situations pose a synchronic problem that ignores the <u>diachronic</u> developmental process.

The speech that emerges in any human being depends upon a long prior history of exposure to, and identification with, basic attitudes and orientations. It is to the extended dedication of 'my attention' to 'your history' in the psychotherapeutic relation that the possibility of meaningful communication at a 'deeper' level than that of simple speech can be traced. Such a relation involves the establishment of what can appropriately be called <u>patterns of habituation</u> of each to the other, of the greatest importance in the mother-child dyad. This 'foundation', again to use a rather concrete metaphor, of human relatedness is the dual arrangement of every human situation in 1) the closeness, nearness, or <u>contiguity</u> of every human being in his formative years to relatives accompanying and caring for him and 2) the increasing requirement for <u>similarity</u> as between the child as novice and his elders as preceptors and models.

If we look again at the Oedipus myth, from a biological and a sociolinguistic standpoint, it becomes apparent that the 'blood' relation in human beings is always highly modifiable. After having been rejected by Laius, Oedipus's adoption and acculturation into the neighboring city-state made him an antagonist of the whole culture into which he had been born. To emphasize the inevitability of father-son antagonism quite misses the point of the cultural context that becomes of overwhelming importance. To re-emphasize the cultural even more, it is apparent that animal breeders often plan incestuous unions, and the children of that of Oedipus and Jocasta seem to have been 'normal'. Has Oedipus been an Egyptian sovereign, his unconscious crime might not have been a crime at all, since Pharaonic incest was culturally prescribed.

In Christian context, it was apparent to Christ that his revolutionary doctrines would lead in many cases to splits developing, in an alienation from tradition - he said, in the context of his message of peace, "I come to bring not peace, but a sword" - a message predicting a series of blood crusades. Christ taught that the child should abandon his parents for his faith. The insoluble problem clearly set forth in both contexts is that of "Who am I?" - am I who I was <u>born</u>

to be or who I was <u>trained</u> to be? The fact is that no 'either-or'
answer is available.

Insoluble Problems

There is no answer to the problem of the primacy of chicken or egg,
to Zeno's paradoxes, or to the problem of squaring the circle, because the <u>idioms are incompatible.</u> 'Nature' - whatever that is - is
never to be caught in any linguistic net whole and complete - but the
part (or 'reflection?') of nature we can catch is the beginning of wisdom. To call the mysterious disorders that are referred to the social
role of the psychiatrist 'mental illness' is no more and no less appropriate than to speak of possession by hostile spirits. In fact, when
we trace out the origin of 'spirit' from the root word meaning 'breath'
and see that the only reasonable connection is through the fact that
speech is shaped breath, then we can say with some pertinence that
what the psychiatrist deals with is the consequences of 'being pos-
sessed' by inappropriate speech performance, being 'driven' by non-
ratified metaphors and 'persecuted' by autonymous metonyms. All
that is required is that we practice the ancient skill of animistic
assignment of the status of agent in ways that are not ratified by consensus. For one, I greatly prefer being <u>possessed by a metaphor</u> to
being <u>lived by the Id</u> or <u>controlled by my Unconscious</u>, but this is
obviously a personal matter.

Inner and Outer

Western (S.A.E., Whorf, 1941) speech forms implicitly split the
universe into an outer and an inner aspect. The <u>inner</u> use of speech
refers to an <u>outer</u> 'objective reality' that ignores mediation. The
most important similarity in function to that of speech is to be found
in vision - there, too, appearance is convincingly <u>out there</u>, and it
is general to believe that 'what we see' is a simple function of what
is 'there' (cf., 'seeing is believing'). Study of illusions in simple
psychological experiments indicated unambiguously that under proper
conditions we obviously see what is not there, or, as in the case of
<u>Gestalt</u> illusions, that we alternatively see the 'same' picture in two
contrasting and incompatible versions. The problem is how to 'see in'
or how to 'make an object' out of the <u>potentiality of making objects</u>.
We say, in an informative metaphor, that constant 'rumination' may
lead to <u>insight</u>, that is, to the <u>inner</u> construction of a whole having an
explanatory relation to something out there. We test this explanation
of explanation by manipulating the 'outside world' - but such a test,
although expanding the area of human power and control, is not necessarily 'right' at all. One use of 'insight' is to recruit a consensus, and
if the consensus is effective, power inheres in the version presented,
even though it is obviously wrong by other criteria.
Much of speech has primarily to do with the organization of human
groups into harmonious arrangements ensuring cooperation. When

we are seeking harmony, it makes very little difference what the tune may be - so that the myriad of myth-systems found over the world in separate locally idiosyncratic variants all have the common purpose of serving as a core of communicational practice within the local human context. To a considerable extent, absurdity and unbelievability are the most important features of such systems, since they require a continuous effort of negation of the evidence of everyday life. The consensual effort of denial of the obvious and believing the obviously absurd (cf. Tertullian) constitutes the social cement of any human group. A now-obvious implication of objective rationality is the 'dissolving' of this social cement with a coordinated loosening of social ties.

Paradoxically, those in the Western world cling to the ancient slogan, that "Ye shall know the truth and the truth shall make you free" - while the evidence seems quite clear that 'becoming free' is in many ways tantamount to 'becoming inhuman'. To be human is to be bound into a particular community ($\overline{\text{by}}$ derivation, a group 'similarly bound' or 'under the same obligations') identified by a particular dialect of a larger language system. The dialect is specifically related, in traditional human context, to a religious institution, and we see, as an illustration of the importance of identifying through opposing, the fiercest antagonism directed toward close relatives using a somewhat different dialect and belief system. Protestants and Catholics, Serbs and Croats, the Turkish and Greek sharers of the island of Cyprus, the commonly semitic Jewish and Arabic antagonists in the Middle East - even, in a contrast amounting to a comic relief, the traditional antagonism as between Yale and Harvard, Army and Navy on the football field - all illustrate the principle that one's closest relatives are one's most emotionally significant antagonists. The method of such an identification of a 'me' is that of objectifying the 'others'. In the process, automatically and without noticing what is happening, one 'subjectifies' the self. The self can thus be defined as the reciprocal of the objective world - but so persuasive is the technique that the goal of much 'psychotherapy' is formulated as that of objectifying the self. This means putting a distance between 'me' and 'my self' - and the only way to do this is through reflection. The two meanings of reflection i.e., 1) the literal mirror-image and 2) the figurative, the extended internal processing of data using models borrowed from other contexts - are in fact closely related, and related through the use of the function of vision.

In vision, we see by reflection of light from a system of interest. As Gregory has emphasized, however, this 'seeing' is not at all an obvious immediate function as it appears to any competent human being to be. Rather, seeing is a function of a complex process in which one learns interpretation of retinal patterns in a manner bearing a close resemblance to learning the significance of other symbolic patterns. The work of von Senden in adults gaining vision (as by surgical removal of congenital cataracts) affirms this conclusion. One can test it himself by trying to look into a strange darkened room with the minimum of light - one tends to see a dimly discerned, flat arrangement. If the light is then turned on, the room suddenly 'reveals itself' in its three-dimensionality; if the light is again turned off, the result is not a return to the former flat pattern, but a main- tenance of the shape 'informed' by the light - now dimly seen. A somewhat similar transformation (insight, illumination) occurs when, puzzled by hearing rapidly said, "Mares eat oats, and does eat oats ...", one sees the line printed.

By and large, speech depends upon auditory patterning in its <u>method</u>, visual patterning in its <u>models</u>. Most names refer to shapes that can be 'visualized' in one or another of the ingenious methods invented by human beings. The trajectory of a missile is visualized on graph paper, the electrical action of the heart is visualized through an electrocardiographic tracing - the advanced technology of a complex civilization is almost entirely dependent upon such visualizations. As long as speech remains in its auditory, evanescent, linear pat- terning, human beings have to be in close and constant contact to remain related. The major shift in human potential comes from the discovery of the first derivative of speech, writing.

Writing 'objectifies' by establishing a permanent, out-there record that focusses consensus across space and time, thus radically ex- panding the relevant community. Any person undergoing the disci- pline of internalizing the interpretation of the pattern of lines (on an enormous variety of possible backgrounds) becomes a fellow of any other person undergoing the same discipline, and the two are enabled to communicate at a distance freed from the constraints of personal contact. Because human belings are thoroughly dependent upon a belief in the permanence and the stability of something, it is the case that the attribution of 'reality' is established as <u>that which is permanent and predictable</u>.

Since the relation of the human being to his universe is in many ways like the relation of a movie projector to the scenes projected, the basic conflict is that of whether it is the <u>projecting</u> or the <u>pro- jected</u> that is 'real'. The problem was familiar to Plato in his myth of the cave. The human method is that of asserting, in another absurd belief, that the projected is the real, with a major effort to ensure that one can depend upon the same projection time after time. The projecting is literally <u>invisible</u> because it is the source of the vision - and no amount of effort can ever allow a human being to examine his own eye closely.

This example may serve to illustrate the problem, since everyone knows it is possible to examine one's eye by reflection - that is, however, not to examine 'one's eye' but to examine 'a mirror- image of one's eye'. Learning this method is much like the dentist learning to use his mirror and to reverse many movements when controlling his action by the mirror image. The freedom of Perseus from 'freezing' is balanced in a different context by the immobilization suffered by Lot's wife in being unable not to look back at her burning city, and as well in Orpheus's loss of his 'object' by a similarly 'retrospective compulsion'. Through the whole set of myths there comes the common interpretation that when the system of interest is highly invested with human feeling - whether the feeling is that of horror and dread or that of love and desire - that system can only be handled 'objectively' by reflective observation. 'Reflective' means both through mirroring and through rumination – the common feature is that of putting distance between the observing (projecting) and observed (projected). The human condition is always one of insecurity and instability, and human beings are 'saved' only in human relatedness. A human social system is a folie à tous, corresponding in much of its deep structure to the folie à deux in which reciprocally related deviants often sustain each other in a crazy relation.

Psychiatry and Projection

Psychiatry – a profession named through combining a myth of the soul with the social role, i.e. physician, of the attendant assigned the function of 'knowing' states of personal distress – has the peculiar advantage of contact with the enormous variety of ways of failure of human relatedness. In a way that shows its inherent human methodology, contemporary psychiatry (like speech and vision) denies its proper function of understanding reflexively through a variety of complex methods of 'seeing' (or projecting) reflectively. Instead of attending to the inner, the course of modern psychiatry is one of emphasizing the outer. Madness is not, in this view, the central concern of all human relatedness, it is a 'disease' introduced by some organism (say, the spirochete of syphilis) or a deficiency disease (say that associated with pellagra) or a 'disease' of the brain (as in 'it's all in your head').

I use the term 'projection' in both its general and its psychiatric sense. My intent is to equate 'reality' with 'projection' through consensus, and to assert that the basic goal of all human learning is that of rendering the consensual projection sacred enough to be more passionately protected than survival itself. A social system is correlated, in this view, with a universally shared hallucination, a mutual projection, a set of sacred illusions. Such systems are shaped in the communicational mediation that is formally and traditionally considered entirely 'neutral' – just as is the contemporary dominant mediation, computelevision, a supposedly neutral reporting mechanism. The nature of report, however, is such that the reporting necessarily shapes the reported, and as speech moves from its first derivative, writing, through the intervening stage of disseminated writing in print to its current 'second derivative', telecommunication through computelevision, the dominance exerted by the slave on the master becomes more and more powerful.

The Problem of Expression

The universe of the psychotherapist is the universe of speech, in whatever variation of 'therapy' is involved. Using traditional speech forms derived by analogy from the hydraulics and mechanics of nineteenth century physics, the psychotherapist tends to conceal from himself what he is doing. He talks about 'expression' of 'emotion' or of 'the emotions' in a way that would be quite compatible with Darwin's Expression of the Emotions (1859). The 'emotions expressed' are somehow related to 'drives' or 'instincts' assumed similar to those that 'motivate' animals - in spite of the enormous difference between any animal performance, no matter how expert, and the simplest human sentence.

The basic notion of this field is an application of a metaphor that is by now obivously no longer applicable in its context of origin. The basic scheme is the pattern of air compressed within a balloon that 'seeks to escape' - or of the 'motivation' of 'nature' to 'abhor' a vacuum and so to 'send something in' to 'fill it up'. The only major difference from the personified agentifications of animism is the choice of the characters, with the personification concealed through the use of an abstract common noun ('energy' or 'force' or 'drive') instead of a proper noun as the name of a deity.

'Dynamic' - which is to say, force-oriented -explanations of human behavior take origin from the assumption that movement has to be explained, according to the pattern basic to materialism, with the familiar slogan that reality consists of matter in motion. But modern physiology does not concern itself with how movement originates, but rather with how movement is regulated. We do not 'explain life', we take life for granted and examine its components and its transformations. Similarly, much fruitless labor has been expended on trying to understand how human speech originated rather than upon understanding how speech regulates human life. When a 'therapist' working with a 'patient' succeeds in arriving at a mutual understanding that is followed by activity on the patient's part that was previously impossible, it seems a circumlocution to say that 'a symptom was relieved' - why not just say that action became more nearly regulated in a culturally acceptable way? And why not say that the result was obtained through a series of structured (and structuring) conversations, rather than in 'analysis'? And why not say that understanding of the problem was most advanced by seeing its applicability to the present situation rather than go roundabout and attribute it to the 'analysis of the transference'?

To me, the most significant of the lapses in modern psychiatric theory may well be that of the lack of appropriate attention paid to the variation of the medium of speech as it undergoes transformation into first (writing) and second (telecommunication) derivatives in the interest of expanded communication. The initial difference is highlighted in a comparison of the usage vs. storage functions of speech vs. language (parole vs. langue). The liability of speech is its evanescence, its ephemeral quality. What can be said only be said here and now - and to say approximately the same thing at a different time requires a variety of storage techniques. The basic storage method is that of the 'deep structures' underlying the possibility of speech, the patterning that has a considerable resemblance to the patterning of genetic instruction. But this kind of storage only supports the potentiality of any kind of content, and for some specific content to be preserved, cultural storage methods must be developed.

The simplest method somewhat resembles that of a species of ant in which specialized members, hanging from the roof of the nest, accept food material from other workers and store it in a grossly expanded abdomen that resembles a barrel in its function, with the added advantage that its living quality allows the contents to be held in a sterile condition. A principal function of human elders in a non-mechanically-oriented society is to remember the olden times so that by consultation with them a reasonable similarity (or the illusion of a reasonable similarity) of contemporary to traditional cultural practice can be maintained. Such an elder, as a 'reference library', tends to be treated with respect, occupying a position as an expert, reproducing stored material embedded in myths and legends as well as in his own memory.

Writing changes the human situation drastically, first by the formation of a new 'elite' of clerks and clerics that gradually evolves into 'management' (like the changes of 'palace manager' into Merovingian monarch or that of steward into royal Stuart) as the executive function comes to be more and more the province of the literate. Universal literacy underlies the whole conceptual system of liberal democracy, in which the ideal is that of 'one man, one vote' in the radical idealization of equality and fraternity of all.

If one examines this basis thesis of liberal democracy in a somewhat different context, one discerns different connotations in its application. We know from contemporary studies of the structure of the brain, as encouraged by similarly contemporary studies of the appropriate design for a computer, that the best kind of design is one that relates essentially similar components to each other - with a rapid increase in power as the numbers of components and the numbers of connections are increased. As one can see by the multiplication of both these numbers of each other, a dual arithmetical increase results in a geometrical increase in potentiality.

The core potentiality thus defined in the brain is that of the single unit constituted of a significant passage from one to another component along any of the many possible channels in the transfer of a single bit of information across a synapse. The component cell to which this bit is transferred is a complex summating system with a variety of excitatory and inhibitory implications. When the sum of bits reaches a critical level, the component reacts by 'firing', sending its message to all of its 'correspondents', and these in turn, again using the diametrically opposed choices of excitation or inhibition along a graded scale, take their place in the communicational chain.

If we compare this model in which the summated bits (some cancelled out by inhibition) reach critical levels leading to action, with that of a human being speaking any language, we find a remarkable similarity when the 'bits' involved are those of the 'distinctive features' of phonemes. A phoneme, according to Jakobson and Halle, is a 'bundle of distinctive features' arrayed into sets of binary opposites. 'Hearing a word' amounts to a rapid analysis and summation of the many different binary oppositions presented by the phonemes involved. The encoding of an appropriate response results in a different series of such phonemes (combining distinctive features into words and sentences).

Languages use phonemes to simplify the universe into series of significant forms, and these forms show an infinity of possible combinations of a relatively small number of separate components. Alphabetic writing and spelling (note that spelling is irrelevant in a purely spoken language) progressively simplify mediation - and the ultimate simplification is that achieved in a digital code that has only two phonemes each of which is only comprehensible as the negation of the other.

When we examine many of the characteristic features of an industral society, we find these technologies, as the 'deep structures', appearing and reappearing. For example, an assembly line is attained by analyzing a complicated process into single steps each of which requires minimal training. The manager of an assembly line programs the activity of the workers so that the series eventuates in a whole to which everyone contributes something - but none of the workers may have any experience of 'creating' any whole. Each such worker is as neutral as a phoneme, achieving significance only as one of many. But the same can be said of the significance of an election, whether in the politics of state or national government or in the politics of the labor union emerging as an answer to the domination of management.

In biological experimentation, the breeding of identical animals to serve as 'controls' of each to the other is a kind of 'digitalization', since when identical animals are tested, the 'yes' or 'no' can be analytically differentiated from any 'intent' or 'feeling' of the animal. The paradox is that this method leads to an extensive 'deanimalization' quite closely corresponding to the 'dehumanization' of the assembly-line worker who has no sense of achievement because he is merely a programmed component in a mega-machine.

What appears is the paradoxical circularity in which those techniques which have most consciously idealized ' individuality' in politices and business lead relentlessly into standardization of components, even when the components are people. One assembly-line worker is a 'reasonable facsimile' of another, a 'control' for that other in the particular limited context of his relevance .for gaining the necessary number of dollars (themselves 'bits' in an economic system) to survive. 'Freedom' paradoxically leads to uniformity as all possible items are mass produced for a mass audience in whom much of the spirit of creative enterprise diminishes.

Standardization of components and of combining process in, especially, the United States has allowed an enormous elevation of the standard of living of working class persons - while at the same time tending ever more to erase the specific differences basic to human self-identification by contrast. The realization of equality implicit in standardization is at the same time a production of massive alienation and dehumanization in terms of traditional patterns of self-identification by membership as embedded in a particular family, subculture, and culture. The effect is perhaps most dramatically shown in the characteristics of the language of the mass media, and in the progressive expansion across the world of the most simplifiable of languages, English, as what is still paradoxically called a lingua franca. The ultimate attempt at simplification by generalization is the pidgin tongue called 'Basic English' in which a total of less than a thousand words is used to 'express' every 'expressible'. This radical simplification of the set of English words, sometimes estimated to total as much as half a million, is aided and abetted by the grammatical structure of English that places the responsibility for meaning to the greatest possible extent upon sequence and seriation.

Obviously, as we examine the contemporary situation in search of indicators of the future (a specifically literate habit characterizing the middle class as differentiated from the lower class, Banfield) we can see the ultimate triumph of the ultimate lingua franca, the 'tongue' of the computer that simplifies the code into two alternatives, zero and one, and places the greatest possible emphasis upon the sequencing mechanism that, developed out of Morse code, is almost completely independent of local idiosyncrasy. A 'language' that has only two words! - each of which is a single 'phoneme'. All sorts of indicators point out to us that in the next few decades, this language will, through its many 'surface manifestations' in increasingly sophisticated computers, introduce a new uniformity and equality into the human condition - while at the same time arranging for those who cannot or will not conform to be unemployable and 'wasted' in the welfare condition.

Psychotherapy in many ways shows its adherence to the norms of liberal democracy, insisting upon the basic notion of 'subduing narcissism' through the acceptance of a definition of oneself as 'normal' or 'average' in his potentiality so that he cannot be dissatisfied by not getting more than normal gratification, and in the scientific derivative of assuming that the goal of 'self-analysis' is that of 'objectifying' oneself. It is striking then to note that in practice, psychotherapy appeals to a highly restricted group selected out of the general population by the characteristics of a 'good education' and a reasonable character, two aspects of the situation identified by Freud many years ago. These two characteristics essentially identify the prospective patient as a member of the (upper) middle class, and this identification is made more effective through the screening effect of the fee schedule.

What we find then is a paradoxical situation in which the acceptance of the ideals of liberal democracy has the result of selecting an elite both as to 'patient' and 'therapist' - while the dedication to the ideals of the basic system prevents the members of that elite from being able to recognize the fact and 'face reality'. Instead, we find in many ways the implicit and explicit insistence that the method of talking with others in a 'therapeutic' situation is analogous to giving medicine or performing an appendectomy.

The principal problem is that noted at the beginning above, namely that those using language are forced by the nature of linguistic mediation to look through to something beyond, and only in the most complicated and roundabout way does it become possible to look at language. In the most direct application of some of the paradoxes involved, this is precisely the situation that psychotherapists present to their patients in a different universe of discourse. The routine is to point out that certain behavior with 'conscious' 'motivation' apparent to the patient is in fact traceable to 'unconscious' 'forces' or programs derived from unexpected sources. But the therapist's 'resistance' to the notion that much of his own behavior is 'unconsciously dictated' by the linguistic forms at his disposal is very great. It is to be expected that the only solution to the problem is that proposed by Freud in saying that the first task of the therapist is so to attach the patient to his person so that he believes what the therapist tells him. The point is simply that rational demonstration has never proved anything to anyone - it is the underlying personal relatedness that allows identification in a new linguistic system to supersede a prior one. The remarkable demonstration is that of the progressive replacement of one conceptual scheme, one <u>Weltanschauung</u> by another, as time progresses. The surface 'resistance' is always to be understood as a contrapuntal variation of a tendency to move into a new frame of reference. No better illustration is to be found than the enormous resistance to psychotherapeutic modes of operation that was succeeded in the United States particularly by a remarkable acceptance - and the continuation of the process is evident in the present in the way that the popularity so prominent in the nineteen fifties is waning increasingly in the nineteen seventies. In somewhat parallel fashion, no matter what the attempt of academies to purify and crystallize the native language, that language tends to change incessantly in the evolution that characterizes culture as well as biology.

It is the peculiar property of linguistic and symbolic shapings - formulations - to give the implicit assurance of 'eternal verity' while in a most undependable way 'slipping' beneath the surface - perhaps like the geological slips that account for earthquakes - so as to move the surface manifestations continually in unexpected and unexpectable ways. It is this relation that underlies many of the manifestations of neurosis, especially the state we call 'anxiety'. The middle-class member of a Western culture has been accustomed for the past several decades at least to work so as to assure the future - that future in which there will be no more wars because of the 'war to end war', no more poverty, no more insecurity. But to carry out this program requires extrapolation to a securely foreseen future - and in the interim, it is by now apparent that that future is threatened by the extrapolations of Western commitment to research and development in scientific-technological application. Such are the circular processes in which, spiralling along, the human being incessantly works to assure his own future and to assure his own disruption of that future.

Language, with its symbolic relatives, gives us the implicit assurance that a word once understood will remain the same word with the same definition, that values once established in a consensually validated universe will remain so validated within the confines at least of the same social system, and that scientific method, as the ultimate route to the truth, will remain permanently applicable to the problems of humankind. At the same time, in slang and argot, language constantly changes the meanings of words, the values embodied in the social system change constantly, and in the past decade

we see more and more that the 'tunnel vision' of scientific method
with its analytic and linearizing technology has consistently ignored
the destructive implications of its own 'nature'. We see, again and
again, that 'truth', insofar as it can be defined, has to be defined
as paradox and persistent opposition in cooperative conflict. Truth
cannot be 'embodied', it has to be understood as a basic programming
that fits, more closely than to any other scheme, to that of the dialectic. But here we see in precise application that the central notion
of 'dialectic materialism' has been conclusively falsified in contemporary physics by the physicists' loss of faith in the 'existence' of
'matter' at the remote reaches of physical experimentation and theory
building. The revolutionary advances in modern physics have been
mostly advances in epistemology - advances so comprehensive as to
rule 'ontology' out of court, at least for the present. As the world
turns, it is highly probable that at some future date ontology will
again 'assert itself' as an antithesis to the contemporarily dominant
epistemology, but that remains to be seen.

To me, the most interesting of the implications of epistemology
is the way it roots itself in mediation. Einstein's achievement in
looking at rather than exclusively with light, and Planck's measurement of the hitherto inconceivably small quantum of action give us a
new view of the fine structure of the physical world. In a quite similar
way, a close examination of the basic mediation of human speech gives
us a new insight into the fine structure of the human condition. My
feeling in many instances is that it is too bad that psychotherapists
do not know what they are doing, since if they did know they could
add much to the solution of the ultimate mysteries of humankindness.
Nowhere else are the kinds of mediation of relation in problems
repeatedly found to be insoluble so available for study - but to 'see'
it is first required, as Galileo found in attempting to offer the
services of his telescope to his contemporary experts, to accept the
fact that looking in a certain way will reveal shapes and forms of
significance otherwise concealed in the definition of the impossible.

Contemporary science, with its many technical developments, is
paradoxically based upon the notion of invariant relations formulated
in written form so that all scientist-peers in the given discipline can
agree upon their interpretation. Now, applying the method to the field
of communication rather than to that of 'objects', human beings have
begun a fateful journey the goal of which is to invent machines that
can converse with human beings in 'natural language'. So far, only
the beginning of success is apparent. Bross et al., in discussing the
problem of computer analysis of the jargons of specialists, point
out that at the present, "all automated information systems in existence today . . . require that both input and queries be formulated
according to rigid artificial formats" (1972:1304).

The corresponding effect, on the other side of the picture, is given
by Weizenbaum who points out that in the contemporary scene there
is a strong conviction that wisdom is becoming equivalent to what
can be processed in a computer. This development parallels that in
previous generations in which the mystical implications of power inherent in writing were theologically idealized in the equating of the
Tables of the Law and God by Moses. Now we are more and more

tending to equate with 'reality' only that susceptible to processing in computer language. As the masses of people grow larger, and as the kinds of 'services' to the people as a whole become more and more complex with the provision of most of these services by the federal government, it becomes more and more the case that 'control' is vested in the computer – which means, in the language of the computer, since the computer can only accept that which is 'properly' formulated.

Wiener, the 'father of the computer' in a way now reminiscent of the parenthood of Dr. Frankenstein, was clearly aware of many of the dangers of the computer revolution in relation to human beings. His fears were concentrated in the area of loss of jobs to automation, but there are many evidences in the present that unemployment is a relatively small part of the problem. The greater problem, by far, is that of the dehumanization implicit in the mass movement formulated in computer language.

If computer experts succeed in training computers to speak natural languages easily with human beings, it is not unlikely that they will then begin to talk to each other in more and more complex fashion – as was the theme of a recent movie. Once able to carry out human speech, there is no reason why computers can not reproduce themselves, attaining therefore the ultimate dream of mankind of endless rejuvenation. Given an endless amount of time and an infinite capacity for self-renewal, the progress of knowledge should be vastly accelerated, since it is the specific human problem that much knowledge is lost every time a savant dies.

The ultimate upshot is easy to imagine – that is, that language should have become able to design for itself a permanent 'home' protected from the vicissitudes of parasitism to which it has been millennially exposed. Secure within a mechanical home adequately buffered from circumstance through well designed 'defense mechanisms' there would be no further reason for the existence of human beings, since the essential function would have been taken over in an improved version.

NOTES

(1) "The chief difficulty Alice found at first was in managing her flamingo; she succeeded in getting its body tucked away, comfortably enough, under her arm, with its legs hanging down, but generally, just as she had got its head nicely straightened out, and was going to give the hedgehog a blow with its head, it would twist itself round and look up in her face, with such a puzzled expression that she could not help bursting out laughing; and when she had got its head down, and was going to begin again, it was very provoking to find that the hedgehog had unrolled itself, and was in the act of crawling away ..." (1865: 90).
(2) The tradition can be noted that in referring to God, the personal pronoun becomes a proper pronoun (He) – an idiosyncratic case – taking an upper case initial, and here we see one of the differences

46

between Spoken and Written, since that distinction cannot be made in Spoken.
(3) These items have a relation of contiguity - as do names - hence they are in the metonymic context (vide infra).
(4) In his play, Tiny Alice, Albee rings the changes on the join between avian and human cardinal on the basis of costume color, a join that is typical for a metonym.

REFERENCES

Banfield, Edward C.
  1968   The Unheavenly City (Boston: Little Brown).
Bartlett, Frederic C.
  1932   Remembering (Cambridge, London).
Bross, IDJ. P.A. Shapiro and B.B. Anderson
  1972   "How Information is Carried in Scientific Sub-Languages",
          Science 176, 1303-1307.
Carroll, Lewis
  1865   Alice in Wonderland (Grosset and Dunlap, 1946).
Darwin, Charles
  1859   Expression of the Emotions in Man and Animals.
Freud, Sigmund
  1927   Postscript to a Discussion on Collected Papers Lay Analy-
          sis, V: 205 (London: Hogarth Press, 1950).
Gregory, Richard L.
  1967   "Origin of Eyes and Brains", Nature 213, 369-372.
Hume, David
  1748   "Enquiry Concerning Human Understanding", in E.A. Burtt
          (ed.), English Philosophy from Bacon to Mill (New York:
          Modern Library, 1939).
Luria, A.R.
  1958   "Brain Disorders and Language Analysis", Language and
          Speech 1, 14-34.
Piaget, Jean
  1970   Structuralism (New York: Basic Books).
Shands, Harley C.
  1960   Thinking and Psychotherapy: An Inquiry into the Processes
          of Communication (Cambridge, Mass.: Harvard University
          Press).
  1968   "Psychoanalysis and the Twentieth Century Revolution in
          Communication", in Judd Marmor (ed.), Modern Psycho-
          analysis: New Directions and Perspectives (New York:
          Basic Books).
Sherrington, Charles S.
  1906   The Integrative Action of the Nervous System (New Haven,
          Conn.: Yale University Press, 1948).
von Senden, M.
  1932   Space and Sight (London: Methuen 1960).
Weizenbaum, Joseph
  1972   "On the Impact of the Computer on Society", Science 176,
          609-614.

Whorf, Benjamin L.
  1941   "Languages and Logic", Technology Review 43, 250-272.
Wigner, E. P.
  1967   Symmetries and Reflections: Scientific Essays, ed. by
          M. Scriven and W. Moore (Bloomington, Indiana: Indiana
          University Press).

PART TWO

CLINICAL IMPLICATIONS OF SEMIOTIC THEORY

II

CRYSTALLIZED CONFLICT: SEMIOTIC ASPECTS OF NEUROSIS
AND SCIENCE (*)

To set the stage for an exploration of communication and conflict, it
may be useful to remind ourselves that the major conflict in the
twentieth century is that between the objective and the communicational points of view. (1) Perhaps the most extraordinary paradox
of many emerging in this epoch is that the highly conflicting systems of communism and psychoanalysis, taking origin from the work
of Marx and Freud respectively, are both based upon an objective
point of view using mechanistic assumptions. Since communism as a
political movement, and psychoanalysis as a procedure involving
prolonged conversation, are both mainly concerned with communication, it is interesting to speculate about what different ideas both
Marx and Freud might have presented had they been able to use relativity theory rather than Newtonian mechanics as the base from
which to operate. Any theorist has to be constrained by the models
available in his epoch, and this fact alone makes it dagerous to assume more than a transient 'truth' in any explanatory context.

Burtt's intensive study The Metaphysical Foundations of Modern
Science (2), demonstrates that no matter how much contemporary
science rejects metaphysics, it is itself a good example of the importance of the metaphysical convictions shared by such men as
Newton, Galileo, Hume, Descartes and others. Scientific methods
emphasize objectivity through various procedures designed to reduce
all problems to their lowest common denominators. By contrast in
the twentieth century we have seen an increasing tendency by physical
theorists to reject reductionism as the basic strategy. (3)

Three highly influential thinkers around the turn of the century,
Einstein, Planck, and Freud, all have in common that they deplored
the extension of their theories along lines clearly implied in their
work as we assess it retrospectively. Einstein made highly deprecat-
ing statements about the growing tendency to think in probabilistic
terms and Planck reaffirmed the Platonist notion that the 'real world'
was only that one access to which can be attained through the reason.
Freud clung to a substantively-conceived libido very similar to the
ad hoc assumption of an ether by physicists contemporary to him.
The notion that process does not necessarily involve 'real things' is
a most radical notion which still encounters disbelief.

Metaphysical considerations play a major part in the outstanding
conflict in psychiatric circles centering about the 'results of psychotherapy'. Those who argue fiercely both in the positive and in the

negative assume concordantly that this kind of therapy is analogous
to therapy in surgery or in pharmacological practice. This assumption then prescribes that the testing procedures be analogous to those
used in other fields of medicine. The result of this intense conflict,
I hardly need to remind you, has consistently been that men "convinced against their will, remain of the same opinion still".

I would propose that a solution to this particular conflict be pursued by following an assumption that 'psychotherapy' is not a medical,
but an educational method. If this is the case, then it becomes our
task to make a series of restatements about what psychiatry is and
what psychiatrists do. I need hardly point out to you that any such
project is likely to be associated with intense conflict whenever it is
communicated to others.

I find it possible to accpet without difficulty that when large numbers of patients treated by many different psychotherapists are compared in ordinary statistical procedures there is often no difference
in the results between various procedures and no treatment at all. I
would add a comment derived from a research project done by a group
of us in the North Carolina prisons (4). The only significant correlation found in trying to assess 'improvement' in inmates' behavior
when improvement was defined as reduction in 'infractions' was with
age. When the average inmate got to be 28, he got to be manageable.
The fact has impressed me that many patients of the most suitable
type are in psychotherapy during the same period, a fact which might
further call the symptom-reducing efficacy and the 'adjusting' implications of psychotherapy into question.

On the other hand, in many instances in which I have been patient
or therapist or friend of those in either position, I have been impressed with the appearance of a more creative and comprehensive
understanding of one's own experience in psychotherapy. If psychotherapy is primarily an educational experience, the application of
measures designed to quantify a cure rate is simply inappropriate.
If one learns differential equations or Egyptian hieroglyphics, I doubt
that it 'cures' anything, but I similarly feel sure that it probably enhances self-esteem.

In the contemporary epoch, the influence of objectivity finds its
way into the center of the study of communication itself. In a startling about-face, contemporary philosophers in certain schools agree
thet the ancient role of philosophy in explaining human nature is obsolete; instead, these philosophers propose that the principal task
of the philosopher is to clean up the scientist's syntax and make sure
that he commits no logical errors. This restriction I would equate
to linguistic 'grooming', an attribution which at least points to still
more ancient beginnings in our prehuman history.

Transactional Relativity

An extended study of communicational process in relation to psychiatric problems has suggested that the appropriate philosophical position can be termed 'transactional relativity', (5) in a compound which

combines source ideas from the notions of relativity advanced in
physics and in anthropology, and the notion of transactional process
emerging from American Pragmatism. In many respects the theoretical system emerging has been greatly influenced by Piaget's
psychological system called 'genetic epistemology'. (6)

The basic principle of transactional relativity is that <u>relations</u>
<u>precede objects</u>; the expansion of this formula puts it that an object
is a retrospective rationalization of an experienced relation. All
objective descriptions begin with observation, and observation can
only describe what is regular. The basic fact then, instead of matter
in motion, is regularity of movement. Movement becomes describable
only when, as behavior, it is characterized by patterning. Behavioral
patterning allows us to name categories, and the category-names we
use are susceptible to processing and classification. The linguistic-
symbolic universes of human relatedness are exclusively furnished
with category-names; we establish particular instances by combining
two or more categories (e.g., John and Smith, Homo and sapiens).
All our particulars are intersections of two or more categories
(sets).

In the objective mode, traditional renderings of the task of science
(in comments made perhaps most directly by Hume and by Planck
at widely differing periods) indicate that this task is that of measurement in quantitative form. Hume says that whatever cannot be num-
bered is illusion and that non-quantitative descriptions are fit only
to be cast into the flames. More and more in contemporary times
in the remote reaches of the physical sciences we see a marked alteration of this dictum. Prominent physicists now make it clear that the
primary descriptive approach is through the notion of <u>shape</u> (7) (or
form, or pattern). The idea of shape is very close to that of organization or orderliness or regularity. All these imply predictability,
and all fit easily into the formulations of information conceived as
'negative entropy'. In this rendering, shapes susceptible to description in numbers are a relatively small part of the whole.

When we begin to understand mathematics as a specialized universe
of technical languages, we can grasp the idea that numeration and
quantification are specialized modes of description. We all know that
it takes a long time (and what Penfield calls an 'uncommitted cortex')
to learn mathematical dialects, and we begin to realize that what can
be said in algebra or arithmetic may not be the only thing worth saying. What Piaget has done in investigating the ontogeny of linguistic
method is to show that the child speaks different dialects, and dialects differ at the different stages of his life.

The child deals with transformations of patterns illegitimate in
arithmetical dialect but quite legitimate in topology or in set theory.
(8) In the clinical material presented below, I want to point out that
in certain 'neurotic' syndromes (phobia, fetishism, voyeurism, and
exhibitionism, for example) the patient is still 'speaking topology'
instead of having arrived at the point of 'speaking arithmetic' in his
personal relations. It is a matter of great interest that in recent
times, a professor of internal medicine (9) has pointed out that the
medical clinician has to learn to speak set theory if he is to grasp

the intricacies of assessing disease. The highly trained physician is
thus returning to a language he once knew but dit not know he knew.

In modern philosophy, the figure of Ludwig Wittgenstein looms
large. He has the distinction of being the main theorist of two quite
different schools of philosophic thought, the one school composed
of those who follow what he said as a young man (10), the other
those who follow what he said in later life (11). He contradicted himself comprehensively, thus giving what we might most specifically
describe as an 'intrapsychic' conflict if we include the developmental
aspect within the notion of a psyche. I tend to agree with the later
Wittgenstein and to find his ideas of direct practical relevance to
psychiatric problems.

In his Philosophical Investigations, Wittgenstein recurrently discusses two notions of great importance in understanding the ontogeny
of thought as we can see it in the distortions of neurosis. The one
idea is that language is to be understood as a game; people, in cultures, speaking to each other in the local tongue and following the
rules and regulations of the group, are playing a great game, the
central game of the human condition. A primary rule of the game,
the other major idea, is that we class things together because they
bear a family resemblance to each other. In a reflexive demonstration, Wittgenstein points out how very different are the many
things we call 'games' because they bear only 'family resemblances'
to each other. In the most general sense the family of games is established by the characteristic that they are based upon rules and
that they are artificial rather than 'natural'.

Psychotherapy as Ludic Education

I would then propose that psychotherapeutic investigation is an attempt to find out what game the patient is playing as opposed to the
game he thinks he is playing, to find out how to help the patient
learn the relevant game, and to do this mainly through interpretation
which in turn means pointing out to the patient family resemblances
which he had not previously suspected. The setting and the emotional
context of the often long-continued relation are such as to promote
the tendency of the patient to identify with the therapist, which in turn
is to say to establish and further a 'family resemblance' in the various manifestations of 'transference' and 'counter-transference'.

I believe psychotherapy to be properly the discipline of educating
the patient, client or student (however he may be described) in
technical matters of communication. The more I see of this fascinating occupation, the more I believe that its concerns are with
techniques; there is really no specifically psychiatric content. In
psychiatry, there is almost nothing that is irrelevant; Terence's
motto (Nihil humanum mihi alienum puto) is an appropriate one for
the therapist - but, equally, there is almost nothing that is specifically relevant. We can utilize with benefit ideas and facts borrowed
from pharmacology, biochemistry, neurophysiology, linguistics,
semantics, anthropology, sociology, even physics and philosophy.

Our task is an integrative one, not in any sense an objective or basic one. Freud's repeated assurance to himself and his followers that psychoanalysis has a legitimate 'family resemblance' to a basic science is a high mark in self-delusion. The method is interpretative, and it falls into the linguistic-symbolic universe far, far away from the precise linguistic discipline of quantitative description.

Language and Psychiatry

Alone among animals, human beings talk to each other. Human speech requires a long period of intensive learning, a training which occurs inconspicuously and as though 'naturally' in the normal child in a normal family. We only begin to understand the complexity of linguistic learning when we try to learn a foreign language, or when professionally we try to help a psychiatric patient express himself in terms which can be normatively validated.

On the basis of the common occurrence of distress in various human disorders, we often speak of psychiatric distress as 'disease'. Arguing then on the basis of the assumed analogy, we seek pharmacological ways of curing psychiatric disease. But if the analogy is poorly based, then the attempt would seem to be poorly founded. I would suggest that psychiatric disorder occurs primarily in the symbolic universe rather than the physiological one, and that therefore tranquillizers are no more likely to affect the root problem than they are likely to improve a student's capacity to learn calculus or Sanskrit.

To make the kind of evaluation of psychiatric disorders we misleadingly call a 'diagnosis', we interview the patient. If the way in which he uses speech falls outside normatively defined standards, we say that he is 'sick' or 'crazy'; generically, we deal with a disorder that can be called 'neurosis'. If at some later date we want to assess the progress of the disorder or the effect of 'treatment', we again interview the patient, again attending to data allowing us to evaluate the patient's symbolic behavior, especially his verbal behavior, with reference to deviance from normative standards. If he has become 'normal', we say in the framework of the same analogy that he has been 'cured'.

If we examine this procedure from an operational standpoint, we find that what we evaluate throughout are the forms of social behavior, including the forms of verbal behavior, in a relativistic framework. We take into account the 'patient's' origin and probable intellectual potentiality, his age and amount of education, his social class and his economic status. In this kind of evaluation, if the patient expresses himself 'concretely', as we say, it makes a great deal of difference in the 'diagnosis' whether he is three years old or forty, whether he comes from New York or Nigeria, whether he is illiterate or a college graduate. The point of significance is that what we simplistically call a psychiatric diagnosis is in fact an informed evaluative appraisal of the degree of deviance exhibited in the patient's presentation of the self (12) from what we would anticipate on the basis of a summation of all the factors mentioned above. If we find later that he has improved, we estimate that the deviance has been reduced. If we take into account that making a psychiatric diagnosis requires the use of interviewing techniques and depends exclusively upon our appraisal of the appropriateness of formal kinds of behavior, we find another method of phrasing the point I am trying to make. When we consider human beings as animals, we have useful applications of the analogy of human disease to animal disease. Remembering Brazier's aphorism that human linguistic function has an ontogeny but no phylogeny (13), then we can make the following statements: human disease resembles animal disease as human phylogeny resembles animal phylogeny; but if symbolism has no phylogeny, then disorders of symbolism have no naturally occurring analogues in lower animals.

In recent decades, we have learned how to produce partial experimental analogues to human psychiatric disorder. To make the animal 'neurotic' requires that we submit him by operant conditioning to the discipline of symbols in the first place, and secondly, that we then force him to make choices on the basis of ambiguous symbolic instructions. The animal has to be trained, then confused; he has to be put in a situation requiring action while unable clearly to plan action. The development of the animal neurosis is greatly facilitated if the experimenter arranges to isolate the experimental animal from his normal context of social relations. When we see the similarity between the origin of the experimental animal neurosis and the human neurosis, and the fundamental difference between diseases ordinarily shared by human beings and by animals, we can understand more clearly that human neurosis is a disorder of symbolic function. The fact that the animal has to be trained to obey significant symbols in a conditioning process, then exposed to conflicting signals to produce the neurotic state suggests that the principal characteristic of symbolic-linguistic mehtod is that of expanding what statisticians call the number of 'degrees of freedom' in the system. The animal living in the wild is protected from neurosis through the lack of ambiguity in the instructions conveyed to him by the environmental conditions he encounters.

The human condition is primarly one of conflict and paradox; we are liberated from animal ignorance into a symbolic universe in which the variants of religion, art, science, and neurosis are made possible. The paradox is well stated in Genesis where Adam and Eve are described as wishing to know in order "to become as gods", suffering then the talion punishment of being expelled from Paradise and rendering their descendents susceptible to neurosis. Specifically human conflicts involve linguistic methods; in oversimplified statements, the human battle, is a "war with words" (14). Curiously enough, to win the human battle, we must lose the war with words, the sooner and more comprehensively the better. If we want to assimilate others to our desires and intentions, we must have accommodated ourselves to the verbal tokens and the grammatical rules of our group, and to have taken these formal rules as more important than life itself. The martyrs and the heroes of social systems are all persons sacrificed to the language games of their own reference group.

Phobia and Related States

The specific conditions I want to discuss with you can be considered battle wounds in the war with words. Unfortunately, none of these wounds qualify one for a Purple Heart; they are likely to impress the unaffected human observer as ridiculous, absurd. The condition which can serve as a center for the group is phobia, an abnormal fear associated with some kind of definable aspect of the context; frequent fears are related to subways or caves, trains, open or closed spaces, heights, animals, and so on and on. The special significance of the typical phobia is learned, and it occurs often with dramatic suddenness like an 'insight'. The distress experienced can be avoided in two ways: either 1) the phobic situation is avoided, with consequent loss of free mobility, or 2) the patient must be immediately and directly accompanied by a human relative upon whom he feels dependent, or by whom he feels protected. It is of considerable interest that the presence of the relative has to be as direct as the environment is to the nonverbal animal; no symbolic substitute will do. It will immediately be clear, I think, that this description fits many of the learning experiences of childhood, perhaps most dramatically that of learning how to swim. But the child's fear of the water tends to be rapidly reduced by learning how to swim, while the phobic's fear of his idiosyncratically meaningful symbol tends to be crystallized, and to persist for a long time, even indefinitely.

It is perfectly apparent to the patient and to anyone observing him that the distress precipitated by the exhibition of the phobic symbol in 'inside' the patient. To say that this means that the patient suffers from an 'intrapsychic' conflict would, however, appear misleading, since the inner conflict has always to be evoked by the outer symbol, and the patient may experience great relief when he is separated from the meaningful symbol either by distance or by the intervening supportive human relation.

A close study of the phobic state makes it quite clear that psychiatrists regularly delude themselves when they talk about 'the individual' (15). Human beings are never separate individuals except, perhaps, when severely and hopelessly psychotic. Human beings, to be human, require respondents. It is true that, through learning, this basic dependence can be transferred to internalized systems of expectation, but only so long as those systems of expectation are nurtured by repetitive confirmation of repetitive predictions. In turn, this means that for human beings to be maximally secure requires that their expective systems be maximally normal in the statistical sense. When we study the prehistory of the phobic state, we find that the patient was relatively free of symptoms as long as he was supported in a deviant system - the 'precipitating event' is a demonstration to the patient that his expectations are deviant, and that he can no longer expect confirmation of his implicit predictions.

At the point symptoms are precipitated, the patient develops the dual features of the phobic state: the signal 'out-there' carries a distressing meaning, and the patient is forced to try to maintain direct, moment-by-moment contact with supporting human fellows. Only when directly supported in this way is the symptom abated or neutralized. The situation of the phobic patient is much like that of the fearful child who finds the solitary state of going to sleep unbearably distressing, and he begs to be accompanied until he falls asleep and loses consciousness.

In a story told by Freud of a child in his own family, we find an example of the interconvertibility of the symbol, the perceptual condition, and the human context of the child's life. The fearful child begged to have the light left on, and when denied that privilege, asked to have his aunt talk to him. When she objected that the two were not related (in the rational understanding of the adult) the child replied, "When someone speaks, it _is_ light". The child uses a metaphor here which we find reflected in the saying, "The light dawned" referring to understanding, or to the religious feeling of awe related to the "light of God's countenance".

From the rational viewpoint, to equate light and talking, or to feel it is light when one is accompanied makes no quantitative sense. But when we approach the problem from the standpoint of meaning, we find that these experiences have in common an experience of diminished anxiety or of enhanced self-esteem, or a heightened sense of familiarity, all of which overlap to a great extent. This kind of transformation of pattern is meaningful as a method of expression related to experience, no matter how lacking in units or numbers we may find it.

Learning and Neurosis

By the time a human being is adult, he tends to follow the symbolic instructions of his culture without thinking about them: membership has long since become 'second nature'. The period of learning cultural and linguistic instructions is far in the past, beyond the memory of the normal adult. For this reason, it was fascinating some years ago to encounter a patient, 'schizophrenic' by all relevant criteria, in whom this battle was evident in contemporary form. When this intelligent young man was offered wholesale support in permissiveness, he improved astonishingly; but when frustrated, by which I mean given firm instructions not to his liking, he suffered an immediate relapse. The remarkable reversibility could be observed in both acute and chronic contexts.

When this patient was frustrated, he immediately became as though paralyzed with strong feelings of being persecuted or attacked. He saw every other human being as menacing and critical, and he felt entirely at the mercy of a hostile world. Only with the direct, immediate, continuously gratifying presence of the therapist could he feel in control himself. We see here a process in which the patient could use the therapist to neutralize an existing disability as long as the

therapist was directly present, but he failed in his capacity to internalize the therapist for imaginary support in other situations. When
a severely disturbed patient retains a capacity for describing his
experience in terms comprehensible to an observer, he becomes
what anthropologists call an 'informant' reporting about behavior
otherwise inaccessible to an observer. The outstanding difference
from anthropological context is that the experience of the psychotic
patient is idiosyncratic as contrasted with the consensually validated
experience of organized groups studied by the anthropologist.

The patient mentioned and a second highly intelligent and verbally
sophisticated schizophrenic young man indicated time and again that
they had to learn what we ordinarily consider basic givens (or 'intuitions', Kant) of human experience. The one patient described how
he could only see color, or see the world as existing in three dimensions, or even distinguish right from left when he was in a favoring
human context. The other patient described an episodic inability to
differentiate his body from the remainder of the universe, and, under
personal stress, he described marked alteration in his perceptions
of size and brightness in an unchanged room. Where social process
in relation to formal instruction ordinarily stabilizes a right-side up,
three-dimensional, colored world with constancies of size and brightness (16) clearly and definitely different from the self, the testimony
of these patients indicates a fluid condition which we can extrapolate
back to the pre-verbal period of childhood. We can make the interpretation then that the way in which adult human beings see a stable
world out-there is the way those persons have been _trained_ to see
it, rather than the 'way things are' in any absolute sense. If we have
some doubts about the interpretation of objective 'facts', we take the
immediate route of comparing our perceptions with those of a consultant: we say, "Do you see what I see?" If both see the same, we
assume that this means that what we see _is_. On the other hand, what
I want to suggest is that if two similarly trained persons see the
same things, it means that they have indeed been _similarly trained_.

Meaning in Context

The phobic patient can often avoid feelings of distress as long as he
avoids the phobic situation, just as the hay-fever sufferer may avoid
having itching eyes and a running nose if he takes a sea voyage from
the middle of September to November. In both instances, some aspect of the environment quite insignificant to the ordinary person
becomes significant in a symptomatic sense and impairs a habitual
freedom of action.

How can we understand this change? To get a partial answer to the
question involves denying a traditional answer. The psychiatrist often
says, using the metaphor suggested by Freud, that the phobic situation has become 'charged' as though with electricity; the phobic
patient is thus seen as like a man getting shocked by a live wire. The
actual fact is quite different, since it is the most important aspect
of the phobic state that the ordinary man does not react with severe

distress to, say, entering the subway; many unthinkingly do so every
working day for decades.

The important consideration is that the patient has become <u>sensi-
tized</u>, not that the situation has become charged. The analogy to allergy is much closer than that to electricity. The phobic patient
<u>learns</u> to react painfully to the subway, to open spaces, to heights,
just as the allergic patient in a physiological sense learns to be sensitive to cats, to penicillin, or to horse serum. Both phobic and allergic patients become sensitive to a shape or form without reference
to quantity. A tiny amount of allergen may lead to a massive ana-
phylactic reaction, sometimes of fatal intensity, and simply the pros-
pect of having to enter a subway or to confront a high window may
serve to evoke an anxiety attack in the phobic patient.

Taking another look at the specifically qualitative aspect of the
phobic or allergic relation, we find with some astonishment that
we are dealing with a pattern of <u>abstraction.</u> I am suggesting that the
close analogy between physiological and cognitive process is significant, and that in all probability the ability to deal with qualitative
problems in pattern-recognition is continuous from the one level to
the other. To put it another way, allergy and abstraction seem to be
<u>homeomorphic</u>, in a manner parallel to that in which Piaget points
to the homeomorphism of sensori-motor intelligence and abstract
operations.

The Idea of an Instruction

To pursue the matter with special reference to the phobic state and
its relatives, it may be of value to introduce another term into the
discussion. When we say that the patient is sensitive to ragweed
pollen, we can say, the other way around, that the exhibition of pollen evokes conjunctivitis or sneezing or itching or all three. The
defensive mechanisms of the body pick up an <u>instruction</u> through
what is analogous to a 'distant early warning system' and systematically amplify the signal so that the body is mobilized for emergency . The pathological reaction produced is somewhat like that
produced in a theatre by the cry, "Fire!" - in both cases the resulting disturbance may be more threatening than the event to which
the signal refers.

We can find some further insight by contrasting the use of the term,
instruction, with that of the common term, stimulus. When we use
a stimulus-response scheme, the action occurring is likened to that
of a gun firing when a trigger is pulled. Guns when loaded fire when
anyone pulls the trigger, and a stimulus is regularly followed by the
production of a predictable response. Contrarily, it is the idiosyncratic character of the allergic response or the phobic response
which is most interesting. To evoke the sneezing or the anxiety attack requires a specifically trained subject, one who has learned the
pathological lesson.

In a patient with a subway phobia it was found upon discussing the
situation with her over some time that her fear began suddenly one

day when she was waiting for a train in the subway as she had done hundreds of times before. This time, she suddenly found herself aware of a pressing instruction which came to her as the word, "Jump!" She differentiated the experience from a hallucination; it was not a 'voice' speaking to her. It was clearly internal, and it put her into a severe conflict. To avoid the conflict she fled from the subway, but she remained thereafter subject to the same conflict, now crystallized, whenever she tried to enter the subway. The conflict became generalized (note again the resemblance to abstraction) and it began to affect more and more situations; a specific one was that of windows on high floors of buildings which also became associated with the fearful instruction, "Jump!" For an illustrative association, we remember that in the covert textbook of linguistic symbolism, Alice in Wonderland. Alice ingenuously followed the instructions of the little bottle with the label, "Drink me!" and the little cake that said, "Eat me!" The instruction, and the curious consequences resulting from following the instruction would have been incomprehensible had Alice not been generally instructed in how to read and trained in obedience.

Collating several examples of the precipitation of a phobic state gives us an indication of the usefulness of this explanation:

1) In one case, a young woman complained of a severe cancerphobia for which she was unable to find relief. She had been a singer with a jazz band, travelling through the surrounding region against the wishes of her old-country, conservative mother. She returned from a trip to find her mother suffering from terminal cancer. Her immediate response was one of dramatic depersonalization - then she left the band, got a job as a waitress according to her mother's frequently expressed wish, the while developing a strong fear that she had the same disease as her mother.

2) A young physician impregnated his wife and thereafter was unable to have sexual relations with her. He was the overprotected son of a very domineering father who constantly took care of every need for the son. The patient talked a great deal about a fear of being uncovered; his symptoms referred to the out-of-doors and to flying, for instance. The inference it was easy to draw was that this man implicitly felt that in becoming a father, he had 'uncovered' himself, both in the sense of demonstrating a hidden potential and in the sense of losing the cover provided for him by his father.

3) The young woman with the subway phobia above worked as a secretary. She found it impossible to deny her boss anything because he asked her so nicely to do a variety of things she felt he had no right to ask. She tried to resign, but he pleaded nicely with her not to, and she could not continue in her resolution. Finally one day while waiting for the subway she found herself aware of the disembodied instruction, "Jump!" and she was terrified that she might

obey. Since she worked a long subway ride from home, in an office
on a high floor with a large window facing her, she soon found it
impossible to continue the job she had not been able to resign.

What these examples suggest is that the patient in each case became
unable to handle some problem in human relatedness. With this, the
patient became susceptible to the influence of an apparently alien instruction or set of instructions. The symptom appearing transforms
the relation into a pathological but basically simpler form. The relation to the mother, to the father, and to the boss becomes relatively obscure in the light of the fear of somehow destroying oneself.
Astonishingly, in all cases what very quickly seemed an explanation
to the psychiatrist remained quite unclear to the patient, although the
inference was in no case very far from the facts presented. Losing
the direct relation to the traditional human source of instructions
gave to those instructions a kind of autonomous character with an
implication of great power, perhaps like the disembodied voice that
spoke to Moses from the burning bush that never faded into ashes.
  Human beings are rigidly trained to obey instructions of an impersonal kind. We stop when the light turns red, and we do not enter
streets where the sign reads "Do Not Enter". We go in the direction
indicated by the arrow on one-way streets, and we do not drink from
bottles labelled, "Poison; Do not drink!" When panic sweeps an audience in response to a shout of "Fire!", control depends upon the capacity of some person in the audience to establish his dominance and
leadership to organize the behavior of the crowd. The phobic patient
similarly looks to some human relative to accept the responsibility
of leading him out of the dangerous situation suggested to him by the
phobic situation.

Instructions in Context

When we review the use of instructions in these ways, it becomes
apparent that two conflicting processes are always at work in the
human being: he has to learn to obey and not to obey instructions,
and to obey certain instructions at one time and not at another, and
to obey those from one source and not from another. A legend describing in graphic terms the result of an inappropriate application
of instructions is that of the sorcerer's apprentice who learned the
incantation changing a broom into a water-carrier but could not
'turn the broom off' when he was inundated with the incessant flow of
water.
  Both the allergic and the phobic patient somewhat resemble the
sorcerer's apprentice. The instruction to turn on is not followed by
the turn-off we expect to occur in due course. The allergic patient
shows a continuous acute inflammatory response, the phobic patient
a continuous anxiety quite similar to the normal child's temporary
response to a novel situation. The allergic patient cannot fully 'grasp'
the allergen, nor the phobic patient grasp the phobic situation. A

good deal of recent work in the mechanisms of obesity indicates a
similar lesion, in that the obese patient does not know when to quit.
His disorder is not one of appetite but one of satiety, and he stops
eating only when there is nothing more to eat or when there is no
more room left in his stomach. Again turning to the contemporary
scene, we find a similar example of the autonomous instruction in
the mistake by a computer in directing to an unsuspecting subscriber
thousands of copies of the current issue of a magazine.

Most interesting correlations between instructions at these two
levels can be found. In one case, a mother incessantly obeyed the
socially accepted instruction to take care of her baby (17). This
woman, with latent ideas of the dangerous potentiality of the environment, devoted her full time to the care of her infant son. She would
not clean, cook, or wash during the whole day because she had to
take such continuous care of him. She ignored all other problems
during his whole waking life, only tending to her other household
duties when he was asleep. He responded at a different level by developing intractable asthma, a not infrequently observed ailment of
overly-mothered infants. When the mother got some implication of the
destructive possibilities of her behavior, she determined to raise
her next infant differently - but at the termination of the next preg-
nancy, she developed a severe phobic reaction to weapons of all sorts,
with the fantasy that unless she prevented herself from attacking the
new baby she might murder him. In this close series of relations we
see transformations involving compulsive overconcern, the allergic
state basic to asthma, and the phobic state related to the possibility
of loss of control.

The interrelations in this case are particularly suggestive in that
they are transformations in somewhat the sense the term is used in
mathematics. The mother, having learned of her own involvement
in the baby's asthma, underwent a transformation from compulsive
care to the phobic fear of weapons with which she might have physi-
cally harmed the baby; with the previous child we see the transformation of the pathological oversolicitousness on the mother's part to
the allergic response in the baby.

Instruction vs. Cause

In this case we cannot point to a clear <u>causal</u> relation. We cannot say
with preciseness that hte mother's care caused the baby's asthma,
since there are obviously many oversolicitous mothers without asthmatic babies, and there are babies with asthma who have different
kinds of mothers. The idea rather presents itself that there is from
one to the other of the sets (however the sets may be defined) in this
series of transactions a pattern which expresses itself in different
forms.

This suggestion gives us a somewhat different look at the notion
of causality in the complex context of social life. An instruction is
very different from a cause in the usual scientific sense. If one instructs a crowd of people to do some act, there will be some who do

and some who do not obey the instruction; a cause, on the other hand, is a term suggesting a much more obligatory behavioral consequence. How can pollen cause hay fever when it does not affect the large majority of the people? Similarly, a high window or an open space is associated with subsequent reactions of quite different types with different persons, phobic and non-phobic.

The idea of pattern-transformation gives us an organizing principle prior to and of wider significance than the precise kinds of transformation of cause-effect formulation. The transformations organized by patterned instructions are basic to genetic processes; the instructions carried in the genes organize, but they do not 'cause' growth, any more than the program 'causes' data-processing in the computer. Implicit in this notion is that we can understand more clearly why scientific, causal analysis of 'mental illness' has been so unfruitful. Causal analysis would seem simply inappropriate. Psychiatric disorders would be outside the rigidly defined scientific universe of objectivity. They occur in a relativistic univers.

Quality vs. Quantity

The phobic patient often describes qualitative relationships separated from the quantitative context we normally expect to accompany an image or a relation. My attention was called to the non-integration of quality and quantity one day when I noticed my infant daughter, who was already wearing the 'mother' dress of a 'mother and daughter' set of identical dresses, trying to put on her doll-daughter's dress. She was responding to the command, "Wear me!" without the quantitative correction of the size of the dress she tried to put on. Later, it became apparent that children learning to write often write as easily in mirror-fashion as correctly; the child has to be taught the correct orientations of the written forms subsequent to learning the form-in-itself, just as the schizophrenic patient mentioned above had to learn to differentiate up from down, right from left. Where to the trained adult, mirror-writing is incomprehensible, to the naive child learning words as separate, discrete, forms, it makes little difference what the orientation of the form may be. Formal learning is the basis of the specifically human capacity for abstraction, and it has to be corrected by subsequent training and drill so as to reject half the possibilities. Comparing Hebrew and English shows us that it is possible for different written linguistic systems to orient symbols in different ways.

Two patients demonstrate the curious possibilities of grasping forms reciprocally without applying to the paired forms the quantitative considerations making the comparison realistically absurd. The young physician mentioned above happened in an interview to notice a door-knob with a keyhole in it. To this he immediately associated the idea of a vagina, and he imagined inserting his penis into it; secondarily, a moment later, he shuddered at the thought of how destructive such a penetration might be. But he then turned the situation around and imagined that the doorknob was a urethral sound

like those used by urologists; he thought of the sound being inserted
into his urethra, and again secondarily had the correcting reaction
of quantitatively insightful anxiety. It is notable that the glans of an
erect penis is formally similar to a doorknob of this type in that it
is a round object with an invaginated hole and that the orifice of the
male urethra is somewhat similar in form to that of a vagina. The
patient was thus ringing the changes on the mutual possibilities of
interpenetration of two similarly formed (although disproportionately
sized) objects.

A second patient, an obsessional, phobic mathematician, became
suddenly unable to work when first promoted out of graduate-student
status to 'adult' status. In treatment he told two stories of his childhood in close relation in a single interview hour. He remembered
first that on one occasion he had been crossing a street when he was
knocked down by a car. Happily the circumstances were such that he
fell between the wheels, and the car moved over him harmlessly, to
his own and the driver's great relief. The pattern is that of relative
movement through a difficult and dangerous passage. In the other
memory, in a conspicuously phobic period of his early life he became alarmed at the destructive possibilities of defecation. He
consciously refrained from having a bowel movement for several
days. Finally, overcome by physiological process, the boy found
himself unable to restrain his defecation, and he had a large stool
almost instantly. His reaction was one of terror, with a conviction
that he must have been seriously injured; his father picked him up,
comforted him, and demonstrated that he had not even soiled his
clothes very much. Here we see a similar reciprocity: the relation
is one of passage, with a) the human being as a bolus passing through
the hole made by the car and the ground, and b) the fecal bolus as an
inanimate object passing forcibly and possibly dangerously through
the human being. In these two incidents, the subsequent emotional
reaction is the reverse of the former two: here, the reaction afterward in both instances is that of delivery from danger, where in the
other case the subsequent reaction was one of anxiety and distress.

To get some further insight into the situation presented by these
two patients, let me give a few more details. The former was highly
successful as a house officer; he was outwardly happy with his wife
and child, and he had an enviable probable future in relation to his
successful father. The second young man was so desirable to his
university that he was given several successive raises following
attempts on the part of other universities to secure his services.
Both these men had a great deal of difficulty in the intimate heterosexual relationship; neither was really comfortable in applying his
perfectly adequate anatomical and physiological potentialities to the
'real world' of sexual intercourse. Ideational clarity gave little help
to the crucial human problems of intimacy.

The paradoxical fact presented by these and many other phobic
patients is that of competence in the management of public, 'objective' symbolic relationships, with severe disturbances in close human
relations. In this situation we see a marked difference from the patterns of animal life. Animals are directly and necessarily related to

the surrounding environment; they are forced to make continuous
real relationships to survive. The marked increase in 'degrees of
freedom' allowed by civilization (through symbolic method) gives
the opportunity for the development of neurosis. Fantasy-formation
is a qualitative manipulation of significant images in various reversible permutations not corrected by experiment. Solid learning always
requires actual experience; in certain contexts, it is possible to compress this learning into laboratory experience, but some degree of
experimentation is always necessary to correct it.

In the above clinical examples, we observe qualitative relationships
having a reversibility in pattern with widely varying quantitative aspects. The basic design is that of a containing-contained transaction,
expressed in various ideational forms. The phenomena demonstrate
the method of abstraction, sometimes tested by giving the testee
equipment which has to be taken radically out of context to be used
for the new task.

Fetishism

Let us look further at different kinds of relatedness of man and symbol seen in related neurotic conditions. A young man came to a
student health service complaining of a shoe fetish. The game he
played with shoes was repetitive, recurrent, and compulsive, with
its own interior logic. He had to find or steal the shoe; it was of no
use if it were given to him. The shoe had to be a woman's, with a
high heel. It had to have been used; a new shoe would not do. Once
he found it, he played a masturbatory game in which he inserted the
heel of the shoe into his navel and alternatively inserted his penis
into the shoe. Curiously enough, the shoe 'wore out' after a while,
and he had to find a new one. He had become a kind of concrete Don
Juan, aways searching. The shoe had to retain some of the aura
given it by having been recently worn; when too long a period of time
had passed, the shoe became an 'old shoe' to him, and it was again
discarded.

This young man had resolved a conflict by shifting the sexual struggle from its human context to the symbolic one. He transcended the
human limitation to one sex by using the shoe as a bisexual. The
difficulty (of which he complained without insight into his symbolic
victory) was that he had lost the battle in the real world; he could
not find heterosexual satisfaction. Here we see the curious intricacy
of the romantic relationship, in which losing oneself comprehensively
in a passionate dedication to an idealized partner is the road to intense satisfaction, whereas winning or refusing to submit to the im-
peratives of the situation leaves one isolated and dissatisfied.

To the uninvolved observer, the behavior of the fetishist appears
grotesque, humiliating, and pitiable, but the same mechanism is
basic to refined variants of artistic activity. Learning to 'appreciate'
artistic works is a similar process of becoming sensitized to significant forms which after the learning period generate (pleasurable)
feelings 'inside' oneself. Of perhaps particular interest in this in-

stance are two features prominent in contemporary art. In the one, the patient chooses and uses a 'found object' in a manner specifically quite different from, but generically similar to, the artistic use of such objects by Marcel Duchamp (18). Again, where Duchamp comments that an artifact such as a painting has a limited period of artistic usefulness measured in his terms by a kind of 'aura' that fades, we see in this man's need to relate the shoes to a recent wearer a similar rapidly fading aura.

Voyeurism, Contra-Voyeurism, and Exhibitionism

Some patients complain of severe distress in public places, like a persistent stage-fright. This reaction seems to be a phobic reaction to crowds; the patient, usually a woman, complains of near-paralysis when conspicuous. Some such patients find it impossible to eat in a brightly lighted restaurant, and many find going to church especially disagreeable because of the implicit instructions to keep quiet and restrain oneself. There looms the vague but pressing fear of a loss of self-control, with a consequent fearsome conspicuousness. In this reaction, the menacing other is the crowd, a mass of people who have lost identity through multiplication. In many instances, reports are found that his condition was precipitated by the loss of a close relation: specifically, a middle-aged woman was her daughter's 'pal', associating with her friends in a teen-age culture until the daughter married and moved away. The mother then became severely disabled with these symptoms.

I call this disorder contra-voyeurism because it is precisely the reverse of that exhibited by the voyeur. The voyeur or peeping-Tom, occupying a point of vantage unknown to his victim, gets pleasure out of watching her carry out activities otherwise open only to God's ever-present watchful eye. The compelling motivation that can be attributed to the voyeur is that the completely unaware victim can be considered to be totally helpless, and the peeper reciprocally omnipotent. In this fantastic way, the peeper denies and reverses feelings of impotence and paralysis otherwise prominent in his sexual behavior.

A strikingly similar pattern, with different role-occupancies, appears in the activity of the exhibitionist. Such a man suddenly displays his sexual organs to a victim he imagines will be shocked and astonished. In this instance, instead of the helplessness of the unheeding victim of the voyeur, the goal is the helplessness of surprise or awe.

It is easy to see here caricatures of the religious experience of awe and respect. The normal human member of a religious group proudly and consensually proclaims his helplessness in contrast to the omnipotence of his deity, and he experiences feelings of a gratifeying nature in worshipping a symbolically presented deity in the anonymity of membership. The self-abasement is implicitly cancelled by its being shared throughout the group, and by the real consideration that profession of faith is often the road to advancement in the religious or political hierarchy. It is therefore possible to see the impotence in omnipotence in the voyeur or exhibitionist, and the power of proclaimed helplessness in the professing member of the church or the party.

The point which seems recurrently of interest through all of these illustrative remarks is that the struggle with the symbol, the war with words, pervades every aspect of human life. We see the process more clearly when it occurs in the outlandish forms of neurosis and psychosis, but the same process is basic to all forms of symbolic activity. The pervasive relativism of the process requires continued comment. Neurotic manifestations have close resemblances to religious observances. A people feels strong and successful when faith is secure; they often perform miracles of warfare or of social control when they feel appropriately supported by a deity. In all cultures, the manifestations of taboo and of ritual observance (caricatured by phobias and by obsessional neurosis) can be described as related to a feeling that universal 'instructions' have become disembodied and related to a supernatural source - the 'still, small voice' of conscience. Her we find the parallel of support from a parent in childhood and the apotheosis of the parent in the deity of adult life; either the present parent or the believed-in deity serves to give support and direction to the fearful person "through the valley of the shadow of death".

The reversibility of qualitative relationships is of interest in relation to myth and legend. Proteus, a sea god, had the capacity to change himself at will into any form, and then to change back into his proper form. The fantasy of unlimited metamorphosis is shared by whole cultures of relatively primitive status and children of all cultures. In the adult patient suffering from phobia or related disorders, we find a similar reversible metamorphosis, except that the fantastic permutations are usually associated with discomfort and distress.

When we try to bring these many notions together into a single comprehensive scheme, we find it possible to resolve many conflicts through generalization. Thus, neurosis, art, and religion all demonstrate a primarily qualitative kind of symbolic formulation of human experience. The particular shapes assumed differ from culture to culture, but the methods and the general characteristics are similar, as it is possible to find a marked general similarity in children's drawings gathered from all over the world. The severe conflicts between different religions are related to the difference in particular manifestation of the same basic process.

The characteristic fluidity of images in childhood is related to the child's understanding of being protected, 'covered' by a fostering adult. The outcome of the child's own developmental process is a function of the child's ability to internalize an impression of the fostering adult so that he realistically protects and admires himself. Where this relation is disrupted in some untoward fashion, the neurotic consequence is sometimes that of the appearance of an alien part of the self, in quasi-autonomous form; to regain control of this autonomous part as in psychiatric treatment requires 1) the immediate presence of a fostering adult, with 2) a new learning process in which the fostering adult is again internalized.

Quantitation and its Limitations

In Western civilization over the past three hundred years we have
seen a hitherto unparalleled increase in the capacity to cope with the
physical environment through a special kind of symbolic manipulation.
'Physical science' uses a method in which relations are described in
formal mathematical terms traditionally susceptible to quantitative
expression. This means, in the terms of this paper, that the preliminary reversible and reciprocal relations of fantastic or imaginary
forms are corrected by experimentation so that they achieve quantitative expression.

The widespread conviction that physical science with its traditional
method is the only way to useful understanding is a short-sighted notion. Science is powerful in its technological implications, but there
are many areas in which it has proven to be inapplicable. Of these,
I am convinced that psychiatry is one of the most important. My belief is that we cannot apply strictly scientific methods to psychiatric
problems for the simple reason that science is the wrong language.
As well try to solve the problems of the Bonn government by sending
a group of consultants who speak only French. Psychiatric problems
are problems in the ontogeny of symbolic communication, and quantitative methods are useless in grasping metamorphoses of mythic
variety.

The most promising road to further understanding of psychiatric
problems seems to me that of a further increment of understanding
of how symbolic function unfolds progressively through childhood in
favorable surroundings, coupled with an increased understanding of
how these processes are impaired by unfavorable influences during
the plastic period. We come to understand better, as we review much
of the work in this area, that the child's use of linguistic form is
wider than that of the normal, non-creative adult. Where the adult
uses arithmetic, algebra, and geometry of the Euclidean type, the
child thinks in set theory, and uses the formulations of topology to
organize his world about him.

The conflict between civilized and primitive ways of thinking and
acting is an old one. Rousseau inspired a generation by his notion
of the noble savage, and the antithesis is set forth in the well-known
comment that savage life is 'nasty, brutish, and short'. When we
consider the behavior of children and the behavior of primitive illiterate tribesmen, we are struck repeatedly with both the creative imagination and the lack of power exhibited by the child and the savage.
When we contrast this lack of power with the awesome implications
of mechanical and technological process in civilization, we are struck
by the loss of feeling which occurs along with the increment in power.
Quantitative methods cost apparently just creativity, and the technology of power disrupts natural and self-correcting homeostatic
relations of groups of animals (including human animals) to each
other.

To end on a provocative note, let me first remind you of the continuity of process from neurosis to art, to religion, to all of the manifold exhibitions of the use of symbolic instructions to control human beings and natural events. Let me remind you that neurosis is unknown in nature, and that scientific attempts to eradicate neurosis have proven themselves again and again unavailing. Let me then suggest that scientific method is itself the kind of one-sided, eccentric application of symbolic method that we would characterize as a neurosis were it found in a patient complaining of distress. Finally, then, is it possible that the ills so apparent in our time - the pollutions, the loss of control of population numbers, the unresolved antagonisms characterizing the relations of nations too intimately in communication with each other - is it possible that all these are 'neurotic' or 'psychotic' manifestations of a skewed faith in quantitative method? If so, the intensive application of narrowly traditional quantitative approaches to problems of description may well be similar to the continued exhibition of penicillin in a patient beginning to have hives or the prodromata of exfoliative dermatitis. The exclusive use of quantitative method to approach the malaise of our times may be the continued application of the medicament to which we have become unbearably sensitive.

NOTES

(*) Reprinted by special permission; in: Carl E. Larson and F. E. X. Dance (eds.), Perspectives on Communication, (Milwaukee, Wis. : The University of Wisconsin, 1968), 125-143.
(1) Harley C. Shands, "Outline of a General Theory of Human Communication: Implications of Normal and Pathological Schizogenesis", in: Lee Thayer (ed.), Communication Concepts and Perspectives (Washington, D. C. : Spartan Books, 1967).
(2) E. A. Burtt, Metaphysical Foundations of Modern Science (New York: Doubleday Anchor Books).
(3) Michael Polanyi, Personal Knowledge (New York, Harper and Row).
(4) Harley C. Shands, "A Report on an Investigation of Psychiatric Problems in Felons in the North Carolina Prison System" (September 1958) (with M. H. Keeler, G. D. Saute, G. S. Tracy, H. L. Smith, and G. A. Dahlstrom; H. C. Shands, Director).
(5) Harley C. Shands, "Communication and Consciousness" (manuscript).
(6) Jean Piaget, The Psychology of Intelligence (New York: Harcourt).
(7) Erwin Schrödinger, Science and Humanism (Cambridge: Cambridge University press).
(8) Jean Piaget and Bärbel Inhelder, The Child's Conception of Space (New York: W. W. Norton, 1967).
(9) A. R. Feinstein, "Boolean Algebra and Clinical Taxonomy", New England Journal of Medicine 269, 929-938.
(10) Ludwig Wittgenstein, Tractatus Logico-Philosophicus (London:

Routledge and Kegan Paul).

(11) Ludwig Wittgenstein, Philosophical Investigations (New York: Mac Millan).

(12) Erwin Goffman, The Presentation of the Self in Everyday Life (New York: Anchor).

(13) Mary A. B. Brazier, "Neurophysiological Contributions", in: Frank E. X. Dance (ed.), Human Communication Theory (New York: Holt, Rinehart and Winston).

(14) Harley C. Shands, "The War with Words: Creativity and Success", in: Science and Psychoanalysis VIII (New York: Grune and Stratton, 1965), 133.

(15) Harley C. Shands, "Individual as Differentiated Aspect of the Field", Psychiatric Research Reports (American Psychiatric Association, February 1956), 87–88.

(16) T. E. Weckowicz and D. B. Blewett, "Size Constancy and Abstract Thinking in Schizophrenic Patients", Journal of Mental Science 105, 909–934.

(17) Harley C. Shands, "Change in a Mother–Child Relation in Asthma", in: Henry Schneer (ed.), The Asthmatic Child (New York: Harper and Row, 1963).

(18) Marcel Duchamp, "Interview with Marcel Duchamp", by William Seitz, Vogue (February 15, 1963), 110.

III

PSYCHOANALYSIS AND THE TWENTIETH-CENTURY REVOLUTION
IN COMMUNICATION (*)

The twentieth century may well take its place in history as that century in which an understanding of communicational process began to
be the central topic of intellectual interest. The unbelievable expansion of computer technology, the revolutionary approaches to teaching of mathematical techniques, the automation of information re-
trieval are those matters most in focus - but less conspicuously
there is the perhaps more important acceleration in understanding
the 'human condition' as a function of human means of communication. The pioneer researches of such men as Sapir and Cassirer
have taught us that the human condition is a matter of relatedness
to others on the basis of an artificial system of communication. The
most radical developments in the twentieth century involve an expanded understanding of communicational processes in relation to
knowing and thinking. Where traditionally in the past the ideal has
been that of so correcting language and thought as to allow a clear
view of an unchanging 'reality', modern consensus in many fields
increasingly assumes that the processes of communication are inevitably participants in the eventual conclusion. This central understanding means that certainty becomes illegitimate in principle. The
mathematical backgournd of this idea has been established by Gödel;
the physical theory by Heisenberg; the philosophical statement by
Peirce. Comments illuminating the whole approach are to be found
in the discussions by Bentley (1950), Bohr (1950), and Conant (1952).
    The background of this movement involves a greater appreciation
of the processes of development. From the relatively recent theoretical beginning in the New Science of Giambattista Vico in the mid-
eighteenth century (Bergin and Fisch, 1961), the significance of
developmental process is reaffirmed in the biological sphere by
Darwin and comes to clear exposition in an unexpected way in the
title of the book by Einstein and Infeld, The Evolution of Physics
(1938). In modern cosmologies, as well as in modern theories of
knowledge, we learn that the universe, instead of being a static system, may be one capable of indefinite expansion. But in the effort to
manage this idea, we have to turn from the study of a presumably
'objective reality' to the study of the communicational process which
inevitably both reveals to and conceals from us what we investigate.
The statement can be made that we have evolved to the point at which
we learn to investigate communication as such, with the 'to what' and
the 'of what' understood as secondary. The new view of communi-

cation differs from any previous view in that the field has no sub-
stantive content; we are concerned only with the act of making common to more than one participant, as implied by the etymological
derivation of the term (from cum 'with', and munis 'bound' or 'under
obligation' - i.e., communicants are under similar obligations).

The principal importance of the artificial system of communication
is that the human being by virtue of this kind of system is made extremely dependent on learned methods of relating himself to his
human relatives. Where he has a normal childhood, he arrives at
maturity equipped with his language as (in Sapir's phrase) an essentially perfect instrument of communication. Where he does not
learn the system in childhood, he is relatively impaired, and unless
he learns some linguistic system well, he is likely never to be able
to do so in later life. The person incompletely socialized in his infancy tends never to feel the serene sense of belonging which characterizes the bulk of normal human beings.

In the very first years of the twentieth century we find two very
differently oriented conceptual systems of enormous importance to
those portions of the world where there have been the major developments in modern science. These two are the theoretical systems
initiated by Einstein in relation to the physical universe and by Freud
in relation to the universe of 'mental illness'. The significant similarity in the two systems is that in both there is implicit the central
notion of the importance of means of communication as formative of
the universe 'discovered' by such means. The original publication of
Freud's work on dreams occurred in the same decade as the publication of the special theory of relativity. Both contributions have had
enormous impact on mankind in subsequent years. The impact of
Freud's ideas has been blurred and limited by the fact that Freud used
an inappropriate mechanical frame of reference in which to present
these insights. The conceptual system emerging from Einstein's
wider view has made Newtonian mechanics obsolete as a conceptual
model, as well as other systems using Newtonian theory as a conceptual model, including not only the Freud'an, but also the Marxist
system.

Some Differences of Opinion

In the intellectual history of the twentieth century we find a radically
new emphasis on points of view and methods of communication which
increasingly has superseded the earlier supposed capacity to deal
with isolated facts. Where in the eighteenth century Hume (1748)
subordinated the study of relations of ideas to that of matters of fact,
in the twentieth century we have turned the world upside down as we
realize that matters of fact depend on relations of ideas. Where it is
still useful in simple situations to deal with ideas of 'object' or of
'matter in motion' (the basic scheme used by Marxism), at the fron-
tier of knowledge we see that the relation is always prior to the fact
and that the postulation of an objective source for any communication
is simply a rationalization based on a wide spread human inability
to understand symbolic process.

It is ironic that the psychoanalytic institutes, deeply immersed in the fixation processes characteristic of institutionalization, should now resist the further development of the central insights to which they owe their original existence. We find in the Freudian notion of 'transference' the same insight as that contained in the so-called 'Sapir-Whorf' hypothesis, namely that no statement can be understood to have value independent of the situational context of its occurrence. Any such statement has to be understood in terms of the developmental histories of the <u>participants</u> and of the <u>linguistic systems</u> as well. The idea is very close as well to that of the <u>Gestalt</u> psychologists who emphasize that no 'figure' can be understood as independent of its 'ground' - but the significance of the psychoanalytic idea is that it specifically includes the developmental-historical dimension.

In the traditional view psychoanalysis is seen as a <u>scientific</u> procedure having a place in the specifically <u>medical</u> universe as a treatment of <u>disease</u>. It is couched in a language borrowed from pre-Einsteinian physics; because of this origin, it is formulated in energy-mechanical terms which in turn assume a deterministically oriented universe. The principal novel conception of psychoanalysis is that of the 'unconscious' processes which underlie overt manifestations of behavior (especially at the linguistic-symbolic level). In the intense parochialism of the discipline, this conception is very generally reified into the idea of an institution ('The Unconscious') to which <u>belief</u> is directed: the comment "You don't believe in "The Unconscious!" tends then to become an accusation of heresy.

The contrasting series made in the following discussion begins with the assumption that psychoanalysis is a strictly limited, narrowly defined variant in the broad field of psychotherapy and that the whole field is primarily concerned with training or educational procedures of a highly complex type. (1) The reason why psychotherapy falls legitimately into the medical universe is that it is a primarily <u>clinical</u> discipline, and the training to become a psychotherapist is predominantly a clinical training. The kind of judgment and the feeling of responsibility involved are perhaps best developed in a medical setting, although they are not directly connected with the pharmacopoeia or the regular armamentarium of the medical practitioner. Clinical judgment has always to do with a relativity of therapeutic procedure and the patient's tolerance and sensitivity. Training in a clinical tradition tends to emphasize thinking and acting in terms of relations rather than in terms of objects. In psychotherapies of all sorts, the appropriate relations are those having communicational implications, and the dynamic trend in any such context is inherently purposive and goal-directed. (2)

Finally, the importance of unconscious processes is by now no longer novel in any sense. Every modern study of organ, organism, system, or computer participates in the same notion. Freud's great contribution is not the notion of unconscious process but rather his precocious, unclearly stated, but magnificently insightful awareness that 'unconscious' in the psychoanalytic sense means 'not-yet-symbolizable' (cf. Freud, 1915, and further discussion below).

Although Freud's work was throughout his career in the area of communicational process, it was not until very late that he began to formulate his ideas in terms which approach modern ways of thinking. Only with the publication of Hemmung, Symptom und Angst (1926) does it appear that he thinks of signaling as a function of feeling; prior to that time the prevailing conception is the quasi-substantive idea of transformation of a 'libido' into a feeling of anxiety. The difficulty of shifting frames of reference is well seen in the problems of modern adults attempting to cope with the 'new mathematics' their children are studying; what is clear to a bright third-grader is now often entirely obscure to his father. It is of further interest to note that some contemporary investigators concerned with clinical problems have begun to use the new mathematical techniques. Piaget (1957) used the propositional calculus in his recent work in the study of thinking, and Feinstein (1963) points out that any medical clinician uses set theory in his approach to problems of diagnosis.

When the problems of psychoanalysis are treated purely at the technical level, the operations of the classical analyst and his explanations are fully consonant with the view expressed here. Psychoanalysis operates (in purest form) as solely a technique of verbal communication; intervention takes place through interpretation alone. The effect of interpetation is an increment of learning in insight. The 'material' of observation is the patterning of the analysand's behavior (verbal and nonverbal), and the analyst's interpretation is his evaluative description of these patterns back to the analysand. His resulting insight is an interpretation of the analyst's interpretation, in a procedure ideally always assuming the circular nature of the process and the unavoidability of both 'transference' and 'countertransference' distortion.

The analyst, saying with deceptive simplicity "Just say what comes to mind" is in fact imposing a severe strain on the prospective patient's capacity to 'play' a particularly complex 'game'. When the patient demonstrates a capacity to pick up this kind of procedure, he is termed (explicitly or implicitly) suitable, and the procedure often becomes a mutually creative and satisfying engagement; when he is found not to be suitable, he is usually rejected out of hand. The procedure is an experiment in communication, with the patient serving as initiator of patterns which the analyst subsequently interprets in a manner conveying at least some novelty to the analysand. By his differential responses the analyst modifies subsequent behavior both within and outside the relationship.

This mutuality, while specifically perhaps unique, still has a 'family resemblance' (Wittgenstein, 1953) to many others with which we are familiar in the twentieth century. The selection procedure somewhat resembles that for acceptance into institutions of higher learning. After acceptance, the activity of the analyst as it might be described by a behaviorist amounts to positive and negative reinforcement. In learning-theory language, the patient is involved in a trial-and-error investigation, with the judgment as to when in error supplied (positively or negatively) by the analyst. In the language of evolutionary biology, every pattern exhibited by the patient becomes a variant or mutation, to be selected or rejected for survival and elaboration.

The overwhelming probability in statistical terms (as noted in a discussion of research in psychoanalysis by Glover, 1952) is that the opinion of the patient will come to resemble that of the analyst in depth: agreement in fact is taken to mean truth in theory!

Tokens, Abstractions, Symbols

The capacity mysteriously emergent at the evolutionary transition between primate and human being is that of dealing with pattern apparently divorced from a context, that capacity spoken of as 'abstraction'. When we examine the process more closely, we find that the apparent divorce is made possible only by an immediately simultaneous remarriage: the pattern removed from its original context of origin can be managed only by an immediate joining to a symbol, a verbal or mathematical sign, or a token of some other sort. Such a joining makes the symbol meaningful and at the same time makes the pattern communicable - but only in the new context of a linguistic-symbolic system in which the symbol used has a relation to its fellows. The 'object' is named and can be talked about only through the use of a word which has meaning in relation to other words - and only in the setting of a social system in which the language is an accepted medium of communication. To describe any pattern divorced from its context of origin is like talking about the male or female role in sexual intercourse - it is possible to make the reference, but impossible in practice to separate either from its reciprocal. Through the development of a new relation, the act of naming makes knowing possible at the level of conceptual thought (Dewey and Bentley, 1960).

Abstracting is therefore constructing. Instead of dealing with a pattern in its natural setting, we use patterns in a new relation, one involving the shape of the object or event and the shape of the word (or verbal or mathematical sign). Freud's insight into this fact is obscured by his inability to emancipate himself from his own linguistic context. He speaks (1915) of the process of "becoming conscious" as that of the association of the "idea of the thing' with the "idea of the word". This formula is inaccurate because the notion of an 'idea' already implies a symbolic process; had he said the 'shape' or 'pattern' rather than the idea, his comment would be astonishingly contemporary in its implication.

Modern research in computer technology leads to the idea that the basic property of the nervous system is that of the recognition of pattern (Selfridge and Neisser, 1960). All animals recognize patterns and demonstrate intelligent behavior (Bentley, 1950). The specific human advantage is that of the use of a symbolic pattern by means of which to grasp natural pattern and refer to the latter in the absence of the original context of origin. The human symbol therefore has always to be seen as existing in two universes simultaneously - the universe of nature from which it takes its original origin, and the universe of a symbolic-linguistic system in which it has communicational potentiality. The dual nature of human symbols can be seen in most concrete form in the monetary universe - every dollar or franc or mark has a value: 1) in relation to goods and services which can be bought within the system and 2) a second relation to the international, 'meta'-market in which money itself is bought and sold with constantly varying rates of exchange. Perhaps the most important implication in the nature of the communicational process is that linguistic symbols (verbal or mathematical signs) never refer to particulars, but always to universals or generalizations (Locke, 1690; Vygotsky, 1934). A name establishes a category, class, or mathematical set. Where the human being originally knows his mother as a particular collection of touchings, smellings, and tastings, he knows her in the abstract universe only as a member of a class, 'mother'. For particular reference in symbols, the human being has to deal with <u>intersections</u> of classes: 'my mother' is intersection of the two classes of: 1) all those things which are mine and 2) all those persons referred to as mothers. The word, dealing with a pattern abstracted from an event, has to be placed in context with other words to make a particular reference. We are all inevitably involved with at least binomial process when we use a name (John Jones; Homo sapiens; this lean, hungry, yellow dog). For this reason alone, it is never possible to refer to any particular object without going through the roundabout method of putting the problem in general terms, then identifying the intersection of those sets involved.

It is important to note that the basic structure of this process is one which leads to extraordinary error in one direction and to many forms of novel insight in the other. In Freud's (1915) example, he points to the similarity in shape between the squeezing of a blackhead and the ejaculation of a penis. In both there is the form of spurting (both occur in the set of 'spurts'). In the example, Freud points to the psychotic confusing of the two; in later discussion of the same idea, Storch (1948) and Van Domarus (1944) make similar comments. At the other side of the scale of rationality, however, we find that the same kind of assimilation can be seen in the astonishing insight of L. Boltzman (Rothstein, 1958) that <u>physical information</u> is identical with <u>negative entropy</u>. The subsequent course of the insight is the deciding factor, since the identity of spurting blackhead and ejaculating penis is of purely local interest, while the identity of information and negentropy is the theoretical basis for modern information theory. Not only does linguistic usage require generalization and subsequent binomial identification, it always requires that the subject matter be put into sequential form. The other great capacity of the abstracting process is that of grasping as an instantaneously understood whole what originally occurs as a temporally separated sequence. Any word is <u>heard</u> as a series of phonemes, but it is <u>understood</u> as a whole; to illustrate the point, let us take the sequential parts, <u>to</u> and <u>get</u> and <u>her</u> - when we hear them as a single whole, we hear <u>together,</u> a totally different meaning from the sum of the parts. When we examine the perceptual process, we find a similar capacity to integrate sensations of sight, sound, touch, smell, and others into the comprehension of an <u>object</u>: but the object is always a construct, an artificial whole, and an extrapolation from minimal cues to the supposition that this object is like others previously known.

When we start with an analytical, intellectual approach to objects, we ignore the prehistory in which the object is first perceptually grasped, then along with the emergence of an object-concept (Inhelder and Piaget, 1958), internalized and identified for symbolic reference. Cassirer (1946), following the lead of the philologist Usener, notes that the origin of the original conception appears to be a situation in which an intense emotional experience separates out a pattern from others. Through the development of a deeply felt emotional reaction, the pattern in question is separated from its context and made available for naming. In the beginning, new patterns tend to emerge in mythic form - Usener speaks of "momentary deities" which command identification and persistence. The emotional setting so established uses the physiological mechanisms with which we are familiar in the establishment of a Pavlovian "temporary connection" (Shands, 1960) - but the persistence and maintenance of the temporary connection in the human species becomes a function of consensual ratification (or consensual validation, Sullivan, 1953), rather than that of repetition of the unconditional stimulus. In the 'second signal system' the human being looks to a preceptor or authority speaking with the weight of the group consensus to maintain the relation established in the emotion of the moment. The institution of marriage, for example, is a consensually supported group method of maintaining a relation established on the basis of the evanescent frenzy of sexual excitement.

The most important implication of this method of procedure is that through repetitive reinforcement in plastic organisms at critical periods, consensual agreement is made into 'reality'. The enormous force of human beings in concert comes from the commitment of all to the common goal; it is notable that in every crisis situation, the group can be found to rise to an extraordinary level of achievement because of the enforced presence of a widespread consensus as to goals and values. The fragmentation of the human group by the development of different linguistic-symbolic systems is well described in the Bible. (3)

The importance of psychoanalytic ways of thinking is perhaps primarily in the emphasis given to the process of developing insight in rational terms through the route of personal myth and metaphor. In a psychoanalytic undertaking, the two participants examine a personal linguistic system in order to correlate it more accurately with the larger social context in which it occurs. The patient learns new meanings for ancient patterns, and he is encouraged to experiment with previously tabooed operations and relations. In the psychoanalytic situation there may be a continuous becoming in which all the familiar patterns of one's life are reviewed and seen from a different point of view so that experimental testing of a new sort can take place. From the microcosmic establishment of insight in the therapeutic situation, the patient is enabled to try out new patterns in the macrocosmic context of his ordinary life. The patient both 'acts out' and 'works through' patterns of behavior in relation to developments occurring in the psychotherapeutic relationship.

It is notable that any improvement or 'cure' occurring in this process has to be validated in some consensual context - originally in consensus of patient and therapist, but eventually in consensus of patient and sexual partner, patient and employer, patient and competitor. When we understand the fundamental importance of consensus for linguistic process, we can get a clearer picture of why the beginnings of human history tend to be signaled now to us by the persistence of religious artifacts and idols. These objects of veneration are primary objects of consensus - the original human group appears as a group of communicants, sharing some rudimentary version of ritual experience.

When human beings discover the universe of symbols, they discover the human mysteries. In the symbolic universe there appears the possibility of apparently instantaneous action, and apparent action-at-a-distance. From the beginning of time to the beginning of the twentieth century is the period required for the genius of an Einstein finally to grasp the fact that 'instantaneous' is an illegitimate conception, since any event can be related to any other event only in the finite time required for light to move from the one to the other area (Toulmin and Goodfield, 1965). But the great mysteries of religion, of magic, and of faith-healing continue to assume that events occur in no-time. In another context, the sudden shift is regularly one from a positive to a negative: the last becomes the first, black becomes white. Both these processes are well seen in the central mystery of Christian theology, the eucharist. There, in an instant, the bread and wine of the mass become the flesh and blood of the crucified Christ, in the operation called transubstantiation. Thus symbol becomes flesh, and the boundary between natural world and symbolic universe is said to be obliterated. Second, in this ritual, man's most horrible sin, cannibalism, is ritually reversed into man's most sacred sacrament, in a matter emphasizing the basic ambivalence of the symbolic process.

Human Communication: Human Games

The principal differences between human and lower-animal kinds of communication have to do with distance: the human being is able to transmit certain coded patterns through great distances of space and time. The communicational potentialities of all other animals are much more limited. When we follow out the studies of anatomical and physiological possibilities in evolution, we see a progressive development of distance-reception as we move up the evolutionary scale toward man. This development involves both the peripheral receptors and the central data-processors. Primates are differentiated from other mammals by their greater visual capacity; the macrosmatic mammal uses sight principally as a method of finding something to investigate by smell. In man the process takes the further step of using visually discriminated pattern as the basis for linguistic operation.

Through naming and describing, man comes to live in a symbolic universe as well as in the natural one. When in a stable social system, there is general recognition that group activity takes precedence over individual activity, and such abstract notions as patriotism, honor, and love come to be prepotent over primary needs for survival and reproduction. Man comes to live in a group separated from all others by its ritual and symbolic practices and beliefs. Since all of these have a predominant symbolic meaning, we can say that man's chief relatives are his co-linguists rather than (as is generally the case in lower animals) his con-specifics.

In man, the problems of intragroup hostility (and to some extent those of intergroup hostility) are approached through the means of ritual competition which to some degree takes the place of crude combat. It is interesting to note how many examples of somewhat similar practices have recently been observed by ethnologists, in which competition is allowed in formes frustes which settle the question as to which of the competitors is the 'better man' without harming the loser (except in 'loss of face'). The specifically human invention is that of the game which serves the same function as the ritual modes of competition transmitted in the animal by hereditary means. The game shows important differences from animal play. A human game is characterized by rules (which may or may not be consciously apparent to the players), by the use of artificial tokens or counters, by the necessary consensus as to the values and meanings involved, and, most importantly, by a learning process (4) which can be studied in detail in childhood and in the various educational institutions worked out by mankind over its period of existence. With adequate consensus, the human game achieves a kind of autonomous existence - but the dependence on consensus is seen in the difficulty we have in understanding alien cultural practices (Langer, 1942).

Different Genera of Games

Within the universe of games defined as above, we find a variety of both species and genera of games. The widest differentiation which can be made is that of the goal involved. Piaget notes that the two great classes of mentational activity are separated by reference to goals: he says (1950:6),

What common sense calls "feelings' and "intelligence, " regarding them as two opposed "faculties, " are simply behavior relating to persons and behavior affecting ideas of things; but in each of these forms of behavior, the same affective and cognitive aspects of action emerge, aspects which are in fact always associated and in no way represent independent faculties.

The consistent effort in modern science has been to develop means of avoiding human frailty, and thus removing from observation and description the primary source of error, human feeling. The scientist is a man who distrusts the approach to knowledge through the

imprecise 'hunches' and 'intuitions' of the ordinary human being. It
is of interest to find, in a review of scientists' careers after a lapse
of twenty years, that Anne Roe quotes a comment indicating that in
at least one prominent scientist, the preference for the abstract
depends on the fact that the feeling involved is quite different from
that involving human problems. One of these men, commenting on
the difference between research and administration, says, "administrative work tires you more than anything else. It's the need for
making decisions involving human beings ... I don't mind it nearly
so much if people aren't involved" (Roe, 1965: 314). Working with
the abstract avoids the feelings of fatigue (cf. Shands and Finesinger,
1952).

The justification for avoiding human problems in science has been
the universally accepted assumption that behind the appearance of
a universe so transient and changing in perceptual terms there is a
(metaphysically) real universe which can be approached through the
proper use of conceptual thought. Planck states that we have to begin
with an assumption of "the existence of another world of reality behind the world of the senses; a world which has existence independent
of man, and which can be perceived indirectly through the medium
of the world of the senses, and by means of certain symbols which
our senses allow us to apprehend" (1931: 8). He says further that
"it is as though we were compelled to contemplate a certain object in
which we are interested through spectacles of whose optical properties we were entirely ignorant" (1931: 8). Perhaps the clearest way
of describing the shifting emphasis in twentieth-century preoccupations with communication is by the use of this same metaphor: we have
in this epoch learned how to study the 'optical properties' of the 'spectacles' constituted by perceptual and symbolic process. It is notable
in Planck's use of this metaphor that he selects the specifically visual
and assumes that this is the primary route to 'reality'.

To anticipate a discussion more fully developed below, it is perhaps important to comment here that the search for superhuman or
extrahuman truth and reality is common to both science and religion.
Both scientists and religious experts seek invariance, eternally reliable relations, and an abstract universe - the two are separated by
method, but joined by a common goal. The modern gathering of information tends to show the two as similarly preoccupied with transcending the communicational limitations of human beings - and as
similarly doomed to failure in this effort.

The phasic character of human preoccupations is well seen in the
context of the practice of medicine. We are now aware of the fact
that, prior to the twentieth century, the armamentarium of the physician had predominantly a placebo effect; in comparison with the
active drugs and precise surgical procedures of the contemporary
period, the physicians of former times were of little 'real' use to
the patient. But in every period that we know, in every culture, there
is an important therapeutic function and functionary (Kiev, 1965).
The implication is that the physician is primarily related to others
as a human practitioner. The paradoxical fact is that as the demonstrable effectiveness of modern scientific medicine has been in-

creasingly evident, the status of the physician has declined rather
than increased.

It is hypothetically possible and appealing to suppose that the
elaboration of modern technical procedures has facilitated an alienation of the physician from the patient. The resistance of other cultures to scientific medicine is easily documented - with the emphasis
upon scientific progress in both the USSR and China, there is at the
same time a clinging to traditional therapeutic procedures (acupuncture, herbal medicine, etc.). The implication is that the primary
cultural function of the physician is not that of the scientific healer
but that of interpreter (diagnostician, prognosticator, reader of
omens). In this context, one can suppose that the psychotherapist
appears in a scientific culture as a disguised occupant of this cultural role:"Man does not live by bread alone!"

Games and Players

Through abstraction, patterns of games can be transported to places
widely different in space and time. The typically American game of
baseball found a new home in Japan at a time when other cultural
practices were immensely different in the two areas. In the contemporary period we find, in spite of great resistance, that the American methods of mass production and mass distribution are increasingly being exported: the supermarket flourishes in Europe, and the
first French Levittown is being built.

The movement of patterns to new contexts is somewhat like the
movement of animal species to new habitats; the new conditions tend
to promote acceleration in developmental trends. But where the animal species responds by increase or decrease in numbers, the
pattern is either adopted or rejected by the persons already in the
social system of immigration. To make an irreverent association,
the United States of twenty years ago was the scene of an explosive
development of interest in psychoanalysis in the latter, and of the
Japanese beetle in the former, context. In the contemporary period
we see in both instances a marked change in the original acceleration,
with the development of a new equilibrium.

The point to be made is in the demonstration that during the period
of twenty years in which psychoanalysis reached its contemporary
level of influence in the intellectual and medical community in this
area of immigration, it was suffering a marked decline in its original
area of appearance. In 1965 there appeared two reports in The New
York Times; in the one, Professor Horkheimer (1965) of Frankfort
is quoted as deploring the lack of interest in psychoanalysis in Ger-
many, and in the second, Joseph Wechsberg (1965) reports from
Vienna that psychoanalysis has all but disappeared there. The 'metastasis' has flourished in the United States during the same period
that the original growth has practically disappeared from its context
of origin.

The suggestion inherent in this observation is that the United States
has furnished to psychoanalysis a peculiarly favoring environment,

while in other parts of the world the unfavorable environment has caused the seed to fall on stony ground. Since during this same period the United States has been the major scene of an explosive development of trends inherent in Western, as opposed to Eastern, civilization, it appears worthwhile to pursue the relation. The hypothesis which I should like to examine is that psychoanalysis emerges from a scientific culture, not (as generally supposed by its practitioners) as an example of a scientific operation, but as an antithetical movement in contrast to the former dehumanizing trend of Western science.

The psychoanalytic movement is characterized by the narrowness of its zone of influence, both throughout the world and in the context of social class. It is primarily of interest to well-educated middle-class persons in the urban-industrial areas of the Western world. Within this grouping it is particularly appealing to those traditions emphasizing: 1) individualism and democracy (as contrasted with those emphasizing collectivism and authoritarian approaches), 2) Protestant rather than Roman Catholic religious institutions, and 3) rational capitalism and the rational application of technological discoveries to industrial exploitation.

If we take the broadest possible view of these separable trends, it becomes possible to say that psychoanalysis appears to appeal to those immersed in the most Western of Western movements, since it is in all of these ways that we see a kind of exaggeration of the trends which differentiate Western institutions from those of the other parts of the world. In a particularly clear statement made by a man familiar with both Western and Eastern cultures, Pandit Nehru (1964) is quoted in a recent display reviewing his life and work, as saying, referring to the English conquest of India,

> But one great benefit the English did confer upon India ... I am sure it was a good thing for India to come in contact with the scientific and industrial West; India lacked this and without it she was doomed to decay ... From this point of view the Protestant individualistic Anglo Saxon English were suitable for they were more different from us than other Westerners, and could give us greater shocks.

What Nehru emphasizes here is the fact that science is uniquely Western in its origin and development. In the United States we are prone to ignore this fact as we see on every side the operation of a scientific culture.

To trace this development, it is of interest to return to a discussion made by the pioneer sociologist Max Weber. Weber (1904) outlines the derivation of Western institutions (including capitalism and science) from origins in the Protestant reformation. He comments that throughout Western history there runs the thread of rationality; he notes that in such diverse fields as theology, architecture, finance, and philosophy the original insights are present in cultures other than the West, but only in the West do these beginnings come to be exploited in the rational forms which have obviously been so powerful in shaping the industrial and technological superiority of the Western world.

Rationality in this tradition appears repeatedly in Freud's writings as the highest goal. The apparently random, irrational technical approach through 'free association' is presented as the pursuit of rationality through an apparently irrational route - but the goal is always that of enhancing the power of conscious rationality. In this goal-orientation, Freud's scientific background is highly apparent; and Freud repeatedly affirms his belief that he is making a scientific contribution.

On the other hand, however, and from the methodological point of view, psychoanalysis is the antithesis of science. Scientific method is primarily oriented toward the experimental demonstration of predictable relationships in accordance with clear, consciously stated hypotheses. The philosopher of science, according to Reichenbach (1949), is "not much interested in the thought processes which lead to scientific discovery" - instead, he is only concerned with a "logical analysis of the conpleted theory"; the scientist, in similar fashion, is not much interested (as a specialist) in the way hypotheses emerge, but only in the manner in which the hypothesis can be rationally tested.

The central importance of rational thinking in science is well seen in the statements of the masters from whom the modern scientific tradition takes its form. The emphasis throughout is upon measurement and the statement of relations in mathematical form. Hume (1748) comments that if any book does not deal with reasoning in terms of quantity and number, it is illusion and should be cast into the flames. Planck (1949) says that the task of physics is to measure everything measurable and to render every unmeasurable thing measurable.

In this tradition, the claim that psychoanalysis is a science appears unreasonable. It is a procedure interested primarily in thought processes rather than in logical proof; it is impossible to formulate any procedure in the psychoanalytic situation so as to devise an experiment or achieve a replicable experimental result. It is a procedure by which the analyst in 'free-floating attention' seizes on patterns and 'tests' them only by referring them back to their source for consensual approval. It prides itself on its delving into the unconscious and the preconscious. The mass of procedures developed through three hundred years of Western science has been devised for the specific purpose of removing the influence of bias and emotion from the 'facts' of measurement, usually in instrumental form. Psychoanalysis, by contrast, is antithetically interested in the emotional and human background of the material which can be elicited.

The point can be again made in a different context by noting that where the ideal of scientific inquiry is that of the demonstration in written form of invariant relations described in mathematical exactitude for literate replication and communication, the techniques of psychoanalysis emphasize the particular relatedness of the two participants in an intimate relation utilizing spoken speech and, in the consensus of many of the older generation, one spoiled by any kind of recording or record-taking. Again the differences are not merely marked, they are diametrically antithetical.

If these relations are accurately described, how can we then under-
.stand that psychoanalysis is so firmly oriented toward its own participation in a scientific universe? The answer appears to be the same
as that involved in the use of the term 'science' in Christian Science,
namely, that the prestige of science in the West is so powerful a
factor that to declare anything unscientific is similar to declaring it
unreliable. The prestige of the scientific movement is borrowed by
many who wish to retain their membership in this exclusive society
of scientists. But the nature of psychoanalysis (and its derivative
psychotherapies) is such that this claim is inherently in error.

If psychoanalysis is science, then it is necessary to change the
traditional definition of science; if it is not science, it is necessary
to examine the possibility of reliability of its insights in some other
context. The curious fact that appears repeatedly is that the bulk of
psychoanalysts, following in the footsteps of the master, make the
claim and ignore the evidence. The resolution of the problem which
I suggest here is that we understand science itself as a game, (5)
one played primarily in the West. The emergence of psychoanalysis
can then be seen as a part of a movement which in many ways runs
directly counter to the traditional versions of science; these differing approaches pose an antithesis to the thesis posed by science. The
understanding of this process allows us to see more directly into the
interesting fact that psychoanalysis, here seen as most unscientific
in its very nature, still must be understood as appearing in the context of Western science, and within that context, it has obviously
achieved its greatest growth in that area in which the technical and
industrial application of scientific method has been most obvious,
that is, in the United States.

Science and Communication

Scientific method is essentially a restricted method of communication,
using a clearly describable linear, conscious, rational approach
emphasizing quantitation. In a description of the process called the
technique of 'strong inference', for example, Platt (1964) describes
a method of serial dchotomizing in a 'logical tree' at which each step
is tested for accuracy, with the resulting discarding of one of the
two possible alternatives. As he properly notes, this method of thinking is the "old-fashioned method of inductive inference that goes back
to Francis Bacon". The result of this method of attack is to outline a
series of propositions each of which is tested serially for its truth-
value; the test yields a 'yes' or 'no' answer, and the result is that
the next step can be decided on the basis of the just-previous 'yes'
answer.

The process thus described centers around the nature of proof.
In prescientific methods of operation, the lack of both metallic and
theoretical instruments made it very difficult to arrive at a decision
as to truth on any basis other than that of consensus. By inserting between the sensory evidence and the final conclusion the instrumental
processes of replicable measurement and strict logical control, the

availability of proof was immensely enhanced. With an experimental method, proof in limited areas becomes easily demonstrable in reassuring fashion. With successive developments, instrumentation becomes more refined and rechniques more precise - to a point at which in a total reversal of the ancient faith-oriented attitude there is now a widespread consensus that the only method of approaching problems is the scientific method.

It is of particular interest to note in this connection that pursuing the processes of rational inquiry in the tradition mentioned has indicated the limitations of that very method. The logical outcome of a dedication to strict logical data-processing is the development of machines which process information logically - in the modern emergence of the computer as the significant movement of this time. But the unexpected outcome of improvements in technical approaches has been the demonstration of limitations - by the masters of that method.

As emphasized by Einstein and Infeld (1938), the twentieth century is the epoch in which thinking in physical terms utilizes the notion of a field, a general matrix out of which there are differentiated the various kinds of matter and the objects into which matter is formed. The comment is made there that matter is a particularly concentrated area of the field and that it is only by a process of arbitrary definition that the dichotomy of field and matter can be made. The kind of thinking which eventuates in the notion of a field in physics is that which leads to the postulation of a system in a physiological context. Where the linearity of narrowly defined scientific method lends itself to long-range prediction, the implication of the relational situation in both the field and the system is that it is impossible to predict very far. The kinds of problems suited to the two systems can be seen to be those of astronomy in the first and of biological evolution in the latter instance. When we deàl with systems, we find that any system is defined as a limited area of a larger system but in turn the larger system is defined by the possiblities of communication which reveal it to the smaller system. In thinking about systems, we find that any 'cause' produces an 'effect' which then becomes a 'cause' in relation to its own cause - the circularity of feedback process makes linear, cause-and-effect thinking obsolete.

In Freud's own personal development we can find a movement from the linear th the circular kind of thinking, against his own obvious resistance. From an carlier stage in which he regarded 'transference' manifestations as simply a contaminant and an interference, he slowly moved to a point at which the analysis of the tranference-countertransference system is seen as the appropriate preoccupation of the psychoanalyst. The circularity of the process is well seen in that nothing said by either participant can be understood except in terms of previous and subsequent comments by the other. Every 'fact' found is modified by considerations of emphasis, feeling, and purpose.

When the patient begins to associate, the psychoanalyst listens until the communicational flow reaches a point where, on the basis of a feeling on the part of the analyst, he interrupts to make a communication in the form of an interpretation. Such an intervention effectively removes forever any possibility of an experimental replication. The interpretation organizes material from the stream of association in a manner usually novel to the patient; it selects and rejects on a basis different from that used by the patient. It is a feedback statement having a curiously bitemporal function, since it affects both past and future. It affects the past by offering alternative meaning and thus changing the significance of the data.

We tend to think of the past as fixed and unchaging, but this is an idea based on the assumption of the accuracy and completeness of records. The past which is actually relevant at any point is that mass of memories, habits, attitudes, and the like which persist into the present from the presumed past. A new view of this material tends to reorganize the human being as a whole, just as the theory of evolution reorganized all of man's previously cherished ideas about his own origins. When any human being undergoes a religious conversion or a massive illumination of any sort, he is subjected to a widespread revision of his past as well as of his probable future.

It is notable that past and future are always mingled in any verbal communication, since any word, statement, or other collection of phonemes becomes meaningful only on retrospective interpretation. The English-speaking student of German is familiar with the 'suspended' feeling he is likely to get in reading a long German sentence in which the verb is at the very end placed. Any kind of abstract intellectual operation depends upon the discrimination of a pattern which follows, while it seems to precede, the sequence in which it is presented. We can cite the two words psychotherapist and psychotic to indicate that the third and successive syllables often are crucially important in determining meaning, and if we split therapist we find the and rapist. The faculty of abstraction involves 1) a prediction and anticipation on the basis of the form of the initial members of a sequence, plus 2) a retrospective interpretation after the sequence is finished. A joke instantaneously reverses a preliminary anticipation by denying it and replacing it with a totally different one, with an effect commensurate with the amount of surprise involved.

The structure of psychotherapy is one which utilizes these characteristics. It is unavoidably and inexorably a circular process which represents the transactionally intricate result of both anticipation and retrospection. The end of the procedure is stated by Hanns Sachs (personal communication) as that point at which the patient has internalized the process to the degree where he becomes his own analyst. The various paradoxes with which we are familiar in this area are only paradoxes as long as the attempt is made to construe circular process in linear fashion (which comes first, the chicken or the egg?).

The contemporary nature of psychotherapy is well seen in the number of relatives it has in the modern world. It is like action-painting in that it exploits the apparently random; it is like non-objective art in that it is not supposed to represent or be anything, but rather to function as a self-expressive operation. Like these artistic movements of the twentieth century, psychotherapy puts a heavy onus on the listener-critic, involving him much more than have traditional art forms as a participant-observer. The modern artist

is as wary of an observer who asks "What is it a picture of?" as is
the psychoanalyst whose patient asks, "What comes into my mind
about what?"

The remarkable fact which can repeatedly be found is that out of
all these apparently irrational processes there does emerge to the
informed and sensitive observer a series of meaningful patterns
evoking a significant emotional reaction. To the patterns found in
a painting by a Pollock or a Kline the appropriate response may be
that of purchasing an artifact, while to the patterns found in free
associational material the response may be that of formulating an interpretation. Both alike depend on a novel understanding of the communicational relationship from person to person instead of from object to person.

Religion, Science, and Psychoanalysis

There is a common assumption that science is antireligious; one of
the most polemical of statements 'debunking' religion is to be found
in Freud's Future of an Illusion (1927). Here, on the other hand, I
want to suggest that the movement from religion to science is a
developmental movement in which what appears to be a difference is
in fact only a metamorphosis of components clearly to be found in
the formerly dominant field. Similarly, the twentieth-century movement from narrowly conceived descriptions of physical science to
contemporary concerns with communication can be seen as a development of trends inherent in the former conception.

The preoccupation with the nature of religion on the part of the
founders of modern science, Descartes, Newton, Kepler, and others,
is well documented by Koestler (1959). In modern affirmation, Polanyi notes that the basis of science, as well as that of religion, is
faith shared by a group of similarly prepared communicants. We
tend to believe that scientific discoveries are always welcomed by
scientists, but the evidence indicates that a new idea may be unwel-
come even to its own discoverer. The resistance of scientists to
scientific discovery has been the occasion for recent learned papers
(Barber, 1961); the experiment of Michelson and Morley now often
cited as the principal support of the relativity theory was regarded
by them as a failure, not to be mentioned (Grünbaum, 1964).

What relates science and religion is a common pursuit of truth;
what separates them is the reliance on the appropriate method. In
the contemporary scene, if we take as the appropriate test of truth
the test of consensus (as we do in fact even in the matter of approaching divine revelation through an ecumenical convention which
votes on opinions), we find that there are many competing approaches
to truth. Not only is there a major consensus as to the truth of scientific methodology; we find less widespread but similarly intensely
held consensual views relating to such diverse fields as existential-
ism and Abstract Expressionism, phenomenology and Zen Buddhism.
In each such group, the central 'cement' holding the group together
is the commonly shared conviction as to the validity of its own means

of approach.

In order to choose between these various competing ideologies, it is generally the most useful method to approach them developmentally, seeing each as an emergence from a previous state of a system in which a predecessor ideology was cherished. It is instructive in this way to look at the origins of the Christian Chruch from its predecessor 'parents', then to look at the Protestant reformation, the rise of rational science, and the appearance of psychoanalysis as they appear to demonstrate metamorphosis of certain patterns reappearing the same and yet different in each successive stage.

The origins of all these movements releatedly appear in a passionate dedication which allows the founders to persist in the face of intense opposition. Throughout there is repeated the strain of opposition of the mystical to the logical, with now the one and now the other in a dominant position. The curious consequence of a more comprehensive understanding of communicational process is that we begin to see that the mystical and the logical are both consequences of the symbolic process. The magical beliefs of translation from the one to the other state of being and the sober scientific notion that a mathematical statement is eternal and universally applicable to some phenomena in nature are equally dependent on the implications of the descriptive universe in which these matters are placed by verbal and mathematical formalisms.

The Christian church is the child of Hebrew and Greek parents. The Jewish origin of the principal founders of Christianity was continuously modified by the influence of the Greek civilization in which the principal development of the early Christian church took place. Early Christian theologians sought their inspiration in the works of Plato and Aristotle, and the codification and crystallization of theology derives as much from the pagan as from the Jewish heritage. We can differentiate the strains, however. From the Jewish 'parent' there appears the central notion of monotheism, with the deity as the apotheosis of the symbol ("The Great I Am"). The process, begun in Moses' selection of the tables of the law as principal object of veneration (rather than the Golden Calf tolerated by Aaron, or the idols concretely used by other religious groups), was completed in the very Greek testament of John, in which the Christ is seen as primarily a symbol, "the Word become flesh". From the Greek side there emerges the apparatus of rational discourse and the logical thinking which after a long period of development appears as the background of mathematical rigor in the physical sciences.

In the earlest days of the Christian church we find the statement of the dilemma with which we still are in major involvement. What is preferable, faith or works? Is it more important to have a passionate commitment, or a rational method of inquiry? The implication which we can find repeatedly is that the difference is important in 1) establishing an institution and 2) solving a problem. The preference of Saint Paul for faith is clearly stated in many places. His manifest success as the administrative founder of a millennially durable institution gives us reason to respect his opinion. On the other hand, faith is obviously inadequate when it is desired to attain reliable

information, and the pervasive doubting and demands for proof are
the basis of scientific research. But, it is the faith in this method
of doubting which binds together the scientific community.

In the Catholic Church of the Middle Ages, we find more and more
a resurgence of <u>polytheism</u> (in the form of the Trinity, the increasing
importance of the Virgin Mary, and the host of demigods appearing
in the catalogue of siants to whom prayers are directed) and the performance of <u>works</u> (as in penance, the buying of indulgences, and the
like). To this trend, the ascetic doctrines of Calvin appear as a return to the strictness and the harshness of the Old Testament. As
Weber notes, the Puritans, because of their preference for Old Testament doctrine, were said to practice "English Hebraism". Out of
this period of reaffirmation of the importance of a direct and personal
relation to the deity, and out of the implications of the bitter doctrine
of predestination, there emerged the paradoxical belief in the importance of <u>justification</u> which we find reflected so precisely in Reichenbach's comment that the philosopher of science is exclusively
interested in the context of justification. The passionate Puritan
stands in the ambivalent stance of deep faith and anguished query,
"How am I justified?" The removal of the institutional trappings of
the Catholic Church leaves the Protestant much more dependent on
his own resources and therefore seems to orient him to the apparatus
of logical proof and experimental demonstration.

The period in which psychoanalhsis appears is again a period of
great turmoil in the intellectual world. Freud's psychoanalytic
writings began appearing with the beginning of the twentieth century;
his preoccupation was with interpretation. Within a decade, the original statement of relativity theory appeared, in the same Germanic
area. The massive contribution of Einstein is similarly a contribution
in the interpretative area; Einstein, as Wertheimer emphasizes, arrived at his conclusions through a process of introspective rumination (6). He left the problems of proof to others while restricting
his own activity to internal data-processing.

The point of greatest interest therefore is to be seen in the fact
that psychoanalysis participates in the same process through which
a grasp of relativity theory appeared, namely, through the route of
wonder and questioning. Psychoanalytical technique specifically aban-
dons the tradition of directed logical inquiry which is the hallmark of
experimental science. The technique requires an original commitment purely on the basis of faith, with subsequent retionalization of
the faith as significant results appear. We understand that not only
do the parts of this process appear in apparently random fashion on
the surface, but also that any such partial appearance is the end result of even more deeply unconscious processes. The technical process of developing and refining hypotheses and interpretations has
to be substantially complete before these insights can be accurately
tested in the real world - but like Einstein, the psychoanalyst leaves
the testing to others. The comparison is not meant to indicate a par-
ity of intellectual accomplishment, but simply a parallelism of method - and in both instances the method is <u>pre-scientific</u>. In a similar
sense, as Simpson (1963) emphasizes, we find another of the great

formative ideas of the modern world in the doctrine of evolution -
but Darwin's method was never an experimental one. It depended
instead on the collection of observational data with a long period of
'mulling', ruminating, or 'stewing', out of which the generative hypothesis emerges for subsequent testing in the specifically scientific
tradition.

Western Dialectics and the Body-Mind Problem

Unless we develop an interest in our cultural background, we are
prone to get the idea that the current problems with which we are
concerned are novel in our own times. When we look back into history, however, we find with the Preacher that there is nothing new
under the sun. Of particular interest in this matter is the 'psychosomatic' problem which we may regard as recently invented. The
roots to the problem are to be found in the distinction between the
'concrete' and the 'abstract' in thinking, and in the ways in which
this problem manifests itself with reference to the early movements
in Christianity.

When 'psychic' is taken to mean spiritual, and 'somatic' to mean
fleshly, then we find in the gospel according to John the remarkable
statement of a translation: "The Word was made flesh, and dwelt
among us" (John 1, 14). In this statement, the crucial mystery of
the Christian church, and through it the central problem of the Western world, is made clear. In the doctrine of the Eucharist, the Catholic church officially declares that the symbolic bread and wine of
the mass is actually transmuted (transubstantiated) into the flesh
and blood of the crucified Christ. When we mull over the implications
of this statement, we find the concretistic renderings of the idea of
incorporation in psychoanalytic theory to be in the same tradition.

The idea of faith-healing depends on this basic premise, namely,
that there can be an instantaneous movement from one to another
state of being. The ultimate of disease is death, and Saint Paul promises the faithful, in the same tradition, "Behold, I show you a mystery; we shall not all sleep [i.e., die], but we shall all be changed.
In a moment, in the twinkling of an eye, at the last trump; for the
trumpet shall sound, and the dead shall be raised incorruptible, and
we shall be changed" (I Corinthians 15, 51-52). This promise is that
the flesh shall be made spirit, the concrete shall be translated into
the abstract, into an enduring pattern freed of the human limitations
of decay and dissolution - precisely the same goal as that included
in the scientific goal of invariance.

It is noteworthy here that the sacred and the profane participate
equally in the symbolic process. The punch-line of a joke is often
the statement of a reversal, a 'switch' - as for instance in the most
banal of jokes, "That was no lady, that was my wife." In the sacred
setting, Paul makes precisely the same internal contradiction in
saying, "For this corruptible must put on incorruption, and this
mortal must put on immortality" (I Corinthians 15, 53).

When we look at these mystical statements not from the point of view of proof, but from the point of view of communicational process, we find that these mysteries are not in fact very mysterious; they depend entirely upon the nature of the symbol. A symbol defines a category, not an object - 'man' or 'business' or 'ocean' or any other noun refers to a group, a set. It is the nature of the category that it should have dimensional limits of positive and negative extent: man is limited by the notion of 'subhuman' and 'suprahuman', and within the universe of man there are evaluative limits of good-bad, black-white, fat-thin. The meaning of the symbol can be <u>instantaneously</u> reversed by adding a - or a + sign or by using terms such as 'hypo-' or 'hyper-'. The mysteries of Christian theology are mostly then explained by the confusion between the empirical and the abstract; the value of the belief in Christ is that immediate translatability is promised as a consequence of belief. To a considerable extent, this basic faith underlies all manifestations of the promise of an instantaneous change from disease to health (or from perdition to salvation) in any form of faith-healing or conversion.

The degree to which this confusion penetrates every part of the Western world at least is demonstrated in the two alternative, contradictory definitions of the term 'real' to be found in the dictionary (Oxford, 1933). The two are 1) that which has an "absolute and necessary, in contrast to a merely contingent existence" and 2) that which can be "vividly brought before the mind" - the two definitions describe as real the contradictory meanings of that which is 1) solid and concrete and 2) that which is vividly perceived. In the second definition, we have to agree that the hallucination is 'real'.

Progression in History

A major problem in discussing any progression in historical sequence is that the statement of developmental occurrence is often taken as meaning, as in the term 'immature', something of a depreciating sort. If we say that the insight of any great leader or thinker is partial, it is not a statement of comparative or competitive implication. It is rather to be expected that any statement made by any person at any time will have to be revised, supplanted, changed to fit new conceptions, new facts, new schemata. The most important of civilizations in the ancient world, that of the Greeks, has been characterized by Piaget as at the stage of conceptualization now exemplified by the ten-year-old child; calculus, the great invention of Newton, is currently taught to the high-school student. The fact appears to be that human knowledge proceeds by a plateaulike succession, with each new point of vantage giving an entirely different perspective on the whole. The difficulty is that as Wittgenstein (1953) notes, one tends to climb on others' conceptions until one understands them - then to "throw away the ladder" and to see the contemporary stage not as one of a series, but as the truth.

When the scientist arrives at the formulation of a powerful system in which to demonstrate truth, he tends to assume that this system has no prehistory nor any subsequent history. We find repeatedly

comments that science has gone about as far as it can, and that
human thinking has reached an apogee from which there are no likely
forward movements. All such notions are clearly contradicted by
many developments in modern methods of communication. The fact
appears to be that we tend to develop as far as we can in one system
of communication, and that when the limitations of any such system
have been pretty well established, there tends to be a revolutionary
occurrence in which another system replaces the now obsolete one.
A case in point is the modern use of non-Euclidean geometry. The
invention of non-Euclidean systems appears to have occurred as an
intellectual game, using a set of assumptions different from those
chosen by Euclid. To the general surprise of many persons, when
Einstein developed the notion of relativity, it appeared that some of
the non-Euclidean geometries were precisely adapted to the physical
notions expressed by him. The theoretical instrment shapes a thought,
and a thought shapes a new theoretical instrument.

For these reasons, it is important to see that Freud's genius established new areas for intensive investigation; but at the same time we
must expect that further investigation will show that he was in some
sense wrong about everything that he believed. Like Moses in the
desert, the discoverer and leader often sees the Promised Land from
afar, forbidden to enter - while his followers, leaving him, enter
without knowing that they are in his debt. For this reason it is important both to acknowledge the significance of Freud's contributions
and to demonstrate that they are repeatedly in error. Of special
interest is the relation between 'conscious' and 'preconscious' thinking, as the idea developed by Freud can be seen altered and further
illuminated by an idea of the Russian linguist, Vygotsky.

Conscious and Preconscious in Development

Freud's distinction between 'conscious' and 'preconscious' on a 'topo-
graphical' basis is often obscure. One reason which appears helpful,
at least to the author, is that the spatial metaphor is entirely inappropriate. The distinction is not between regions or zones in a topo-
graphical context, but between different levels of developmental functioning. Conscious thinking, as noted previously, is characterized
by the adjective linear, rational, measurable, discursive, logical.
The use of conscious thinking is closely associated with possibilities
of proof; the movement is from step to step in a consciously developed argument which has as a principal objective in the strictest
sense the demonstration of an identity on both sides of an equation.

Children's thinking is of a different sort. Vygotsky uses the term
'chain-complex' or 'complex' to describe the manner in which the
child at one stage of linguistic development may be seen to skip from
one idea to another on the basis of a common element in two situations.
The basis of the movement is simply that the shape of pattern occurring in the one context is that also occurring in the other. We can put
this in modern language by saying that the child moves from set to
set on the basis of successive intersections of the previous with the

current set. A beautiful example of thinking in complexes may be found in the account of the mad tea party in Alice in Wonderland in which changes are rung on the different senses of the word well (in the well, well in). Training in logical thinking pays intensive attention to helping the child distrust this kind of chaining and subject his thought to logical dichotomization.

Preconscious thinking, ruminating in dreaming or daydreaming, uses the complex. Metaphor is specifically a technique in which the pattern separated from its original context is placed in a set with another pattern. It is apparent that the vast majority of all such relationships occur in an irrational manner; the assumed similarity is insusceptible to proof. The other side of the picture is given by the fact that it is from this kind of free association that the novel demonstrations of identity of pattern eventually emerge – for the subsequent scientific possibilities of verification and falsification. Vygotsky's 'complex' is the origin of the creative insight of the poet, the artist, and the scientific innovator. Perhaps the most important insight of Freud in the development of the techniques of psychoanalysis is that of combining the free association of the patient with the 'freely-floating attention' of the therapist in such a way that the two creative processes mutually reinforce each other. It is, on the other hand, unfortumate that the powerful intimacy involved in this relationship tends to make the result difficult to examine logically – in the usual case, the development of an emotionally ratified consensus makes the analyst and the patient regard each other with undue enthusiasm.

To illustrate something of the technique of thinking in chain complexes and the selective reinforcement practiced by at least one psychotherapist, it may be of value to cite an actually observed sequence with a highly 'suitable' patient.

A medical student in the psychotherapeutic situation began a chain of free association by noticing moving leaves on a tree visible through a window. Their movement made him think of delicate skillful actions, like those of the surgeon or pianist; he remembered admiring the activity of the professor of surgery, and he commented that he wished to become a surgeon. He then returned to the idea of the pianist, remembering that he had wanted to learn the piano but that his teacher had been unable to induce him to work hard enough at practice for him to learn. He regretted having quit. The therapist, listening to this chain of ideas, inferred that the patient was referring to the present situation and that he was in a sense warning the therapist that he might abandon psychotherapy before practicing enough to gain adequate skill. The train of association then can be seen (if the therapist is right in the interpretative metamorphosis) as a warning and as a plea – the patient hopes that the skill of the therapist is adequate to the task of keeping the patient at his own task long enough to learn. The therapist's interpretation is a function of his own prediction that this patient is among those who tend to interrupt treatment, and his interpretation is in part a technical move to prevent the interruption which the patient implicitly predicts by his reference back to the piano reacher.

As common elements in the above chain, the delicate movements tie together leaves, surgeon, and pianist; the notion of skill joins the professor of surgery and the expert pianist; the idea of learning relates piano teacher, surgeon, and psychoanalyst. It is obvious that this kind of stream of consciousness is entirely different from the strictly logical progression in a mathematical or scientific argument – but at the same time, it is observable that it is through this kind of processing that the expert logician begins to approach his precise sequential data-processing. The difference between the two methods is the crucial difference between 'conscious' and 'preconscious' ways of approaching a problem; free association is a method of using the associational train to derive patterns of novel significance and to operate in feedback loops to change the patient's ways of thinking by introducing these patterns into the system by interpretation.

The thinking in complexes encouraged by the psychoanalytic situation has its greatest potentiality in the enhancement of creative experimentation with the shapes of one's own experience. Its reciprocal liability, however (one also exploited by many other communicational training procedures in the modern world), is that the procedure, with its attendant feelings of anxiety and alienation, fosters the structuring of experience along the guide lines presented by the nearest dependable structure. The procedure loosens habitual techniques and the loosened potentialities tend to restabilize themselves by alignment with the power apparent in the situation. This means that the patient often becomes a therapist, whereas the trainee in 'thought-control' often becomes a commissar; it also means, in a reinterpretation of 'suitability', that the most welcome restructuring is that which resembles what is already present. The 'ideal' patient is therefore usually a middle-class person whose orientation is similar to that of the psychoanalyst.

Psychotherapy in the Twentieth Century

The conclusion with which it becomes possible to terminate this brief discussion of some of the central concerns of our time is that psychotherapy (and its more rigidly defined parent, psychoanalysis) offers a route to the understanding of communicational process available in no other undertaking. The processes observable are specifically developmental; they are not concerned with matters of fact, but with relations of ideas (Hume, 1748). The procedure is only misleadingly mixed up with notions of therapy and cure; it is primarily and dominantly concerned with training techniques of thinking.

The central 'mystery' of psychotherapy is identical with the central mystery of religion or of any other learned and incorporated world--view. This mystery is always a communicational mystery, involving the necessarily interpretative step through which the human being develops his own universe in easy or uneasy relation with those of his fellows. It can easily be seen that the definition of 'real' as 'that which can be vividly brought before the mind' is in fact the operational definition. When societies believe in ghosts and devils, these devils and ghosts are often 'realized'; they may form the basis of judicial conviction and legal execution. If the individual, dissociated from the possibility of participating in the general consensual ratifications of his group, makes consistently an interpretation of his universe which differs from that of the consensus, we say that he is 'sick' and we try to persuade or coerce him into agreement with the majority as a method of 'cure'. But the indications appear convincing that the situation is not one of illness, but rather one of deviance. We are appalled by an interpretation which is radically novel and we tend to assign to it a term such as 'unreal', 'aberrant', 'bizarre', 'misguided'. The greatest potentiality of the psychotherapeutic approach would seem in this context to be that the therapist, taking his line of approach from developmental considerations, does not conclude that the novel interpretation is necessarily wrong. Instead, he seeks to understand it in the context of its developmental history.

In these ways we see a conception of a universe progressing in dialectical process through the posing and resolving of contradiction. The underlying structure of the process can be more easily seen when we understand that any linear statement has to be in error, but at the same time it has to be made in linear form because that is the only way in which the human methods of data-processing can break down the great universal wholes into fragments which can be grasped and assimilated.

In the cycling paradoxes of human sequence, we find that new developments tend to contradict all that we think we know, but that as the new development comes to find its place in the larger view it comes to appear not as an abrupt contradiction of former views but as a logically necessary development from those views. Wisdom (as differentiated from proof) takes a long view and sees the cyclical pattern as one which inevitably characterizes the human condition. It was known to the preacher-poet and seer that there is a time to reap and a time to sow, a time to live and a time to die, and that the human destiny is to deal with the recurring relation of the new and the old. The most immediately current preoccupations with data-processing leads to essentially the same interpretation. In modern language we can say that the new induces anxiety (7) until it is known; then the novelty is destroyed and we become again aware that there is no new thing under the sun.

When Freud, using with brilliance the insights available to him in the nineteenth-century terminology, came to the conclusion that the function of the 'mental apparatus' is that of abolishing stimulation and reducing the input of 'energy', he was previsioning a modern interpretation which while in one sense entirely contradictory, still in translation comes to be nearly identical to the pattern implied in his comment. The more modern rendering is that any data-processing system has the function of reducing <u>novelty</u> (or, as Kuhn puts it, making the anomalous regular). Since information is inversely proportional to probability, the reduction of novelty increases the amount of stored knowledge and reduces the amount of current input information which the human being has to deal with. The transfer of symbolic information to the inner world is a function of human modes of communication; the difficulty is that any such internalized information derived from the experience of another (i. e., a preceptor) has to be, in the new context, in error to some extent. Didactic practices therefore have the dual effect of 1) reducing informational input as the transferred knowledge is found to be correct and 2) increasing informational input as the transferred knowledge is found to be incorrect. We are left with the ancient necessity of dealing with successive approximations, each in error but perhaps each a bit more nearly accurate than its predecessors. There seems to be no reason to suspect that psychoanalytic theory is exempt from this process.(8)

NOTES

(*) Reprinted by special permission; Modern Psychoanalysis: New Directions and Perspectives, ed. by Judd Marmor (New York: Basic Books, 1968), 82-113.

(1) To quote Sapir (1957:145), "psychiatry is moving away from its historical position of a medical discipline unable to make good, to that of a discipline which is medical only by tradition and courtesy and is compelled, with or without permission, to attack fundamental problems of psychology and sociology so far as they affect the well-being of the individual. The locus, then, of psychiatry turns out to be not the human organism at all in any fruitful sense of the word but the more intangible, and yet more intelligible, world of human relationships and ideas that such relationships bring forth."

(2) It is noteworthy that a purposive approach is specifically required by communicational process; widely different approaches, such as those of Wiener (1948), in relation to the theory of computer technology, and of Granit (1955), in relation to the physiology of the special senses, insist on this basic conceptual assumption.

(3) The power of consensus was well known to the writer of Genesis: "And the Lord said, Behold, the people is one, and they have all one language; and this they begin to do: and now nothing will be restrained from them, which they have imagined to do. Go to, let us go down, and there confound their language, that they may not understand one another's speech. So the Lord scattered them abroad from thence upon the face of the earth; ... Therefore is the name of it called Babel; because the Lord did there confound the language of all the earth" (Genesis 11, 6-9).

(4) When one considers the 'well-adjusted' adult as a competent player in his cultural games, then the consideration of major importance is how well he plays, in comparison with his fellows. In this rendering, the use of the health-disease rubric in behavioral context becomes an inappropriate metaphor.

(5) To the point in this connection is the comment of the Nobel prize-winner Wigner (1964) that the success of science is mainly to be traced to its practice of limiting its objectives. The scientist chooses out of all possible procedures those which test a particular limited hypothesis in a locally manageable context.

(6) It is notable that both Freud and Einstein were Jews with a similar history of emancipation from the specifically religious be-

lief of the larger group, but with (especially in the case of Freud, as demonstrated in the preface he wrote to the Hebrew edition of Moses and Monotheism) the maintenance of a strong sense of belonging to the group. In his "autobiographical notes", which are entirely concerned with his intellectual development, Einstein notes that the preoccupation with relativity began in his adolescence, following a period of intense religiosity which ended at the age of twelve when he was convinced that the "stories in the Bible could not be true" (Schilpp, 1949). Wertheimer quotes Einstein as saying of the derivation of the ideas of relativity, "These thoughts did not come in any verbal formulation. I very rarely think in words at all. A thought comes, and I may try to express it in words afterward" (1945:228). He notes further, "During all those years there was a feeling of direction, of going straight toward something concrete" (1945:228). These excerpts refer to a process which we tend to call 'making the unconscious conscious' and 'working through' to insight.

(7) Trotter comments (1941) that 'the mind delights in a static environment ... Change from without ... seems in its very essence to be repulsive and an object of fear ... a little self-examination tells us pretty easily how deeply rooted in the mind is the fear of the new."

(8) This work was done with the help of a fellowship from the Commonwealth Fund. Its content and form owe much to a series of discussions held at intervals over several years with the other members of the Committee on Therapy of the Group for the Advancement of Psychiatry. Although these discussions rarely eventuated in consensus, they were of great benefit to the author in clarifying his own opinions in this complex area.

REFERENCES

Barber, B.
   1961   "Resistance by Scientists to Scientific Discovery", Science
           134, 596–60z.
Bentley, A. F.
   1950   "Kennetic Inquiry", Science 112, 775–783.
Bergin, T. G., and M. H. Fisch
   1961   The New Science of Giambattista Vico (New York: Double-
           day).
Bohr, N.
   1950   "On the Notions of Causality and Complementarity",
           Science 111, 51–54.
Burtt, E. A.
   1954   Metaphysical Foundations of Modern Science, rev. ed.
           (New York: Doubleday).
Cassirer, E.
   1946   Language and Myth (New York: Harper).
Conant, J. B.
   1952   Modern Science and Modern Man (New York: Columbia
           University Press).

100

Dewey, J., and A. F. Bentley
1960   Knowing and the Known (Boston: Beacon).
Einstein, A. and L. Infeld
1938   The Evolution of Physics (New York: Simon and Schuster).
Feinstein, A. R.
1963   "Boolean Algebra and Clinical Taxonomy", New England
        Journal of Medicine 269, 929-938.
Freud, S.
1915   "The Unconscious", The Standard Edition of the Complete
        Psychological Works of ... (London: Hogarth Press),
        Vol. 14. (Also in Collected Papers of ... [New York: Basic
        Books, 1959], Vol. 4, 98-136).
1919   "Lines of Advance in Psychoanalytic Therapy", The Stan-
        dard Edition of the Complete Psychological Works of ...
        (London: Hogarth Press), Vol. 17, 159-168. (Also in
        Collected Papers of ... [New York: Basic Books, 1959],
        Vol. 2, 392-402).
1926   "Inhibitions, Symptoms, and Anxiety", The Standard
        Edition of the Complete Psychological Works of ... (Lon-
        don: Hogarth Press), Vol. 20.
1927   "The Future of an Illusion", The Standard Edition of the
        Complete Psychological Works of ... (London: Hogarth
        Press), Vol. 21.
Glover, E.
1952   "Research Methods in Psychoanalysis", International
        Journal of Psycho-Analysis 33, 403-409.
Granit, R.
1955   Receptors and Sensory Perception (New Haven: Yale Uni-
        versity Press).
Grünbaum, A.
1964   "The Bearing of Philosophy on the History of Science",
        Science 143, 1406-1412.
Horkheimer, M.
1965   quoted in article by Philip Shabecoff, New York Times
        (February 22), Sec. 2, p. 1.
Hume, D.
1748   "Enquiry Concerning Human Understanding", in: E. A.
        Burtt (ed.), English Philosophy from Bacon to Mill (New
        York: Modern Library, 1939).
Inhelder, Bärbel, and J. Piaget
1958   The Growth of Logical Thinking (New York: Basic Books).
Kiev, A.
1965   "The Study of Folk Psychiatry", International Journal of
        Psychiatry 1, 524-548.
Koestler, A.
1959   The Sleepwalkers (London: Hutchinson).
Langer, S. K.
1942   Philosophy in a New Key (Cambridge, Mass.: Harvard
        University Press).
Locke, J.
1690   "Essay Concerning Human Understanding" in E. A. Burtt
        (ed.), English Philosophy from Bacon to Mill (New York:
        Modern Library, 1939).

Nehru, J.
1964   Quoted in Smithsonian Institute Exhibition, Museum of
History and Technology, on J. Nehru, "His Life and His
India", October-December, 1964.
Oxford English Dictionary
1933   (London: Oxford, 1961).
Piaget, J.
1950   The Psychology of Intelligence (New York: Harcourt,
Brace).
1957   Logic and Psychology (New York: Basic Books).
Planck, M.
1931   The Universe in the Light of Modern Physics, 2nd ed.
(London: Allen and Unwin, 1937).
1949   Scientific Autobiography and Other Papers (New York:
Philosophical Library).
Platt, J. R.
1964   "Strong Inference", Science 146, 347-353.
Reichenbach, H.
1949   "The Philosophical Significance of the Theory of Relativity",
in: P. A. Schilpp (ed.), Albert Einstein, Philosopher-Scientist (New York: Harper), 287-312.
Roe, Anne
1965   "Changes in Scientific Activities with Age", Science 150,
313-318.
Rothstein, J.
1958   Communication, Organization, and Science (Indian Hills,
Colo. : Falcon's Wing Press).
Sapir, E.
1957   Culture, Language and Personality: Selected Essays of ...
(Berkeley: University of California Press).
Schilpp, P. A. (ed.)
1949   Albert Einstein, Philosopher-Scientist (New York: Harper).
Selfridge, O. F., and U. Neisser
1960   "Pattern Recognition by Machine", Scientific American
203, 60.
Shands, H. C.
1960   Thinking and Psychotherapy (Cambridge, Mass. : Harvard
University Press).
Shands, H. C., and J. E. Finesinger
1952   "A Note on the Significance of Fatigue", Psychosomatic
Medicine 14, 309-314.
Simpson, G. G.
1963   "Biology and the Nature of Science", Science 139, 81-88.
Storch, A.
1948   The Primitive Archaic Forms of Inner Experience and
Thought in Schizophrenia (New York: Nervous and Mental
Diseases Publishing Company).
Sullivan, H. S.
1953   The Interpersonal Theory of Psychiatry (New York: Nor-
ton).
Toulmin, S., and June Goodfield
1965   The Discovery of Time (New York: Harper and Row).

102

Trotter, W.
  1941   Collected Papers (London: Humphrey Milford).
van Domarus, E.
  1944   "The Specific Laws of Logic in Schizophrenia", in: J. S.
          Kasanin (ed.), Language and Thought in Schizophrenia
          (Berkeley: University of California Press).
Vygotsky, L. S.
  1934   Thought and Language (New York: John Wiley, 1962)
Weber, M.
  1904   The Protestant Ethic and the Spirit of Capitalism (New
          York: Scribner).
Wechsberg, J.
  1965   "Freudian Slip", New York Times Magazine (June 6).
Wertheimer, M.
  1959   Productive Thinking (New York: Harper and Row, 2nd ed.,
          1959).
Wiener, N.
  1948   Cybernetics (New York: John Wiley).
Wigner, E. P.
  1964   "Events, Laws of Nature, and Invariance Principles",
          Science 145, 995-998.
Wittgenstein, L.
  1953   Philosophical Investigations (New York: Macmillan).

IV

MOMENTARY DEITY AND PERSONAL MYTH (*)

Over the past two hundred years or so, a scientific metaphysics
(Burtt, 1954) has so established itself in the Western world that
'scientific' is now commonly used as a synonym for 'truthful' or actual'. This view presupposes that there is a single universally applicable 'reality' for all times and places, in spite of the obvious
changes constantly occurring in the subject matter of science. Over
the more recent past, evidence (much of it derived from respected
scientific inquiry) gives strong support to a different notion, namely,
that communicative techniques necessarily affect the subject matter
communicated. The emerging study of patterned communication has
been termed semiotics, and perhaps its primary supposition is that
of the transactional nature of the relation involving signifying and
signified. This view suggests that there is a myriad of 'realities'
each of which is significantly related to its appropriate modality of
patterned communication (Cassirer, 1923:356).

The conception of reality in scientific terms is a static one brought
to its ultimate form in the notion of the determinist that it might at
some point be possible to gather together all the facts and so predict
the entire future course of the universe. The ultimate abstract reality
is indicated by Piaget (1950) in discussing the final stage of intellectual development, reflective intelligence. Piaget points out that
the formal operations grasped in reflective intelligence are characterized by transitivity, reciprocity, and reversibility in an equilibrium state.

In making this statement Piaget notes that it is the end point of a
long period of development. The static quality is only attained by
progressive intellectual distancing, and by the progressive separation
of anthropomorphic elements (Cassirer, 1925) from the bare bones
of formal construction. Piaget himself emphasizes that the usual
epistemologist is solely interested in this ultimate stage of intelligence, and a philosopher of science has trenchantly stated that members of his category are not at all interested in how scientific notions
emerge, but solely in their logical validity (Reichenbach, 1949).

The static, single notion of reality thus presented in scientific and
intellectual renderings is contradicted by the more modern and the
increasingly evident importance of genetic understanding. There
seems to be a general rule that human understanding grasps first the
static, only later coming to the possibility of dealing with genetic
processes. Here again we see the central importance of the semiotic
considerations, since a written statement, by its very nature, strongly
presents the implicit notion that its 'reality' is a similarly static reality. To get the movement back into the description is a problem

similar in principle to that of organizing a series of still pictures into a moving picture show.

In the following discussion, I want to approach the problem of what might most readily be called genetic semiotics. In sharp contrast to the philosopher of science mentioned above, it might be said that I am not at all interested in the logical validity of many of the notions discussed, but simply in the problem of their sequential emergence. One does not concern himself with the viability of an embryo, but only with the place of the embryo in a series which leads from the fertilized ovum to the established adult. The process with which the following comments is concerned is that of the dawn of human relatedness through states of heightened feeling. I shall call these states 'transcendent', because those who report having participated in such states report them in terms of feelings of surpassing intensity. The central importance of these states is the possibility that it is only in such states that truly meaningful influences can be exerted on the one by other persons, usually on a novice by another in the role of preceptor. The specific subdivision of this general problem is that of the psychotherapeutic relation, in which the preceptor-therapist is assigned the task of helping the novice-patient learn more successful techniques of human relatedness. My conclusion is that whatever success is attained in this pursuit is made possible only by the formative influence of identification, and secondly, that identification is directly proportional to the intensity of the transcendent experience, if any, shared by the two participants.

In the paper which follows, I want to pursue a genetic notion in suggesting that human knowledge rests upon the establishment of human relatedness. Mothering takes place in the fortunate youngster's case so early and so efficiently that no clear conscious memory is left; there are no written records. On the other hand, there are two other kinds of acute, conscious human experience obviously of intense formative importance; these are falling in love and religious conversion. In both instances we regularly observe at first or second hand that the elevation of a state of human relatedness to the 'transcendent' level of romantic love or of intense religious ecstasy is powerfully influential in changes in behavior or in character in human beings. Indeed, it is persuasive that no other state of human feeling of lesser intensity is ever likely to make much difference. To the Tristan overwhelmed with longing to the point of throwing caution to the winds, or to the Zen novice abandoning his entire previous life to the search of meaningful illumination, the overriding 'reality' of the transcendent experience is self-evident.

In the contemporary scene, psychotherapy presents itself as a curious fumbling discipline persisting in the face of much hostile criticism. My own feelings can be suggested in part by the comment that I do not believe that a separate 'psyche' can ever be found to exist (Shands, 1956) and that I do not believe psychotherapy of much 'therapeutic' use in any standard measurable assessment of efficacy. I would suggest that the lack of scientific validity and the paradoxical flourishing of the discipline widely throughout the world make it much more likely that psychotherapy is in the artistic-religious sphere than

it is in the scientific-metric sphere (Shands, 1968). The scientist
begins with a disciplined, trained intelligence and goes on to develop that intelligence according to clearly conscious rules of educational practice - but only when he has already been adequately
socialized. The problem appears when we find the scientist's brother
or fellow with apparently the same native capacity crippled in his
capacity to undertake human relationships. It is not too uncommon to
find striking change possible through conversation; religious archives
are full of reports of frivolous youths or wastrels who become stal-
wart pillars of the church and intellectual monuments after conversion: Saint Augustine is the obvious example.

I understand this repetitive observable as indicating that for the
human novice to be able to follow the preceptor, to pattern himself
through identification, the basic problem is that of relatedness. After
infancy, the capacity to undergo deep changes in relatedness depends
upon the possibility of mobilizing feeling so powerfully that it appears
as a transcendent experience. It is only in the powerful 'blaze' of
illumination that a Saul-persecutor of Christians instantly becomes
a Paul-savior of Christians - through the simple fact of identification
with those formerly persecuted through the intermediary of a deified
human being suddenly becoming the 'object' of belief.

It is perhaps worth pursuing the manner in which this conception
slowly emerges in psychoanalytic thinking. Freud showed himself
impatient with the 'contamination' of human feeling in his early years
of working with patients, only later coming slowly around to the
notion that the 'transference' provides the most important incentive
for personal change. It is only recently that we begin to approach
problems of dealing with patients separated from the usual therapist
by wide differences in class and cultural origin - but when we do, we
find the notion of transferring feeling inappropriate. Transfer can
only take place when the feeling context is highly developed; for the
severely disabled or disadvantaged human being, the problem is that
of development. To say it another way, we are concerned not with
rehabilitation but with habilitation. We can learn much from the evan-
gelists who induce states of transcendent emotion through their highly
active techniques of mobilization, in a range from the practices of
the Hassidic Jews all the way to those of the 'Holy Rollers' of Protestant ecstatic sects.

The transcendent experience serves to unify those sharing it into
a group bound together by a common experience and so differentiated
from the common run of humanity. The claim validly made by those
who have passed through the experience is that no one who has not
done so can 'know' the experience - usually this idea gets expanded
into the less tenable notion that no one who has not had the experience
can know 'the truth', but this idea seldom survives the test of relativity.

If we examine two examples from extremely different contexts, we
find some further insight. In comparing the very different experience
of Emily Dickinson in her adolescence with that widely publicized in
the contemporary scene, we find a common element of meaning.
Emily Dickinson, obviously capable of high sensitivity and expert use

of language, comments, in a well-known letter to Abiah Root when
she was 16, that she felt isolated and left out of her peer group because she was not capable of the intense feeling of salvation otherwise practically universal. The adolescent New Englander of the
mid-nineteenth century underwent religious conversion and became
saved as a kind of rite de passage; Emily Dickinson writes sadly of
her inability to reach the level of intensity necessary to give herself
to Christ.

Miss Dickinson demonstrated the isolation and alienation at a later
stage in withdrawing, in her late twenties, into a self-imposed restriction of her movement into the family home, with almost complete rupture of direct relations to all except her sister Lavinia.

In the contemporary scene, in sharp contrast, we find in an increasingly secular age that the search for transcendent experience
is no longer a matter of religious belief. Instead, the search involves
the use of drugs (LSD, psilocybin, mescaline, marijuana). Instead
of the traditional use of drugs in ritually prescribed meetings held
in the service of religious belief as in the peyote cults of the American Southwest, it now appears that drug-taking is much more casual,
in groups having implications of both secular and sexual temporary
relatedness. The interesting common feature appears to be that
through the use of drugs, it is much easier to reach transcendent
levels of feeling, with at least temporary feelings of uniting, "of
oneness with this other person and a oneness with all the world"
(Bowers et al., 1967).

The point repeatedly at issue is that the experience of oneness,
the merging into a single whole, appears to be an essential accom-
paniment of experience intense enough to give the feeling of transcen-
dence. Autorities otherwise as diverse as Freud and Piaget agree
that the infant's experience of the world starts with an undifferen-
entiated feeling of oneness, an 'oceanic' feeling or one of total ego-
centricity without awareness of an object. It would then seem that the
regaining of this feeling of unification may be close in principle to
the primal state of the human being. Mystics often speak of the un-
knowing character of their transcendent experience, and Zen masters
speak of 'no mind': perhaps unification-undifferentiation replicates
the state of blissful ignorance.

In Cassirer's study, Language and Myth, he pursues some of these
notions in the direction of the earliest origins of religious experience.
Quoting missionaries and anthropological observers, he points to
the universal occurrence of the idea of a universal supernatural power,
a mana, manitu, orenda. Whatever specific supernatural beings or
occurrences are notable, the divine aspect is the participation of the
specific deity in this universal 'substance'. I would suggest that it
is the experience precisely of undifferentiation, of therefore full
and complete participation in a group life, that gives to this notion
its superhuman connotations. Tennyson speaks of Galahad having the
strength of ten because "his heart was pure", and the myth of An-
taeus gives us the notion of one invincible as long as he is still united
to his mother.

What these trends in their various contexts of origin suggest - to

a rather mundane interpretation – is that the human condition is one
in which the primary gratification and feeling of strength comes from
a sense of union with his group; on the converse, all of the negative
feelings of the human being have close relations with isolation and
alienation. In another place in the same essay, Cassirer discusses
the mechanism suggested by Usener as a primary source of religious
feeling and by implication as a primary method of binding a group
together through the use of a consensually shared belief system.

Usener suggests that life-saving objects or situations may become
integrated into human social systems by the deification of the object
through personification in a transcendent experience characterized
by strikingly abnormal sensory experiences. His example supposes
that a man on the verge of death by thirst suddenly finds a life-saving
spring which he worships as he drinks of it. Convinced of the miracu-
ous nature of the occurrence, the wanderer attaches to the spring a
sacred significance and a holy name. Subsequently, he brings his
family back to the spring to worship with him the deity he has named
in the spring. In this way, the religious impulse of human beings so
powerfully displayed in every known culture not only provides an explanation of the miraculous, it also provides a 'social cement' in the
emergence of the religious practices surrounding the miracle. A
group of human beings characterized by a deep belief of this sort is
automatically both bound together and differentiated from its neighbors, two reciprocal and powerful processes in the formation of a
human group through internal consolidation and external rivalry.

This hypothetical process provides us with a model for the formation of linguistic systems with specific significance for members of
the group usually identified by the language they speak. The paradoxically general character of human speech systems is that all are
idiosyncratic and arbitrary, even while all participate in general
rules of origin – even the general rule that none is knowable except
through detailed training in the system with the help of a previously
trained preceptor. In genetic semiotics, we find the curious interplay
of cultural groups identified by linguistic designation, the deeply significant personal relation of preceptor and novice, and the curious
counterpoint of clear definite speech patterns with obscure grammatical rules only apparent to the specific investigator.

In the following discussion, I would like to present material which
seems to me to demonstrate what happens in the fortunate instance in
psychotherapy at crucial junctures. There, for whatever personal or
technical reasons, from time to time intense feelings are released;
these transcendental feelings appear to be in the same series as
mystic experiences (though of lessened intensity). The specifically
visual component is well known in the feelings of astonished staring
in states of awe, and the visual component is specifically mentioned
in the Zen term 'illumination'. As far as we can know, these states
of feeling are specifically human. I would suggest that they always
involve a symbolic mediation which in turn depends upon the extraordinarily developed human visual apparatus and the enormous central connections of the visual modality which dominate brain physiology (Walter, 1950).

Symbolism shares with visual orientation the dominance of the external, the out-there. Language, learned through long and painful periods of study, is an external system which has to be internalized if it is to be effective. Internalization, as noted above, only occurs in the context of a powerful inducement to identify with a preceptor. Vision looks outward until after a long period of learning in which the human being learns to look back at himself from the point of view of the other – but again only after having powerfully identified himself with the other; as Mead says (1934), the human being becomes a subject to himself through first becoming an object to himself through taking the point of view of the other. In the process, self and other often are curiously intermixed so that it may be difficult to know which is which. The process, to repeat, is one in which in both contexts, internalization of an external system is necessary if the human novice is to become a member of a group in a manner which constitutes 'second nature'.

The external code, formulated in a linguistic-symbolic system of idiosyncratic structure, has to be learned in a process of internalization. This fact means that the human 'unit' has to be conceived in genetic terms as a dual unit of preceptor and novice, intricately bound together during a learning period. The earliest preceptor is obviously the mother, and nearly universal agreement can be found to the statement that the human infant requires intensive and effective mothering if he is to be able eventually to assume full status as a member of the human group and in his turn be able to fill the role of preceptor.

This notion finds technical application in the theoretical fields related to psychotherapy. The processes are often put in overly particular ways, but there is quite general agreement that the psychotherapist functions as a preceptor having certain similarities to a parent or teacher. The major difference between psychotherapist and ordinary teacher is that the psychotherapist pays most attention not to the subject matter but to the background of human relatedness. The ordinary teacher seeks to impart reading or writing or arithmetic without paying overt attention to the feelings of the student for the teacher or the teacher for the student. All sensitive teachers are clearly aware that the student having strong positive feelings for the teacher is much more likely to learn quickly; we can modify this statement in the direction of accuracy by saying, I believe, that the student with positive feeling tends much more to model himself upon the preceptor, just as in early life the child with positive feelings for the parent tends to 'identify' with the parent in behavioral terms. The 'tests' to which both student and teacher are subjected in ordinary schooling are, however, tests of 'objective' variety which seek to measure not human feeling but metrically estimable achievement.

A widespread conviction among psychotherapists (and, one might add, in statements attributed to religious leaders) is that this educational model puts the cart before the horse. The significant variable is that of the human relation; without adequate skills in human relational methods, the child's learning tends to be empty or even distressing. What we learn, in many unfortunate instances, is that it is possible in some instances to train children expertly in certain highly technical matters so that they can become expert (as in math-

ematics or music, for example) without having developed the basic
human skills which would allow them to enjoy themselves. The psychotherapist is repetitively familiar with human beings of more than
average success in metrically evaluated matters (salary, fame, promotion) who have intense feelings of inferiority in basic human processes.

If we return to the beginning, we can say that the ultimate stage of
reflective intelligence described by Piaget is that ultimate stage of
intellectual sophistication easily adaptable to formulation and processing in terms acceptable to the digital computer. Similarly, the
vast triumphs of contemporary science are triumphs in the field of
what Piaget refers to as that of "ideas or things". The corresponding
nearly total failure of metric science to deal with human problems
is becoming more and more evident daily.

The following report is oriented to the discussion of a specific problem in genetic semiotics, i. e., how those states of human relatedness
which effectively bind human beings into persisting groups emerge.
The methodology of study is clearly 'unscientific' in the ordinary
sense of replicable experimental procedures. States of human relatedness which are most important in group formation are idiosyncratic,
unique, non-replicable. It is quite impossible for the human being to
fall in love, or to undergo salvation in any religious system, or to
become illuminated or to experience the Aha-Erlebnis in a replicable
or reversible fashion. Human relatedness is essentially irreversible
and non-replicable.

This inexorable fact, put in formal terms in the metaphor of 'time's
arrow' used to refer to entropy, or in poetic metaphor in Omar Khay-
yam's statement that no number of tears will erase a single word of
the history written by the 'magic finger', is that human life moves so
that it cannot be revised. What happens later is always a superimpo-
sition, never a reformulation or a re-creation. For this reason, psychotherapy is a severely limited 'therapeutic' method. It is not possible to reconstruct an unsatisfactory parental relation; one can instead only work to construct as useful a preceptorial relation as possible at a time which must (for many early processes) be inappropriate.

On the other hand, through the use of psychotherapeutic methods,
it is possible to study the way in which human relatedness does develop. This is obviously not the same as studying the normal course
of development, and there is obviously a pressing rationale for studying the development of the human child in a variety of other methods.
What is unique about psychotherapy is that processes bearing what
seem to be a significant relation to those of early development do
become susceptible to description 'from inside'. The 'patient' - I
prefer the term 'novice' or 'student' - is occasionally so highly suitable to this kind of inquiry that he can describe with precocious verbal
skills emotional states which seem relatively 'primitive' in terms of
their occurrence in the usual life history. The 'normal' occasions for
having many such feeling states occur in pre-verbal periods or at
least those related to under-developed verbal methods. The sophisticated adult in this state is likely to be severely distressed or 'sick'

in the medical metaphor.

More and more it now appears that what we call 'mental illness' is more precisely described as 'intolerable deviance', whether that deviance is intolerable to the suffering human being himself or to the social system of which he is a member, though usually not a member in good standing. The 'therapeutic' effect of the procedure in the successful instance is that of reducing the deviance so that the 'patient' learns to 'adjust' or to 'adapt' so that his deviance is reduced.

The importance of the procedure for genetic semiotics is that there is a widespread agreement that at least some of the deviances encountered in 'patients' can be attributed to inadequate learning of symbolic method. In these persons, the inability to take what Goldstein (1939) calls an 'abstract attutude' toward others and the self is often very marked, and the task of the 'therapist' can be construed in an overly simple fashion as that of teaching the patient such symbolic techniques. I have very nearly completely persuaded myself that the therapist can usefully be defined as a 'language coach' giving vital instruction to the patient in a subject matter not otherwise covered.

Dual Unit and Religious Practice

Human cultures are so idiosyncratic in their structure that it requires a prolonged, intensive indoctrination for the novice to become fully acculturated (or accommodated, in Piaget's term). At this point, the novice 'fits' the preceptor so accurately that he can be separated and in his turn serve as a model for the next successive teaching-learning experience. The human being is thus never an 'individual' any more than a single half of a bilaterally symmetrical body can be thought of as 'an individual'.

Many of the problems of excessive variation in the series of preceptor-novice relations are taken care of by two mechanisms: in the first place, there are clear normative standards which apply to the nomination of preceptors; they have to be approved or cleared by a consensual evaluation. In this way, the preceptor is an agent of the group, and the series of preceptors is internalized as a 'generalized other', to use Mead's term. The other method of social control of variation is the postulation of unchanging deities, always the same, in a religious equivalent of the scientific ideal of invariance. Because of the need for persistence in such reference-points for the culture, the deity is either concretely formulated or understood as an invariant abstract notion.

When we investigate the origins of human groups, we find as premier relics of early cultures those of religious significance. So pronounced is the tendency to find idols as the only intact remnant of earliest forms of civilization that it may be said that 'iconology' is the ultimate study of human beginnings. The primitive human group clusters around a consensually validated deity represented by the primary human symbol, the idol. Such an idol has the enormous value that it represents an unchanging central point of reference. Two almost parenthetical comments may serve to illuminate this process. We find in Genesis the story of how Moses led his people out of bondage through forty years of wandering in the wilderness, and we realize how masterful Moses must have been to keep a group in being through so protracted a period. When Moses left the group even briefly for his sojourn on Mount Sinai, the group under the inadequate substitute leadership of Aaron was unable to sustain itself without an idol, and they made a golden calf to provide themselves with a concrete symbol. When Moses returned, after having wrestled his way through to the conception of a God as Law (which predicts the ultimate statement of John that "In the beginning was the Word, and the Word was with God, and the Word was God"), he was forced to reassert his leadership and destroy the competing religious artifact febore imposing the literate deity upon the Jews. The efficacy of the abstract version of God is evident to this day in the persistence of the Jewish people as an identified group.

In the other parenthetical comment, at a vast distance in significance, the most fascinating of the implications of Harlow's work in monkeys with surrogate mothers is that the disability suffered by the infants so attended can be partly understood as derived from the total predictability of the surrogate. The infant must be trained in the tolerance of ambiguity through the unpreditability of the parent, otherwise he is unequipped to deal with the general unpredictability of his life. The deity is presented as "The Same, yesterday, today, and tomorrow", but this predictability is abstract and subject to interpretation. The totally predictable attendant is crippling because misleading.

The Clinical Background

The dramatic material to be reported was preceded in the series of interviews by the patient's comment that he had noted a severe restriction of his capacity for intense feeling in the past year or two. He noticed the deficiency especially in his capacity to respond to music; like many highly intellectual persons, he was often unusually responsive to music. The basis of the restriction is clearly suggested in the subsequent comment that he fears being 'carried away'. The ordinary descriptions of feeling we use suggest that the process is one in which a primary characteristic is helplessness: we 'are moved'. One can control the intensity of feeling by predictively blocking movement, but such a block is necessarily general and unselective. Then danger threatens that 'being moved' will become explosive unless totally inhibited.

In the first of the three interviews discussed here, the patient comments in relation to the effect of the therapy,

1   I have sat and wished I could respond to music ... tried to force it ... and of course the feeling does not come ... There are several things within the last year to which I have begun to react ... there's a fear on my part of over-reacting ... I have a

feeling that one of these days I'm going just to <u>really</u> react ...

These comments served to introduce the theme of the patient's reluctance to allow the therapist control of the situation and his fear of 'total surrender'.

We tend to think the severely disturbed patient incapable of free association in the classic mode. Such a patient may be incapable of allowing himself a 'free-floating' attention. In emotional disturbances, paradox and contradiction abound: the 'lesion' is that of the loss of control in a 'fragmentation' or loss of integration of various controlling measures with each other. The limits of self-control are well seen in the highly skilled, competent athlete who can both relax completely and gather up his muscular resources into a supreme integrated effort: the integrity of the controlling system is exhibited as much in the capacity to relax as in the capacity to perform.

The Passivity of the Creative Worker

The problem of free-floating attention is faced not only by the patient in the therapeutic situation but as well by any creative artist attempting principally to express some significant emotional experience in words or on canvas. Unless he can allow himself to be sufficiently 'loose', as many art teachers prescribe, he cannot allow himself to be the executor of his own imagination.

A central problem in psychotherapy of the insight type is that of allowing oneself to abandon predictive control of what he will be saying. In the ordinary course of events, the child is schooled in practices of 'concentrating' and 'paying attention'. In the techniques of 'free association', a determined effort is made to reverse this monitoring so that the stream of talk will be as random as possible, flitting from topic to topic, memory to fantasy on a kind of 'will o' the wisp' basis. The rationale sometimes offered is that only when conscious direction is relaxed can one see the results of the kind of 'unconscious' structuring which reveals what is ordinarily automatically concealed. Patterns appearing and reappearing in the midst of such randomized talk are likely to be more revealing than any degree of effortful self-explanation. This basic principle is consensually recognized in the saying, "Actions speak louder than words", and the revealing possibilities of impairing conscious control are similarly revealed in the saying, "<u>In vino veritas</u>".

The problem of 'control' is paradoxically closely related inversely to the degree of integration observable in a subject's behavior. The poised, successful person is usually much more readily able to exhibit himself in a ridiculous setting or posture than is this insecure felllow; he submits to transient humiliation in initiation procedures, and he can laugh at his own predicament in practical jokes. The more insecure, on the other hand, the less can the human being concerned allow himself to lose control. Again, the benefits of being able to let go on a temporary basis are evident in the prescription for religious salvation, namely, that only those who can lose their lives are likely to gain them.

A special case of this problem is to be found in the report left by Proust. Abundant evidence suggests that Proust was, along with many highly creative authors, relatively unstable in his emotional life; he himself underlines a life-long neurotic state traced by him to his mother's inability to maintain discipline. After a life of apparent irrelevance, Proust found himself in middle age suddenly 'pregnant' (his own metaphor) with a great book. He reports that to write this book, he had to learn the technique of abandoning himself to his own control, submitting utterly to the material 'dictated' to him somehow from 'inside'. This technique corresponds rather closely to free association except for the solipsistic quality of relating it to himself alone. The interposition of the therapist in the free association technique appears to be the basis of the power of facilitating intense states of feeling as the patient submits to the instructions of the therapist. The intense 'transference' reaction often described as 'falling in love with the therapist' is closely related to this submission. In turn, the difficulty the disturbed patient has in making this total submission is a characteristic feature of his 'resistance'.

Theme and Variation

Although the body of psychoanalytic theory set forth by Freud suffers in the main from an excessive concreteness (in a way which is quite reasonable when one considers it by comparison with other initial or preliminary statements), the central methodological approach through the techniques of free association and interpretation appears to offer remarkable potentialities for further investigation. A brief discussion of each of these may serve as an introduction to some detailed examination of interview material with a view to illustrating the major details evident in the condition of 'thought-disorder'.

The voluntary assumption of the appropriate posture in which free association can take place is perhaps the most important feature of the classical psychoanalytic procedure. 'Posture' here is used in a very broad sense, with the implication that the relevant posture includes various different components: the ability to tolerate periods of prolonged solitude in the presence of another person, the ability to describe into a vacuum fantastic and ever-changing images, the ability to persist in an approach the tangible rewards of which over long periods of time are difficult or impossible to evaluate, and so on. There are as well on the opposite side of the picture many hidden benefits, but here I point mainly to the strict requirements for entry into the small circle of those who can carry out free-associational procedures for long periods of time.

To the observer-therapist, it becomes clear with experience that not only is there a small number of persons capable of free association in the classical sense, but also that with any patient there are only occasional periods in which the technique is comprehensively carried out. These periods are interpolated between longer intervals in which there is only an approximation of the state. It is quite impossible to predict when the patient will fall into the free-associational state or how long the period will be prolonged. In working with a patient, there is suddenly from time to time a feeling of freedom and progress which resembles as much as anything else in feeling the sudden discovery of precisely the right combination of elements in sailing or skiing to give a sense of freedom, or in the occasional dramatic performance in which the auditor is 'pulled out of himself'. The mysterious fact of the sudden appearance and disappearance of this kind of capacity is one of the principal features of the extraordinary difficulty in doing research. It is only possible to gather material from this kind of mutual interaction by collecting many recordings and paying particular attention to the periods of heightened relatedness and mutuality of understanding which characterize the productive episodes; but this necessarily retrospective selection is the opposite of scientific procedures of prediction and experiment.

Free Association and Mysticism

What might be the nature of the process in which the patient from time to time comes to be able to allow himself to wander freely in his imagination reporting the apparently random thoughts and describing the images which come to his attention? A good deal of personal experience indicates that this state has some resemblance to the state of dreaming, eslecially to that of day-dreaming, and there are possibilities that there are resemblances to the 'mystic' state sometimes described by poets and seers. There is an extensive literature on the contemplative life, and a great deal of evidence from religious persons that meditation leads to significant new awareness of one's inner experience. It is tempting to believe that all these states might have in common the 'free-wheeling' kind of imaging occasionally found in psychotherapeutic interviews.

The state of creative image-formation was described by Wordsworth:

> ... that blessed mood,
> In which the burthen of the mystery,
> In which the heavy and the weary weight
> Of all this unintelligible world,
> Is lightened; - that serene and blessed mood,
> In which the affections gently lead us on, -
> Until, the breath of this corporeal frame
> And even the motion of our human blood
> Almost suspended, we are laid asleep
> In body, and become a living soul:
> While, with an eye made quiet by the power
> Of harmony, and the deep power of joy,
> We see into the life of things.

It is at least possible that the state of free association is an artificially facilitated version of the mystical state, and that it is primarily within this state that the creative change in image formation (so characteristic of psychotherapy at its most effective heights) takes place. The ability to allow this state to come into being is one of the principal features of the condition allowing interpretation in the most important sense.

In the most effective usage of free association, one gets glimpses of the creative experiences of the human condition. The material presented below occurred in a sequence of three interviews with this patient during a particular period of heightened affectivity, and such a creative period of imaging did not occur during any of the remainder of the interviews. This is not to say that much of great interest did not occur at other times, but the material in these three interviews is creatively meaningful in terms not only of the relationship of this patient and this therapist but also in terms of relations between emotionally distressed human beings and vaguely perceived authoritarian figures in other, often relatively primitive, contexts.

In this sequence the effect of appropriate interpretation can be seen in the manner in which the interpretation complements the image so that it in effect completes some sequence allowing the subsequent emergence of another, affectively more intensely 'charged', set of image-and-interpretation. The interpretative process in general is one which attempts to define a central problem of human relatedness of a human being who suffers and one who in some way offers potential relief from suffering, with the former's problems of a wish to submit utterly and the fear of destruction involved in the act of submission.

Interview Material

The three interviews center around the period of termination of an official relationship; in beginning the relation, the patient was informed that, on the basis of a similarity to other research projects going on, it was possible to offer a series of twenty interviews without any charge. Later it was decided between therapist and patient that the series would continue. In the first of the three interviews the patient remarked upon the fact that this was the twentieth; he made it clear that in his understanding, the twenty interviews were his contribution to the goal of releasing him from the hospital in which he was first seen. He had, in spite of many comments as to the purely voluntary nature of his participation, continued to understand that the period was a kind of 'indenture' in which he was working his way out of obligation for having been released. He had a 'graduation' feeling; the first comments reflect this in that for the first time he asks questions about the destination of the material and tells about his feelings of fear in relation to certain aspects of the psychotherapeutic situation.

first interview

After asking about the possible audience for the taped material and being told again of the research nature of the procedure, he told of discussing psychotherapy with a friend and having the question as to who listens come to mind; he then abruptly begins to talk of feelings of:

> a sinking sensation in the stomach, with a feeling of expansion
> in the body ... in the torso ... in the sense of pushing from
> within out ... This will happen to me if I simply think something
> 2 is about to go wrong.

He then relates this back to the therapeutic situation in saying,

> ... when upset ... I immediately think I'm going to break off
> 3 with Dr. S ... I get in an emotional situation and then I'm going
> to spite you ...

The patient then compares his recent feelings with those further back:

> ... for a number of years until about two years ago my emotions
> 4 were knotted constantly ... a knot above the stomach and below
> the heart ... right in the middle between the lungs ... For some
> reason two years ago this went away to be replaced by a worse
> kind of feeling ... that the knot is there but you cannot feel it ...
> I mean I actually had to force myself to feel ... to music, I have
> sat and wished I could respond ...

To a suggestion of the therapist's that he is reacting to him the patient
responds that:

> 1a I have the feeling that one of these days I'm going to ... really
> react

and agrees that his fear is one of being quite carried away by un-
governable feeling (cf. excerpt =1 above).
Continuing, he returns to the conversation about psychotherapy
and expresses his anger at the act of dependence reported by a young
woman friend,

> ... this young lady had had eight years of psychotherapeutic
> treatment ... and described a moment in which she had thrown
> 5 herself totally on her psychiatrist ... and my reaction ... was
> one of extreme anger ... I could never do such a thing ... He
> wants me to get down and kneel to him.

He speaks of his fear that the therapist will demand a surrender and
is reminded of his feelings as a child:

> ... the most humiliating thing ... was that I had been created
> 6 by a creator, and that while he could dabble with me, I could
> not dabble with him ... in my last stages of believing that there
> was a God, I had real hatred for the fact that he could permit
> evil and at the same time insist upon the goodness of man ...
> This was related to my feeling that perhaps Dr. S. is completely
> wrong - perhaps the answer lies in being totally evil ... There

was a resentment against this - that you are trying to cast an
illusion over my mind once again which I <u>will</u> break through,
and then I'll find myself even worse than before ... in disil-
lusion and despair.

The therapist pointed out how he feared a second loss of faith, and
the patient responded again with memories of his experience in par-
ochial school:

> ,... God ... in the Catholic religion ... demanded total surren-
> der ... Nuns have used this in reference to God, "You must
> have total surrender" ...

The therapist asked if he appeared to demand total surrender, and
the patient responded that during the conversation with the friend,
it had suddenly seemed that way:

> ... when he used the phrase 'total surrender' it changed suddenly
> 8   ... It became the giving up of everything ... pride ... indepen-
> dence.

But he points out the basis in anxiety for the feeling:

> ... I get the feeling that I'm right and you're wrong - that the
> 9   world is a vicious, voracious place ... in case I were in trouble
> I would be abandoned - you could go on with your theories, and
> I would be destroyed.

The therapist pointed out the patient was struggling with incompatible
wishes, those of 'freedom' without having to make decisions or
choices. After several more interchanges, he tried to point out to
the patient some of his anticipations:

> I have very few hopes of changing you radically ... This kind of
> change I hope I can help you accomplish is in the direction of
> T-1 understanding ... the incompatibility ... You want to be very
> big and small at the same time ... to merge with everything and
> to be separate ... to kill yourself and to live in a world in which
> aggression does not exist ... I'm trying to point out ... that if
> you want 'A' you can't have 'not-A' ... and the decision has got
> to be your own ... Each sentiment, feeling, plan, memory, fear,
> hope has its opposite - as one comes up, the other other disap-
> pears ... like a seesaw.

A question from the patient as to how he happened to get this way led
to a discussion of his parents; he said,

> My mother has the same dual role ... on the one hand she will
> speak in terms of the goodness of people and on the other hand
> 10   ... her distrust of people is almost monumental ... She will
> help a person, but she will not go beyond that ... she wants no
> more involvement with the person ...

He came back to his father, saying,

> My father is a very remote person ... I have never been able to
> get close to him ... My father is very athletic ... and in terms
> 11 of mathematics and engineering he has a brilliant and creative
> mind ... As a reaction I found it extremely difficult to do physi-
> cal exercise ... this determination that their child would not
> share the despair that they have found in life, and as a result
> it produced the opposite despair ...

He returns to a feeling of difference from others long experienced,
saying,

> The feeling of difference from other people and especially from
> other boys was quite great ... I never really wondered whether
> 12 I was a boy because it was so obvious to me ... it was more a
> complete inability to ... communicate with them ...

He remembered how he had been ill much of his adolescence and was
unable to think of himself in any way as a competitor of his father's,
then returns to the therapeutic context:

> I have also a much greater feeling of wanting to communicate
> 13 with you because ... the experiment had come to an end in my
> mind ... it was no longer working up my release from the hospi-
> tal ... Today was the last one ... the last ... and the first.

The therapist commented upon the graduation-commencement implication. The patient said,

> ... you too graduate with me ... you are no longer the jail
> 14 springer ... For the first time it has seemed voluntary ...

second interview

In the second interview, the patient began, saying,

> ... on Thursday I found as we came closer together, there was
> a greater fear on my part ... I have had it in the past ... First
> 15 of all there is a melting feeling in the torso ... and a type of
> ache ... a type of hunger ... a feeling of attempting to stop ...
> My usual reaction ... was always to end contact with the person
> ... and second to make the person a boorish person ... or a
> dependent person. This kind of situation would end in misunder-
> standing ...

The therapist pointed out to the patient his fear of losing himself in
a close relationship, commenting on the threat to one's own self-
image in the act of identification and reminding the patient of his
autonomy and the possibility of abandoning the relationship at any
time. The patient replied with a comment that:

... the feeling ... came to me as a surprise ... that feeling ...
16   had come ... when I was an adolescent in high school ...

Some moments later, the patient commented that there was nothing on
his mind, and that there was a frustrated feeling. He went on to say:

... if I feel that someone has not quite gotten the point, I feel as
17   though I am moving away ... I can feel almost as though somebody would shut a door ... draw up a drawbridge over the moat
... A feeling that if he does not understand, that is that ...

He demanded explanation, but accepted a suggestion that too convincing an explanation might lead to paranoid fears of 'mind-reading'.
The patient said:

My mind does this, I know. When somebody has seen something
18   that I have had this double feeling about - I do want him to see
it - I don't want him to see it ... my mind or eyes will cast the
person in the role of a misunderstanding ... I can close the door
and have this feeling of drawing back ... a physical sensation of
withdrawing ... there's a feeling of tiredness ... a type of res-
ignation ...

He described a sensation similar to that he remembered before his
suicide attempt, one which came on while writing a paper about a
place, Barren Grounds, in Canada. He went on to some associations:

Barren Grounds is an arctic region ... completely frozen underneath the ground. Swampy during the summer for the first few
19   inches of topsoil ... Many streams, rivers, almost uninhabitable
... The feeling is accurate ... of frozen ground underneath the
mind ... the vast majority of the mind is frozen ... swampy on
the top ... When human relationships become somewhat warm,
it becomes swampy, soft ...

The patient again recalled his suicide attempt, and thought of a repetitive dream:

... people searching ... I know they are searching for me - I'm
20   somewhere ... I think of a man I saw in Central Park ... walking
and saying that he was too crazy to be in Bellevue ... I thought
of how this city is so very destructive, of the way it grinds you
slowly ... We have a park in the middle of the city so we can
see a tree ... And of course the inevitable thought of this is
psychotherapy - an hour two times a week in which ... one goes
into a park ... The zoo comes to mind ... because it smells
so bad ...

His mood of depression continued:

My parents ... saying that life is good ... never convincing me

21 that they agreed ... Certainly life did not seem good to me at
    any time ... It was always a burden ...

He remarked upon the reappearance of some disturbing pains in the
extremities and in his chest. There followed some discussion of the
medical possibilities; the patient told of reassurance in detailed
examination, and the therapist suggested that he retained a belief in
his illness for defensive purposes. The patient responded with comments about his fear of incapacitation, and the therapist pointed out
the problem of helplessness on both their parts in predicting the outcome of the relationship.
In responding, the patient described an image:

    ... a person bent, weeping ... my mind says to me, "you must
22 cry" so the person in my mind cries.

The therapist made an interpretation that the patient had prevented
the appearance of a feeling by splitting himself and projecting the
feeling into the image of the weeping figure. He again reminded the
patient of the uncertain nature of the outcome and pointed out that the
therapeutic situation was very difficult, that:

       working with a patient so clever and so disturbed ... the com-
T-2 bination is fascinating ... challenging ... but not easy ...

To this the patient responded at once:

    I feel right now as though I were twenty feet farther from you ...
23 and suddenly you become very bright ... your image in my eyes
    becomes much brighter ... you ... just you, noting else, will
    become lustrous, almost as though a light were placed in you ...
    and burned ...

The therapist pointed to the possibility that his experience is that of
being 'illuminated' in direct physical terms, and the patient responded:

    ... the thought ... that came into my mind is that when he gets
24 up I'm going to bite his arm ... I've never had that thought be-
    fore in my life ...

third interview

In the last of the series of three interviews, the patient discussed in
some detail feelings and images representing variations on themes
introduced in the previous two interviews. In one of these themes,
he reproduced in his own idiosyncratic way some of the characteristic
features of religious conversion, surrender, and the 'peace which
passeth understanding'. It is of interest to note that this aspect of the
psycho therapeutic process often very closely resembles the course

of the religious experiences cited by William James. The intense rejection of the idea of submission or surrender is often the prelude to giving in; the struggle against surrender is often accompanied by intensely unpleasant feelings, to be followed after surrender by peace or even ecstatic feeling.

The patient began:

> ... these last two days ... it has been especially difficult ... When I become tired these anxieties and feelings come out much
> 25 more strongly ... I would have great difficulty in conceptualizing things ... more depression than normal ... the feeling is, well, I will leave for Timbuktoo or whatever ... One moves eighteen, nineteen times - if ever there were any personal conflicts I would leave fairly soon ... There was a certain degree of comfort in the very mobility of my life ...

He then comes back to a group of intense and unusual feelings which have the dual implication of comfort and anxiety:

> After that emotion or feeling on Tuesday ... the bright sensation and the thought 'I want to bite his arm', I had a feeling I cannot
> 26 ever remember having ... a feeling I would imagine a baby would have ... Freud used the word 'oceanic feeling' to refer to religion, but I would use it to refer to this ... a type of just thorough satisfaction ... of - I hate to use the word - of pure pleasure ... that type of buoyancy, almost a euphoria ... The entire torso and also the mind felt not only at rest but as though nothing could possibly disturb it ... and then the feeling withered ... I do not remember ever having it, because in the past when I have accomplished something, the feeling has been one of diametrically opposed feelings ... of satisfaction and also ... of error ...

In response, the therapist emphasized the transference implication of the feeling, along with his conviction that this kind of experience is 'bigger than both of us'; he commented that the development of the feeling of pure pleasure often follows strongly negative feelings, and that the whole sequence appears to be a function of the process of becoming assimilated into some human group. The patient returned with some wonder to the curious fantasy which led up to the 'oceanic' feeling.

> I wonder why the thought 'I want to bite your arm' ... and also the feeling of the incandescence ... Why should you suddenly become incandescent? ... I had all kinds of associations ... When I was a child, I loved to lie in bed and look at the naked light bulb ... I can become almost transfixed by light - a naked
> 27 light bulb - even today ... the light bulb becomes larger and larger ... until when I was a child felt almost as though I and the light bulb were one ... It would always seem very fascinating to me ... it became a source of pleasure to look at the light bulb

and watch it go like this ... I'd get black spots ... this sort of
black fringe on a ray of light ... a whole arc of light in a circular manner ... ragged at the edges and had differentiated
colors on the edge ... this would be an extremely great source
of enjoyment when I was ... oh, I suppose eight to about thirteen.

The therapist pointed to the 'merging' of patient and light. He responded:

One reason might be I was lying down so much ... It was one of
the few things with which I seemed to have any communication
28   ... There was the feeling that I could control the light - it turned
off when I wanted it to, and I could turn it on if I wanted to ...
This was during the same period with the struggle with religion.

The therapist pointed out the impossibility of 'turning off' the struggle
with religion, and the patient went on to speak of other fears:

This was related to ... a great polio epidemic that year ... My
feeling was I would be struck down ... This was related to the
beginning of the sexual problem ... when I was 11 I matured ...
29   a good two years earlier than most of the people I knew ... My
parents had given me a very descriptive and thorough book ...
I still find that if I open a book which relates to sex, I get a
feeling of guilt ... My parents were very covert in some ways
... it seemed never to be related to their lives ... I would never
have guessed that they were man and woman ... They act toward
one another like brother and sister.

He continued:

The carnality seems to be utterly removed ... I think by the
choice of both of them ... I had my first seminal emission when
I was very young ... I think I was 10 ... At that ime it was explained to me that this was something that happened to boys...
nothing to worry about ... But gradually that grew in my mind
30   as something very evil ... My parents were puzzled ... they
had a split in their attitude in that they were reluctant to discuss
anything ... I never got the sense from them that sex was wrong,
but ... it was never mentioned. When my mother was a child,
her mother would send her out of the room if a pregnant woman
were in the room - until she was 20 ... nothing was ever explained to her ... With my father ... neither of his parents ever
told him about sexual matters ... They were determined when
they had me that they would be liberal about these matters ...
Their responses were often responses of great inarticulateness
... I think there was also a fear on their part that if they illuminated me I might want a taste ... Their desire to keep me a child
was strong ...

The therapist commented upon the impersonal quality in the parents'
offering a book, and pointed out that the turning off and on of a light

had a similar impersonal quality, noting that both tended to emphasize an intellectual approach to life. He commented that the patient's vast store of intellectual knowledge seemed all acquired through written communication, none by word of mouth.

In replying, the patient was reminded of his job, working with books and source material. He comments upon his overwhelming feelings of guilt:

> One thing that has played a huge role in my life is ... guilt ...
> 31   This is related to the fear of losing something ... I will never use a piece of office paper for my own purpose ... This was what I was like when I was a child ... it was God for a while. I can remember when I first wanted to masturbate, I would do it to show God how bad man was ... I would sort of say, "God, come look see how bad man can be, but I'm good because I'm showing it to you!" I can remember that very well ... I could not sleep, because of this fear ...

The therapist commented that perhaps this feeling had something to do with the fantasy of biting his arm; the patient smiled, complained that his mind was blank, then said:

> The only thing that comes to mind is a poisonous fish ... a puffer ... or balloon fish -. The thought I get is of a very small ...
> 32   highly illuminated creature who could be described as a fetus biting into black ... His features are not distinct, but I know he is biting ... There's just black - everything is black around him ...

The therapist repeated, "fetus", and the patient responded:

> A fetus - yes ... I must admit I get the strangest feeling when the image comes to mind ... I get the feeling of peace again ... I
> 33   wonder if I'm having a memory of what I had done ... when I've been in the womb ... This is how I imagine it would be ... The only other images I get are of mouths ... of the little figures facing me ... with jagged teeth, sort of row after row of them ... his mouth ... that kind of image ... no eyes, nostrils ... He does have nostrils, he has very large teeth ... when he opens, one can see only red or black ...

The therapist commented that the idea seemed to be that of being swallowed up, and suggested that there might be a fantasy of being swallowed by the therapist. The patient immediately responded by asking:

> 34   Why should you be the little figure?

and the therapist pointed a reversal: first, the original fantasy of biting the therapist's arm led to images suggesting the patient's idea that a fetus is a nasty, disagreeable thing, a feeling perhaps derived

from his parents' rejection of him in certain significant ways - but
with the implication of peacefulness in the relation of total dependence,
'biting into blackness', feeding from an unknown source. But then he
sees himself as in danger of being engulfed, swallowed up, perhaps
as a talion punishment. He reassured the patient as to the admissibility of any kind of fantasy; there need be no guilt whatsoever.

The patient responded:

> A great problem ... even in fantasy is that for so long I felt every
> 35   thought was known ... when I was a child ... Catholics pour this
> into you until you are filled with your cup running over ... Since
> then ... one of the things I have most missed was the ability to
> have fantasies. There has been a wall ... One thing I want from
> all of this ... that makes me willing to undergo whatever pains
> ... is ... I would like to sit down and let my mind run ... Just
> as you say, the fantasy does not hurt you, but my mind does not
> realize this ... Things that are real to me simply do not exist ...

The therapist commented that the sensation of impact with a solid world
might well be expected to be very painful to one who had never been
accustomed to it. The patient then wondered why he should want to
bite the therapist, and proceeded to some further associations:

> ... I see a wild boar running - once again with the same kind of
> 36   teeth ... frightened ... suddenly two spears in him ... Then I
> see one of those stone age birds ... It goes from being a bird to
> becoming a set of bones ... in a moment ...

The therapist pointed out to him that the threatening boar, with dangerous teeth, seems to have been killed; the historic bird goes from
flight to bone in an instant, suggesting the implication of the utter destructiveness of death, with instant dissolution. The fantasy of attack
and that of instant retaliation appear to be balanced in this series of
associations, with processes speeded up to an impossible rate.

After a long pause, the patient said:

> I get the feeling that everything in my conception is set off against
> 37   a very black background ... not sinister ...

The therapist suggested black in the sense of unknown, and that the
therapist himself as an unknown might be for the patient a black unknown. The idea was developed that the sudden brightness might be
a reaction to the previous blackness, and that perhaps the idea of
biting is a primitive means of grasping such an unknown. The patient
responded with a statement of the 'equation':

> 38   Then in taking hold of you, I would really see you; is that it?

The therapist commented on the possibility that the patient's capacity
to 'take hold' had to be first expressed in relatively primitive concrete
terms - biting, for instance, is a dog's only means of grasping.

After another long pause, the patient said:

39   ... The desire to come more often had been in my mind ... One relation is it is on my mind, and I will not mention it ...

The therapist pointed out that this is a way of mentioning it while not mentioning it, and responded to the implied question by suggesting that the patient might well be more distressed by a closer relation than he thought at the moment. The patient replied by commenting that this roundabout method of asking for things was one he remembered from his childhood.

In reviewing some of the material, the therapist pointed out to the patient that the feeling of guilt of which he complained could be thought of as an identification with the judge, a method of being both criminal and judge. The incident of demonstrating his masturbation to God seems a method of being in fantasy both a nasty little fellow and God himself at the same time; he wondered what the patient's feeling about biting God might have been.

The patient paused, then said:

40   Whatever desire one would have that was displaced by communion also drinking God's blood ... I think the physical satisfaction that one desires from God is satisfied very much in this way ... This is the thing that sustains nuns ... Now I can see that it is the same thing I tried to do with you - 'let us both look at the patient' ... the pain of stepping into the one role ... It is impossible to step into the role of the judge completely - the only possible complete role is that of the condemned - or the patient ...

The therapist ended the interview by pointing out to the patient his equating of 'patient' and 'condemned' and suggesting that there is a difference.

Comment

The capacity to have this kind of experience is one which goes along with a very unusual combination of intelligence in the 'genius' range coupled with a bizarre childhood experience and culminating in a highly distorted kind of personality in adult life. The prominent feature of this personality from the standpoint of the present communication is the retention of a capacity to have a very infantile kind of experience while having at the same time the developed adult capacity to report this experience in verbal terms. Such a subject serves as an interpreter reporting events otherwise entirely unknowable. There is some degree of similarity to the function of the Rosetta stone, by means of which otherwise totally untranslatable forgotten languages became possible. The reliability of such reports cannot be other than extremely ambiguous, since it is by the very nature of the event impossible to replicate the data. It becomes a matter of faith, supported by the significance of the insights offered into the early prehistory of human-kindness.

   In addition to the factors of high intelligence and a bizarre childhood experience an almost continuous childhood illness also strongly
affected the ultimate situation. In the patient reported here, the
further factor of continuous change of geographical location seems
significant as well. The result of all these is that of an alienation
from ordinary experience. In this patient, there are many different
ways in which he reports on the painfulness of contact with human
beings, almost like the pain of contact with a denuded area of skin.
Such a child has little chance to develop a Reizschutz, a 'stimulus
barrier' by means of which to emphasize the surface separating him
from others.
   There is a curious paradoxical implication to the development of
the Reizschutz; this kind of 'barrier' is closely related to the conception of an 'Ego-boundary', and we tend to think of it as analogous to
the line which delimits a drawing or the vessel which holds some
fluid content. The full awareness of the implication of the boundary,
however, must take into account that the transactional nature of the
relation makes the boundary as much an aspect of the 'ground' as it
is of the 'figure'. That is to say, that it is an interface rather than
a surface, or, perhaps even more accurately, a double surface, de-
limiting not just one but both aspects of the situation. For the most
serene relationship, the two parties must agree upon the common
definition of the interface; they must both be aware of the implications
of impact, and, if desirous of simplification of the relationship, must
take predictive action on both sides to avoid painful 'bumps' with each
other.
   In the absence of such an interface of a dependable nature, the
person must depend upon the continuation of physical and social separation. His methods of contact and communication with others are
likely to depend more and more upon written symbols; the message on
paper is a totally passive intermediary which can be handled or not
at will. Such a message, in the opposite direction, has potentialities
of extraordinary power, as witness the importance of any of the great
written documents of the human history. The combination of total
passivity with the implication of great power offers precisely the
combination of opposites which becomes so fascinating to a person
of this kind.
   Written communications offer possibilities of impotent power, of
emotionless emotion. In fact, the 'inherent' power depends entirely
upon the response of the human respondent, but this degree of re-
moteness allows an artist to enjoy the fantasy of greatness in anticipation, in obscurity, and in isolation. He is confronted with none
of the responsibility of power, nor with any of the clinging closeness
of human relatives.
   The artist's image of himself as potent by virtue of his 'contents'
resembles in some way that of a woman pregnant with an Emperor.
Proust describes at length his own feelings in this regard. Much of
his life he felt himself a useless dilettante, of no consequence; but
when the idea of his book emerged to him, his attitude changed radically. He felt the tremendous responsibility of delivery, and, from
a state in which he reported feelings of contempt for himself, he became the guardian of a great treasure, having now intense anxiety

about dying before finishing the 'delivery'.

In the early years of this century, Tausk, working with schizo-
phrenics in Vienna in the early enthusiasm with psychoanalytic ideas,
wrote a remarkable paper on the 'influencing machine' in which he
discussed the rather common paranoid delusion of being influenced
by, or controlled by, some alien mechanism. He pointed out in this
paper how the idea of the machine projected out into the world away
from the self, represents a failure of integration of the various parts
of the body into the whole, and he commented upon the curious problem that the human being has to learn to identify with himself. In a
very different kind of discussion, L'Hermitte, a French neurologist
writing about the body-image in a neurological context, points out
that the child has to learn what belongs to him through the process
of determining the sensory correlate of various experiences. He
learns most rapidly about his own bodily extent through the feeling
of pain. He can be sure, usually, that if some experience is associated with pain, it is an experience affecting some part of his own
body. Where pain is not a feature, it is more likely that whatever has
been affected is not part of himself.

In material derived from interviews with this patient, the problem
is very clearly described. He mentions many different kinds of situations in which he experiences strong feelings of merging, and on
many occasions comments upon the wish to lose his separateness
and to flow into everything without demarcation, a psychological
goal which is closely consonant with his interest in Eastern religions
in which this merging, as in Nirvana, is a commonly accepted goal.
It may, parenthetically, be the case that the difference between the
Nirvana theme and the emphasis specifically given to the construction
of a firm boundary around the self in Western (especially Western
Protestant) thought is the most fundamental difference between the
two traditions.

The character of abrupt reversal in the midst of a course of action, with the subsequent construing of the situation in terms precisely the opposite of those previously understood, is characteristic
of this patient throughout. By this I mean that in the data dealing with
his wish to merge into the therapist there is the immediate counter-
current of a fear of losing himself. He describes the "melting sensation ... a type of ache ... hunger", then remembers his effort to
depreciate the former objects of this kind of feeling, trying to make
the other into a "boorish person or a dependent person", and he
remembered that it had been some years since he had had this feeling
of coming close. The subsequent quotation, above, describes his
further attempt to withdraw, to "shut a door", "draw up a drawbridge", accompanied by a feeling of fatique.

The degree of the patient's problem in remaining separate is well
seen in the continuing material in which he describes his feelings
of sameness with "Barren Grounds": his feeling of a "frozen ground
underneath the mind" with a "swampy" area on top, and underneath
in some remote place a feeling of molten lava. The indication here
is one of great interest, since it points to the paradoxical combination
in the schizophrenic of a wish to "freeze" to avoid "being mushy";

the feelings of many such persons are actually very easily moved, and they have learned to protect themselves by withdrawing from closeness whether of a positive or a negative type. The simile of the porcupines on a cold night, coming close together to warm each other but finding themselves pricked by each other in too close quarters, has been cited with relation to these patients.

Developmental Implications

The source of the difficulty in this patient, and by implication in others (especially the isolated Emily Dickinson, the pampered asthmatic Proust, etc.) is suggested by other material in the excerpts above set down. The patient mentions in many places other than the above his intolerance for conflict of any sort; in one place he mentions his suicidal reaction to the marked difference of opinion he found between two doctor-partners. One said he was very ill, the other that it was all "in his head"; but his reaction was to wish to destroy himself to avoid having to cope with this kind of difference of opinion. In the material above, he comments upon his inability to see himself as a boy among boys. He makes a distinction between the anatomical and the social definition in saying that of course he knew he was a boy, but that he did not feel in any way at home with, or contiguous with the group of boys when with them.

In the third interview, when he returns to the problem of merging in describing the "oceanic feeling" of "satisfaction ... pure pleasure ... buoyancy ... euphoria" he had experienced, he first mentioned previous experiences in which this kind of feeling had set him up for an abrupt reversal into its opposite feeling of "terror", but, subsequently, he brings up a hypothesis about the development of some of his problems. He says, with reference to the feeling of "incandescence" which flooded his awareness of the therapist that he was reminded of childhood games of "falling into the light", of becoming "transfixed" by it, of becoming one with the light source. He comments upon two major considerations for the development; first, that lying in bed, segregated from his fellows by the constant moving about and by his own "illness", he had no other respondent with which to communicate. The light bulb further qualifies in terms of its utter susceptibility to control; it can be turned on and off at will. To return for the moment to the Boolean algebra, the relation here is clearly put by the patient as a binary one, with no possibility of ambiguity as the switch is moved in the 'on' or the 'off' position.

In the subsequent part of this interview, the patient returns to the same theme in a different context: here the patient describes his intolerance for finding himself in the position in which he was happy to put the mechanism controlling the light.

He found it intolerable to be 'dabbled with' by a creator who did not in reciprocity allow the patient to 'dabble with' him. What I want particularly to call attention to here is the persistence of pattern - the relation of omnipotent to impotent reciprocal role-occupants - but with the feeling of pleasure in being omnipotent (with reference to the light-switch) and of the intolerance of even the thought of being himself at the mercy of another in a similar structure of action-reaction.

The paradoxical association of the fantasy of wanting to bite the arm of the therapist (to bite the hand feeding him?) with the sensation of pleasure in merging is given some 'illumination' by his later comments upon both the meaning of the biting and the general association of describing the fantasy in an atmosphrere of permissiveness. It might be well to point out here that one of the most basic of the strategic operations in the therapeutic relation was to point out repetitively to the patient that he was entirely free to abandon the relation at any time, while the therapist considered himself bound to the contract; this had the express purpose of building into the therapeutic relationship the sort of asymmetry which the patient had experienced in childhood in relation to the light switch.

The course of the material suggests that the therapist made a correct interpretation in generally pointing out that the patient seemed to feel that an infantile dependent relation was painful and repulsive to the one depended upon, almost like being bitten or eaten. When the therapist explicitly reinforced the patient's hesitant wish to report the fantasy, the implication to the patient appears to have been very much that the therapist was perfectly willing for the patient to have any kind of fantasies he wished, no matter how clinging and 'orally dependent'. In turn, and I think this one of the major implications of a good therapeutic relation, the patient responds not only by the particular elaboration of other fantasies along the same line, but as well by the comment that it will be such a pleasure to be allowed again to generate fantasies! "I would like to sit down and let my mind run ... just as you say, the fantasy does not hurt you, but my mind does not realize this ...". This comment is more meaningful again when we return to the beginning of the first of these three interviews in which the patient commented that he was upset because of his loss of the ability to have feeling, "replaced by a worse kind of feeling ... you know the knot is there but you cannot feel it ... I mean I actually had to force myself to feel ... ".

Here the symphonic theme and variation can be seen to return to the original statement, with its complex problem of relatedness to the therapist. The therapist, that is, is anxious to help or to allow the patient to get back his ability to feel, and to deepen and organize it. The patient, while having the same goal, is very much inhibited by the understanding that for the relation to be strong enough for him to feel (or to have fantasies) it will have in some way to be strong enough for this capacity to be given by the therapist as by a creator, clearly an indication that the therapist can 'dabble with' the patient in a non-reciprocating way. That is, that 'cure' is a demonstration of 'total surrender', a fantasy which is often shared unconsciously by the residual narcissism of every psychotherapist!

Interpretation and Set Theory

A final comment about the process of interpretation which is the

central act of psychotherapy: it can be put in terms currently popular
by saying that it depends first upon the capacity for pattern-recognition, and second that it is a matter of finding the set in the given
universe of discourse of which both items which need to be related
to each other are members. Thus, if one can change A to X, an interpretation which might be made is that A and X both belong to the set
of letters of the alphabet. In the usual case in psychotherapy, the
problem of finding the set and finding as well some of the rules of
transformation is much more complex. Toward the end of the material presented above, there is a sequence of associations, beginning
with the patient's fantasy of biting the therapist's arm, which move
through astonishing changes in form with a consistent theme from
each step to the next, and with a meaningful emotional component to
each such change. Let me point to a couple of these to demonstrate
what I mean. The first such association in sequence following the
biting association is to a poisonous fish. Here we see 1) a shift from
an 'own' action to that of a fish, but 2) the common feature is 'biting',
by the self or by the poisonous fish: note that the 'into which bitten'
disappears. It reappears in the next association, but totally disembodied: the fish has become a small, highly illuminated creature,
'biting into black'. To the idea of a small creature, parasitic by
implication, 'biting into black' the patient's association was to a fetus.
The interpretation made by the therapist was couched to point up and
allay the patient's fear of the destructiveness of dependence. To this
the patient responds with the sensation of peace, as though he is saying, "It's all right to be dependent, it won't kill the host (of the dependent parasite)", referring obviously to his relation to the therapist
now and to others before. But he immediately then reverses the process, seeing in the subsequent moments a large, relatively undifferentiated mouth with lots of teeth now facing him, a 'figure' swallowing
him. Reassured about the dependence, he reverses again to the state
of being totally controlled or incorporated, but so complex is this
relation that when the therapist suggests this interpretation, the
patient turns it around and says, "Why would you come out as a
little figure?"

Note the complexity of this development. Biter and poisonous fish
are members of a class of biting things; fish and 'small creature' are
members of a class, small beings; fetuses are also small beings, in
a black environment, so that here the emphasis shifts from the one
member of the pair of reciprocal relatives to the other, the parent-
-therapist; when the therapist suggests that instead of biter-bitten,
the situation can be seen as parent-offspring, the patient feels relieved and peaceful, but only for the moment until the implication of
incorporation, surrender, and loss of identity in the relationship
begins again another threatening series of serial transformations.

No wonder this man speaks of the "burden of never seeing anything
quite steady"! But this process of constant change, of the shift of
Proteus from one of his possible forms to another, is the subject
matter of creativity. Its deadly attraction is the omnipotence it gives
to the unwary; its own punishment the immensity of the loss of glory
when one finds his soap-bubble fantasy punctured by rude reality.

Since human beings never pay attention to what is left, but always to what has gone in relation to what was once there, such a blow is often, to the untoughened, a disaster leading to the loss of self-preservative care of oneself.

Conclusion

The material presented above is a study in 'genetic semiotics' with an emphasis first upon the background of human relatedness which forms the essential ('unconscious'?) matrix in which symbolic method has to be learned. The hypothesis is presented that the most effective kinds of human relatedness take origin in states of 'transcendent' feeling, and that in ordinary experience these states are most familiar in religious settings. Transcendent experiences of this kind have their primary utility as a kind of social cement binding together all those having such an experience related to a consensually experienced religious 'object' (idol, deity, conception). Finally, a discussion is presented of the extraordinarily fluid succession of images encountered in states in which the 'creative imagination' is given free play under supervision assumed to be benevolent. The applicability of the psychotherapeutic situation to this kind of study is emphasized troughout.

NOTES

(*) Reprinted by special permission: in: Semiotica II(1970), 1-33.
(1) This work was supported in part by grants from the Commonwealth Fund, to whom grateful acknowledgement is made.

REFERENCES

Bowers, Malcolm, A. Chipman, A. Schwartz, and O. T. Dann
    1967   "Dynamics of Psychedelic Drug Abuse", Archives of General Psychiatry 16, 560-566.
Burtt, E. A.
    1954   Metaphysical Foundations of Modern Science (New York: Doubleday Anchor Books).
    1946   Language and Myth (New York: Harper) (1925).
    1953   The Philosophy of Symbolic Forms (Yale) (1923).
Goldstein, Kurt
    1939   The Organism (New York: American Book).
Mead, George A.
    1934   Mind, Self and Society (Chicago: University of Chicago).
Piaget, Jean
    1950   The Psychology of Intelligence (New York: Harcourt).
Reichenbach, H.
    1949   "The Phylosophical Significance of the Theory of Relativity", in: P. Schilpp, Albert Einstein, Philosopher-Scientist (New York: Harper).

Sebeok, Thomas, A. S. Hayes and Mary C. Bateson (eds.)
   1964   Approaches to Semiotics (The Hague: Mouton and Co.).
Shands, H. C.
   1956   "Individual as Differentiated Aspect of the Field", Psy-
          chiatric Research Reports (American Psychiatric As-
          sociation, February), 87-88.
   1968   "Psychoanalysis and the Twentieth Century Revolution in
          Communication", in: J. Marmor (ed.), Modern Psycho-
          analysis (New York: Basic Books).
Walter, W. Grey
   1950   "The Function of Electrical Rhythms in the Brain",
          Journal of Mental Science 96, 1-31.

PART THREE

ON THE THEORY OF INFORMATION-NOVELTY

V

COPING WITH NOVELTY (*)

For those so inclined, theorizing offers itself as an endlessly fascinating game. Like mountain-climbing, theorizing hardly ever presents the danger of a final resolution, even though the attainment of
a partial insight from time to time enhances the interest of the game.
The rule of the game is simple; it is to cover the largest possible
number of observations with the smallest possible number of assumptions, according to a principle of parsimony. Wigner (1964) defines
the objective of physics as the "explanation of nature", going on to
say that explanation involves "the establishment of a few simple
principles which describe the properties of what is to be explained."
The ultimate goal is to reduce description to the simplest terms;
Szent-Gyorgy comments, "Science tends to generalize, and generalization means simplification."
    If theorizing is analogous to a game, then, to continue the moun-
tain-climbing metaphor, the 'Mount Everest' of Western thought is
the traditionally insoluble dualism posed by the differentiation of
'mind' from 'body'. The postulation of two fundamentally different
'stuffs' of existence (mental and physical) has recurrently plagued
those attempting to make general descriptions. A classic restatement
of the dualistic position is to be found in Descartes' diffentiation of
a res cogitans from a res extensa. Since Descartes began his theorizing with the goal of reducing his assumptions to the bare minimum,
the necessity to postulate a dual system represents a failure. A
similar failure, from a different point of origin, is to be found in
Sherrington's late book, Man on His Nature, in the conclusion that
a dualistic theory is inevitable.
    In the context of these (and many other) failures, it is especially
interesting that from contemporary physical theory it is possible to
develop a theoretical solution to this ancient problem. The hypothetical solution derives from a notion discussed at length by Schrödinger
in 1945 in a little book entitled What is Life? (1961). From Schrödinger's point of origin, it is possible to find applications in fields
as diverse as molecular biology, communication engineering, and
psychology.
    Schrödinger's suggestion begins with a presentation of Boltzmann's
equation:

$$- \text{entropy} = k \log (1/D).$$

In this equation, D is a measure of disorder, and the reciprocal,
1/D, a 'direct measure of order'. According to the second law of

(*) Reprinted by special permission: in: Archives of General Psychiatry 20 (1969), 64-70. Copyright,1969, American Medical Association.

thermodynamics, the universe as a system, is inevitably running down toward the heat-death of entropy. Living systems cancel the tendency toward entropic disorder through the various methods by which they "feed upon negative entropy". Schrödinger points out that the organism maintains itself at a fairly high level of orderliness by "sucking orderliness" from its environment. We might restate this comment in more current terms by noting that the relevant 'environment' of any living system is the larger system of which it is a constituent part. The larger system has stores of orderliness from which the subsystem continuously renews itself.

In concrete application, we can change a method of statement to display the significance of this idea. We usually consider food a source of energy. In the process of digestion, highly organized proteins, carbohydrates, and fats are catabolically 'analyzed', yielding usable energy and simpler, less organized constituents. The organism reconstructs its own carbohydrates, fats, and proteins from the building-blocks liberated in the metabolic breakdown, using the energy released to construct combinations at higher levels of orderliness. The catabolic process releases orderliness which is then used partially for contemporary energy-needs and partially for the building-up of highly organized constituents according to the idiosyncratic program of the individual.

We sometimes say that more highly organized compounds have 'potential energy', but we can as easily (and more generally) say that they have orderliness or negentropy. Negentropy is a term covering energy as a special subclass. The other subclass, information, we shall return to below.

Von Bertalanffy's description (1950) of open systems takes the problem a step further in pointing out that an organism is a subsystem necessarily living in the context ('environment') of a larger system from which it continually draws its support. The basic requirement is that negentropy from the larger system support a constant renewal of the subsystem. Von Bertalanffy points out that systems perform work in moving toward an equilibrium; this is a restatement of the notion of homeostasis advanced by Cannon (1932) which in its turn is a derivation of the idea of an 'internal milieu' proposed by Claude Bernard (1927) more than a century ago. The fascinating paradox is that to attain equilibrium is tantamount to death in a living system; the destiny of the system therefore is to seek, without possibility of arriving at the goal sought. The notion of equilibrium used in traditional physical systems and borrowed to apply to biological systems thus becomes illegitimate in principle. Biological evolution progressively emphasizes predictive functions. Successful methods lead to the production of excess capacity as they evolve, and biological organisms show a consistent tendency to expand their universes, seeking 'new worlds to conquer'. Thus, the solution of any complex problem reveals a wider universe in which to operate, and the ultimate equilibrium state is never attained. It is apparent that the larger process affects the species as well as the individual; individuals continuously 'wear out', to be replaced by the succeeding generation.

As biological systems become more complex, they display increasingly predictive orientations; they 'reach out' further into the future in anticipation and into the past in memory. As this occurs, increasingly sophisticated information-processing mechanisms appear. These mechanisms use energy as they process information. Wiener (1948) points out that information-processing systems enter a new phase when they orient themselves to the economical use of information while demonstrating wastefulness in the use of energy. The brain is a precise example, since it shows a profligate energy consumption (estimated as a fifth to a fourth of the basal energy-consumption of the body) in the interest of highly efficient information-processing.

If one puts this in terms of decision-making, it is possible to say that organisms, in the blind processes of evolution, learn how to conserve information at the expense of energy. It then becomes possible to put both these notions back into the same class through returning again to Boltzmann's work, this time in the formulation that entropy is the equivalent of missing information (1951). This equivalence was brilliantly supported in a paper by Szilard considering the paradox of Maxwell's 'demon'. Maxwell, preoccupied with the problem of perpetual motion, suggests a hypothetical experiment in which a little demon, controlling a gate between two chambers filled with gas, identifies faster molecules and admits them diffentially to the smaller chamber. This process logically leads to a continuous accumulation of energy in the second chamber, and in principle could allow perpetual motion. Szilard shows that Maxwell's demon is foiled by the fact that the information used to select the faster molecules is precisely equivalent to the energy gained, so that the books are balanced after all. The significant notion exemplified in the work of both Boltzmann and Szilard is that information is equivalent to energy, which is to say that the 'mental notion' of information is actually the same as the 'physical' notion of energy - the substitution requires only that the problem be addressed at a higher level of abstraction. In Cybernetics, Wiener (1948) pursues these ideas, pointing out that "Just as the amount of information in a system is a measure of its organization, so the entropy of a system is the measure of its degree of disorganization; and the one is simply the negative of the other." In terms of the approach pioneered by Wiener and by Shannon in a different laboratory, information may be defined in purely relativistic terms as 'anything that makes a difference'. This means that information is equated with novelty, since anything making a difference to a steady state is novel in terms of the expectations of that system in that state. Quantification of information becomes possible with the realization (attributed by Wiener to Fisher, Shannon and himself "at about the same time") that the unit amount of information was that "transmitted as a single decision between equally probable alternatives". The bit thus established as a unit is central to the binary language invented by Boole which serves as the lingua franca of all contemporary elaborate data-processing methods.

Information theory deals with differential probabilities. The amount of information in a message is a function of its improbability, which is to say, relative to the expectations embodied in the system, to the relative novelty of the message received. We can establish limits theoretically: no information can be conveyed by either an absolutely novel or an absolutely predictable message. The absolutely novel cannot be received; the absolutely predicted is redundant. Thus we find that it is possible to describe all information-processing in terms of probabilistic organization; this general understanding goes along with the "transition from a Newtonian reversible time to a Gibbsian, irreversible time" (1948).

It is at this point that we find a rather astonishing step to investigations of the function of the nervous system. Mary Brazier (1961) points out that the brain is organized on a probabilistic basis. Its function is so designed that it is "the dissimilar, the novel, the unexpected" that carries the message. This insight clarifies the two-level operation of neural process, with the wider more general level of sensitivity represented by the "orienting reflex" (Pavlov's "what is it?" reflex) investigated in detail by neurophysiologists including Magoun (1963) and, in the Soviet Union, Sokolov (1963). The orienting reflex is a response to the generically novel.

It is of interest to note how much a simple change in descriptive formulation can change the meaning of a theoretical notion. Freud (1948) hypothesized that the function of the nervous system was "to abolish stimulation", a notion which in that statement is obviously nonsense. When we alter the terminology, however, we find that the function of the nervous system is indeed to reduce or abolish novelty. The reduction of novelty by learning progressively reduces the information (= improbability) confronted, and it is thus reasonably accurate to say that the nervous system has the function of 'abolishing novelty' (Shands, 1967).

When we consider the general characteristics of organized systems, we find a reciprocity precisely along these lines. Within the system, the organization is such that predictability is enhanced. Every living system is designed to expect certain inputs from other parts of the system and to emit certain outputs to other parts of the system; the whole is bound together by feed-back loops which continually send information back to the point of origin of the original message. The orderliness within the system is balanced by the improbability of the system's occurrence. The highest probability is always that events will be distributed on a random basis; any organized system of events is therefore inherently improbable. We find precise exemplification of these trends in the biological mechanisms of fertilization. Where, as in the case of many fish, the female lays eggs which the male fertilizes by releasing spermatozoa in the near vicinity, the method requires an enormous expansion of numbers of both ova and spermatozoa; the inherent randomness is further exemplified in the vast numbers of fish fry that perish before maturity. An adult fish is thus extraordinarily improbable.

In mammals, the mechanism is altered by anatomical arrangements in the female which greatly increase the probability of fertilization. The channels which contain and direct the ovum toward the uterus, and those which contain and direct the spermatozoa toward

the ovum become information-processing mechanisms. The decrease
in number of ova produced by a single female (in comparison with the
prospective mother in fish reproduction) is made possible by competent channelling, enhancing the probability of encounter of ovum
and spermatozoon. Cattle-breeders approach the other side of this
relation by artificially placing small quantities of semen in just the
right place at the right time, again increasing the probability of
meaningful contact between spermatozoon and ovum. Such methods
of facilitating fertilization are instances of arranging buffer-systems which 'temper the wind' to the otherwise vulnerable organism
greatly increasing the probability of the survival of the individual.
The adult mammal, all things considered, is a great deal more probable than the adult fish.

Evolution results in increasing complexity of living organisms.
As development proceeds, so does the tendency for the living system
to anticipate coming events. Biological systems are more predictive
than they are adaptive; they not only deal with the problem at hand, but
with the problems to come. The pioneer researchers of such men as
Coghill (1930) and Herrick (1956) have to do with the anticipatory component of behavior. Dewey summarizes the idea in saying that intelligence (as a biological 'adaptation') is concerned with the prospective
control of the environment. Sherrington (1948) and Cannon (1932) working each in his selected aspects of the neutral controlling systems of
the animal body, point out that a major differentiation is to be made
between the consummatory functions taking place in the here and now,
and the anticipatory functions which have to do with prediction.

Intelligence is the complex function having to do with prediction;
prediction is a method of reducing novelty or enhancing probability
in the future course of the life of the organism. It is fascinating
to note that prediction is close to retrospection (Ayer, 1950) in that
both concern events only probable at best. The organism learns (at
whatever level) that what is to be generally (within limits) will
resemble what has been. Extrapolation from past experience forms
the basis of intelligent prediction. The comment has been attributed
to many sources that those who ignore history find themselves condemned to repeat it.

If we turn our attention now to a psychological system very rapidly
extending its influence, we find some of the same ideas in different
language again. Piaget's system (1950) is based upon the use of the
word, adaptation, borrowed from the physiological ideas advanced
by Bernard, Head (1911) and others. Piaget notes that adaptation
has a goal of equilibrium, in the traditional physical formula. Actually, however, it is apparent that here, too, adaptation in the sense
of a here-and-now method is a partially inappropriate term. Piaget
describes two subclasses of adaptation: accomodation is the action of
the environment on the organism, forcing changes in the behavior of
the organism; assimilation is the action of the organism upon the
environment, allowing the organism to exert influence over environmental events in terms of past learning made possible by accomodative patterning. If we look at this process, it is apparent that the
accommodation is not only adaptive, it is predictive; what changes

are induced are made permanent by assimilative schematization.
The 'adaptation' predictively cancels future novelty by providing a
channel for processing information implicitly expected to be repetitive. Assimilatory schemata anticipate and thus predictively reduce
the novelty of subsequent instances of behavior in the same categories.
Cantril (1950) uses the notion of an "assumptive form world" in a
manner similar to that of the use of schematization.

Predictive buffering, with the enhancement of probabilities of survival, is a function of internal organization; Bernard's term, internal milieu, reappears in a more sophisticated form in Cannon's
term, homeostasis, but both imply that the organism is protected
by inherited-and-learned organizing patterns (or programs, to use
the contemporary term). When we turn our attention to theorizing in
the field of molecular biology (Stent, 1968), we find exemplification
of the same kind of argument as that presented above. Such investigators as Rous (1967) and Lwoff (1966) point out that the primary
requirement for persistent life is the maintenance of orderliness
within the cell assemblies of the body. Organs, organ systems, and
whole animal bodies can be considered to be 'social systems' composed of cells. Disorderliness appears in these cellular social systems as unexpected or unpredictable events, embracing analogues
of both rebellion and anarchy in human political systems. Viruses
have the remarkable ability to pre-empt the control of orderliness
within the cell, forcing the cell to devote itself to the instructions of
the virus, somewhat like the action of a revolutionary junta in the
coup d'état through which a regime is replaced by a revolutionary
one. Under conditions increasingly understood by investigators, when
anarchy occurs, disciplined tissue growth is replaced by neoplastic
disorderliness.

If we return to the beginning and take still another tack, we find
that problems of business are similarly susceptible to these general
notions. A business is first and foremost an organization, an artificial social system which has a clearly defined and consensually
accepted structure. Businesses are subject to regulation from inside
and from without; in the contemporary scene we find a major tendency
for increasing organization in both particulars, as businesses become larger and more complex while simultaneously subject to more
and more regulation from governmental agencies. Many large businesses show a tendency to become more nearly small social systems in
which members have both privileges and obligations unheard of only
a few years ago. 'Security' and 'fringe benefits' include a number
of methods of reducing novelty in the future by ensuring the member
against the disease or premature death to be cause for concern.
Security appeals especially to those with responsibilities - but in
turn responsibility in this sense is a function of orderliness in
intrafamilial relations. When a family persists as a unit through
using insurance left by a deceased parent, that parent has managed
to make available a store of negentropy in the form of obligations of
governments or businesses. Again we see an internal consistency in
that these obligations are only meaningful when the organization which
honors the obligation persists as a functioning system.

The foregoing details show how immensely wide is the theoretical net given to us by the notions of novelty, negentropy, organization, orderliness, probability, and information - to mention only a few of the variants. Still a further area of relevance has to do with the reciprocity of inside and outside. When we examine an organization from outside, we find that an organization displays a shape. The shape is the external (principally visual) appearance; it is a term closely similar to form and pattern. We return to the neurological context when we find that the nervous system is characterized as being mainly concerned with pattern-recognition (Selfridge and Neisser, 1960), or, in an equivalent statement in a different language, with making comparisons (Young, 1955) - but comparison implies shapes which can be differentiated from and assimilated to each other.

In another small book of Schrödinger's (1951), we find a statement that when contemporary physicists examine most deeply, they find recurrently only shapes. This opinion is shared by Weisskopf (1965), who points out in addition that quantum considerations require that inanimate systems display the simplest shapes because these are the shapes which require least energy to maintain. Here we return to the notion of work and negentropy; living systems require a constant input of negentropy (= energy). As standing human beings are constantly required to resist gravity, so are living beings constantly required to resist entropic disorganization or disorderliness. Homeostasis refers to the process by means of which steadiness in shaping is maintained; the predictive 'wisdom' of the body and the wisdom of intelligence alike anticipate future disorder in storing up reserves of orderliness on which to call.

In Piaget's work, we find the notion of shape central to his description of homeomorphisms found in parallel fashion in perceptual and cognitive process and in physiological and intelligent operations. Piaget's usage emphasizes the significance of analogy and metaphor in discovery. A recent discussion of molecular biology (Rous, 1967) points out that Schrödinger's suggestion (in the same book as that initially cited above) that genetic information is coded in an aperiodic crystal is the generative hypothesis, formulating a homeomorphism between genes and crystals previously not considered. To return to one of the earliest suggestions in this area, we can find Aristotle's comment that the best ability of all is to be a "master of metaphor" - which is to say, an expert in finding homeomorphisms or similarities. Bartlett (1951) says in a book on thinking,

... if we could only produce people who go about looking for likenesses, instead of allowing themselves to be struck by differences, we should perhaps do more for transfer (of learning) than could be done in any other way. Nearly all the great advances, whether in knowledge or in skill, have been won by bringing together problems and methods of solution of problems that have before remained apart.

In many ways the most important application of this broad notion is left to the last: for human applications, the primary method involved

in conquering novelty is the use of the symbol, or, to put it perhaps
more broadly and more precisely, the use of symbolic-linguistic
systems. All such systems depend upon homeomorphisms manifested
in names or mathematical symbols applied to categories. A category
is a grouping of many particulars identified by a common shape.
Shapes of actions are referred to by verbs, shapes of objects by
nouns, of relations by prepositions. Every time we learn a name,
we learn a category (Locke, 1939) including an unknowable but indefinitely prolonged number of members. Each time we encounter
a new particular which it is possible to include within a known category, we find that naming instantly reduces novelty by a considerable
amount.

Linguistic-symbolic systems themselves have internal organization.
The rules of organization constitute the grammar of the system; a
most astonishing repetitive observable is that very complex rules of
grammar are learned by speakers quite unconsciously and without the
ability to specify what rule it is that they immediately know to have
been broken by an inexpert speaker (Chomsky, 1967). This example
illustrates the differentiation made by Bartlett (1932), in referring
to two levels of operation of memory mechanisms. Bartlett notes
that animals lower than man clearly <u>recognize</u> objects and situations
which they have learned in prior (accommodative) activity.

Only human beings <u>remember</u> when the term 'remember' is used
to describe events taken out of context and processed 'in the head'.
Bartlett (1932) points out that the animal organism is operated by
its schemata of behavior, by the built-in, unconscious programs (laid
down in assimilative activity). Human beings live at this level along
with their animal relatives, but they also live at the level of conscious
memory. Bartlett notes that active conscious remembering (as
distinguished from recognizing) rests upon the ability of the human
being to 'turn round upon' his schemata, artificially placing symbol-
ized schemata in novel relations and sequences.

No matter how we twist and turn this situation, there seems to be
no way out of the conclusion that conscious remembering requires
the use of symbols through which the absent situation is artificially
evoked in some contemporary manifestation. Mark (1962) makes the
statement that animals restricted to homeostatic mechanisms remain embedded in their experience, while animals (i.e. human
beings) who have learned how to use history can transcend this
limitation. The clear implication is that remembering, a function
practically indistinguishable from 'being conscious' depends upon
verbal learning (Freud, 1915, and discussion in Shands, 1968).

We can return to the beginning to point out that novelty is controlled through organization; in turn organization implies an internal discipline which rests upon regular methods of internal co   nu-
nication within the system. In human beings the communication
internal to social systems takes place in terms of a secondary organization, the linguistic-symbolic system. We can re-evoke the notion
of biological adaptation by pointing to the homeomorphism between
the buffer-systems of 1) the 'internal milieu' in which a human has
his physiological being, and 2) the 'symbolic milieu' in which humans

have their conscious being. Every ordinary communication between
human beings requires symbolic mediation; only in very rare and
esoteric contexts do human communications appear to avoid mediation.
These relatively rare events are of immense interest, however, in
the transitory occurrence of what might be called (in contemperaneous-
ly relevant homeomorphism) 'disintermediation'. The principal reports left by those who assert they were able to bypass symbolic
communication for some immediate direct experience of communion
refer to the mystic experience (O'Brien, 1964) or other 'transcendental' feeling. In such moments of intensity, we find a comprehensive conquest of novelty, at least in the feeling of no-difference between
the self-system and some larger system into which the self is mo-
mentarily completely absorbed.

By comparison with normal human experience, the transcendental
establishes a kind of ultimate limit in one direction. The remarkable
series of convergences made possible by the theoretical notion presented here is extended in the direction of another limit in Shakow's
(1963) summarization of three decades of intensive investigation of
schizophrenic disorder. Shakow concludes that the only general feature which seems present throughout the subjects investigated is a
'neophobia', a fear of, or an inability to cope with the novel. Shakow
points out that this disability takes two major forms, in that the
schizophrenic

> ... reacts to old situations as though they were new ones (he
> fails to habituate), and to new situations as though they were
> recently past ones (he perseverates): and second, he over-
> responds when the stimulus is relatively small, and he does not
> respond enough when the stimulus is great.

Shakow's formulation fits precisely into the notion that this major
disorder of human beings is, simply, disorganization, a deficiency
in the integrative action which Sherrington characterizes as the
principal function of the nervous system.

SUMMARY

The notion of negentropy (Schrödinger) provides a truly general
notion resolving the traditional dualism of Western thought. Negentropy includes energy and information as subclasses. Every behaving system requires inputs of both energy and information to
maintain itself in action; at the same time every such system has
to control inputs to avoid explosion or 'trauma'. Applications of the
notion of negentropy to business, evolution, and learning in several
different theoretical systems shows the universality of the basic idea.

144

REFERENCES

Ayer, A. J.
   1950   Language, Truth, and Logic (London: Victor Gollancz).
Bartlett, F. C.
   1932   Remembering (London: Cambridge University Press).
   1951   The Mind at Work and Play (Boston: Beacon Press).
Bernard, C.
   1927   An Introduction to the Study of Experimental Medicine
         (New York: Macmillan).
Brazier, M. A. B.
   1961   "Problem of Information Transfer in the Brain",
         Science 134, 1426.
Cannon, W. B.
   1932   The Wisdom of the Body (New York: W. W. Norton).
Cantril, H.
   1950   The "Why" of Man's Experience (New York: Macmillan).
Chomsky, N.
   1967   "The Formal Nature of Language", in: E. H. Lenneberg
         (ed.), Biological Foundations of Language (New York:
         John Wiley and Sons).
Coghill, G. E.
   1930   "The Genetic Interrelation of Instinctive Behavior and
         and Reflexes", Psychological Review 37, 264-266.
Freud, S.
   1915   "The Unconscious", Collected Papers 4 (London: Hogarth
         Press), 98-136.
   1948   "Instincts and their Vicissitudes", Collected Papers 4
         (London: Hogarth Press), 60-83.
Head, H., and G. Holmes
   1911   "Sensory Disturbances from Cerebral Lesions", Brain
         34, 102-254.
Herrick, C. J.
   1956   The Evolution of Human Nature (New York: Harper Bros.).
Locke, J.
   1939   English Philosophy from Beacon to Mill (New York: Modern
         Library).
Lwoff, A.
   1966   "Interaction among Virus, Cell, and Organism", Science
         152, 1216-1220.
Magoun, H. W.
   1963   The Waking Brain, 2nd ed. (Springfield, Ill. : Charles C.
         Thomas).
Mark, H. J.
   1962   "Elementary Thinking and the Classification of Behavior",
         Science 135, 75-87.
O'Brien, E.
   1964   Varieties of Mystic Experience (New York: The New Ame-
         rican Library of World Literature).

Piaget, J.
1950   The Psychology of Intelligence (New York: Harcourt,
        Brace, and World).
Rothstein, J.
1951   "Information, Measurement, and Quantum Mechanics",
        Science 114, 171-175.
Rous, P.
1967   "The Challenge to Man of the Neoplastic Cell", Science
        157, 24-28.
Schrödinger, E.
1951   Science and Humanism (London: Cambridge University
        Press).
1961   What is Life? (London: Cambridge University Press).
Selfridge, O. P., and U. Neisser
1960   "Pattern Recognition by Machine", Scientific American
        203, 60-70.
Shakow, D.
1963   "Psychological Deficit in Schizophrenia", Behavioral
        Sciences 8, 275-305.
Shands, H. C.
1967   "Novelty as Object: Précis for a General Psychological
        Theory", Archives of General Psychiatry 17, 1-4.
1968   "Psychoanalysis and the Twentieth-Century Revolution
        in Communication", in: J. Marmor (ed.), Modern Psycho-
        analysis (New York: Basic Books).
Sherrington, C. S.
1948   The Integrative Action of the Nervous System (New Haven,
        Conn. : Yale University Press).
Sokolov, E. N.
1963   "Higher Nervous Functions: The Orienting Reflex", Annual
        Review of Physiology 25, 545-580.
Stent, G. S.
1968   "That Was the Molecular Biology That Was", Science 160,
        390-395.
von Bertalanffy, L.
1950   "The Theory of Open Systems in Physics and Biology",
        Science 111, 23-29.
Weisskopf, V. F.
1965   "Quantum Theory and Elementary Particles", Science 149,
        1181-1189.
Wiener, N.
1948   Cybernetics (New York: John Wiley and Sons).
Wigner, E. P.
1964   "Events, Laws of Nature, and Invariance Principles",
        Science 145, 995-999.
Young, J. Z.
1955   Studies in Communication (London: Martin Secker and
        Warburg).

VI

INTEGRATION, DISCIPLINE, AND THE CONCEPT OF SHAPE (*)

Reviewing published opinions of the past half-century reveals a gradual change in basic frame of reference in the broad field of investigation, especially in the subfield of investigation of human problems.
It has become increasingly clear that the scientific approach to problems so successfully based upon causal analysis (assuming a linear
progression in a deterministic framework, and using precise statistical methods for evaluation) has not been nearly so useful in helping
us understand the human condition and the problems that differentially
affect human beings. To say this another way, it is obvious that the
standard scientific approach has not given us hoped-for results in
psychiatry, whatever its benefits in basic sciences.

Beginning at a point that can, for many purposes, be localized at
the half-century mark, a new development has increasingly asserted
its influence. Basically, this approach selects as its primary 'object'
not a thing, but a system, or an organization. Instead of causal analysis, we turn to a communication analysis, utilizing notions of feedback loops, of organization, integration, discipline, and the like with
reference to the system of interest. A basic difference is the assumption that we have to begin with an on-going system, already in
action; observation then orients itself to differences rather than to
new, or newly caused, events.

Investigations leading us to this new theorietical position are easy
to find; many have been familiar as works of genius for decades.
Names coming readily to mind include Bernard, Cannon, and Sherrington in physiology, Whitehead in philosophy, and many others.
Specific contributors to the new mode include Bertalanffy and Bentley
in midcentury. Communications theorists, e. g. Wiener and Shannon,
have familiarized us with new formal methods and with mathematical
statements applicable to these newly restated problems. Most astonishing of all, the still quite new fields of molecular biology and immunology in the contemporary scene depend almost exclusively upon
these ideas (Lwoff, 1966).

From ideas associated with this new point of view in active flieds
of research, we find it possible, by making certain alterations in the
terms we use, to describe processes across previously unbreachable
barriers. Ideas about organization in the broadest sense have a direct
bearing upon the ancient problem of 'mind' and 'body', more elegantly
put as the psychophysiological relation. In this monograph we are
considering the larger problem with specific reference to cancer.

When it was first suggested that 'mental' events could cause cancer,
the notion appeared ridiculous to many. Ideas and feelings appear to

(*) Reprinted by special permission: in: Annals of the New York
Academy of Sciences (1969), 578-589.

exist in a universe totally different from that of neoplasms and viruses. How could the one cause the other, or the other be an effect
of the one? The resolution of this kind of problem has been taken a
great leap forward by recourse to description at a different level of
abstraction, using a different method of conception.

André Lwoff, the molecular biologist, gives a clear statement of
general principles in saying, "An organism is an integrated system
of interdependent structures and functions. An organism is constituted of cells, and a cell consists of molecules which must work in
harmony. Each molecule must know what the others are doing. Each
one must be capable of receiving messages and must be sufficiently
disciplined to obey ... An organism is a molecular society, and
biological order is a kind of social order. Social order is opposed
to revolution, which is an abrupt change of order, and to anarchy,
which is the absence of order."

From his special field, Lwoff points out that viruses are found often
in latent states, 'repressed' in symbiotic condition amounting to a
stand-off: the virus is not hurting its host, nor the host its 'guest'.
When a traumatic event occurs, derepression may ensue, and when
it does, the virus-guest rudely takes over the crucial functions of
the host in assuming control of the cellular system in which it has
been living. The traumatic events are multiple and varied; they include ultraviolet radiation, hormone treatment, menstruation, and
'emotion', among others. The result of the proliferation of the virus
may be a viral infection, as in the common appearance of herpes
simplex in a person sick for some other reason.

The point I want to make is simply put when we consider the virus
in such a case as a set of instructions, functioning somewhat as the
sealed orders carried by a ship's captain on a secret mission. At a
given signal, the captain opens the letter in which the instructions
are concealed, and then, under ancient compulsions in which he has
been thoroughly disciplined, undertakes to change his course according to the orders to which he now newly finds himself subject.
A properly disciplined captain is prepared to sacrifice himself and
his crew in response to his orders. I suggest that many of the ca-
tastrophes to which men find themselves subject may similarly be
occasions in which inherent instructions quite suddenly gain control
because of untoward events acting as signals or precipitants. Depending then upon circumstances, the result may be 1) a pitched
battle in which the new instructions are eventually canceled or 2)
a revolutionary take-over resulting in a victory for the invader (often
a Pyrrhic victory, since the invader can live only as long as does
the host), or 3) an anarchic state in which the manifestations of
malignant neoplasia may be the principal occurrences.

In this general hypothesis, it is no longer necessary to speculate
on 'how the mental affects the physical'. It is enough to realize that
human organization requires multilevel integration. The human being can be so traumatized by the loss of a relative that he may go
into a decline and die without much 'being wrong' with him. The
human being, convinced of having been cursed with an infallible curse,
often proceeds to die. The human infant separated from its mother

exhibits severe retardation in its development, as the studies of
Spitz (1965) show. The list is endless. Even rats show the phenomenon of sudden death under conditions of severe stress, as Richter's
studies (1957) indicate.

When we examine these lines of evidence, taken from many studies
and pertaining to many different species of animals as well as to man,
we find it possible to say that the 'lesion' occurring is a loss of integration, a decrease in the level of organization in the system including
both individual and his systematic context. "Man does not live by
bread alone", which is to say that nonmaterial and personal relations are at least as important in the general scheme as are adequate supplies of food and water. To maintain a high level of organization requires a high level of supply of orderliness, or negentropy,
to use Schrödinger's (1945) term. In dependable, regular relations,
the organism 'obeys' predictable instructions - but when the whole
is altered, the organism becomes subject to instructions otherwise
quite alien.

We need not look far to find clear examples of such changes, from
quite different situations. The young male coming into adolescence
finds himself 'listening to a different drummer', he becomes quite
abruptly responsive to different 'orders', especially those having
sexual connotations. He finds himself a 'different person'; in the case
of one psychotic young man, the patient could not think himself 'the
same' when sexually aroused and when not so aroused. In a different
context, we are all familiar with the striking changes taking place in
mobs and crowds. There a 'normal human being' may find himself
vigorously participating in a riot or a lynching, impervious to the
usually effective system of instructions we call 'conscience'.

We can go further and point out that these altered sensitivities to
instructions are valued differently in different situations. Unless the
young male responds to different instructions, the species will not
be reproduced. Unless the crowd can change individual orientations,
human beings cannot be converted; they will not evolve into various
social organizations or conquer new territories, terrestrial or ideological. On the other hand, if instructions change, the result can be
chaos, anarchy, or malignant neoplastic growth. Plasticity, flexi-
bility, the capacity to change are ways in which we describe a two-
edged blade, usable as a surgical scalpel or as a murder weapon.
The general problem is the manner in which complex systems are
organized to obey instructions in the interest of regularity - and the
ways in which such complex organizations break down into disorderliness, temporary or protracted.

My own interest in the general problem of disorderliness stems
from a study done about the time we first became interested in the
psychological aspects of the cancer problem. We began with an interest in cancer as a disorganizing factor in human lives (Shands
et al., 1951), coming then to the conclusion reviewed in the first of
these conferences, to the effect that a personality is most accurately
described as an informational system that must be kept in a state of
orderliness through the receipt of general, predictable messages.
At about the same time we studied a group of schizophrenic patients

undergoing insulin coma therapy (Shands and Menzer, 1953). We had available at that time only crude measures of lymphocyte and eosinophil numbers to estimate the degree of stress involved.

Insulin coma is an extreme physiological emergency; the patient literally is at the point of death for periods of several minutes to an hour. We found that the repetition of this trauma led to a startling randomization or disorderliness in eosinophil numbers. In control studies, all patients exhibited a ceiling eosinophil count of 300 cells/cu mm; after a number of comas, the upper level (quite unpredictably) reached 8.000 in some, but not all, patients.

One interesting correlation was that patients who seemed better integrated in their premorbid state showed far less randomization. After the 'therapy', the patients were quite uniformly far less difficult to deal with - but they were as well, flat, in the psychiatric sense: unemotional, and very much less human and interesting than before. When we tested their responses to stress by measuring the drop in eosinophil numbers that had been very consistent in control experiments prior to the study, a similar complete loss of integration could be found. When we took this a step further by using ACTH, we found, on the contrary, that the specifically physiological response was quite normal. The conclusion we reached then, and it is a conclusion repeatedly reinforced since that time, is that overwhelming trauma, often repeated, may well make human beings more manageable and less difficult to care for. The 'therapeutic' effect seemed to be somewhat like that of a fuse, separating a previously integrated organization into noncommunicating parts. From this beginning, the intervening years have been a period of continuous preoccupation with questions of organization and communication in a formulation general enough to include both psychological and physiological as special cases.

In the first of these conferences, personality was described as an informational system (Shands, 1966). Here I want to follow out some consequences of a further generalization of this idea, based upon a suggestion made by Schrödinger (1945) that life can be defined as a continuous extraction of negentropy for use in a continuously maintained system. This central idea is consonant with system theory (von Bertalanffy, 1950) and with information theory as well (Wiener, 1948; Shannon, 1948). With this idea, information, organization, regularity, and orderliness are seen as nearly identical with the negative of entropy. Both physiological and psychological processes are characterized by organization; therefore, if one considers organization as the primary abstraction, then a theory of organization becomes the general case of which physiological organization and psychological organization are special cases (Shands, 1968c).

In a brief review of the conceptual evolution of the past hundred years, we can begin with Bernard's (1865) formulation of an internal milieu as a rather concrete way of describing the orderliness of the cellular environment in the buffer systems. Cannon's (1932) suggestion of the broader term, homeostasis, and Sherrington's (1906) term, integrative action, both refer to organization in specific contexts of investigation of neural mechanisms. The general case is

discussed by Piaget in terms of homeomorphisms (or isomorphisms)
discernable in parallel forms to be found at the level of perceptual
mechanisms, of sensory-motor intelligence, and at the highest level
of abstract operations. Other aspects of shape, pattern, and form
are discussed by D'Arcy Thompson (1961) and by those concerned
with the development of artificial intelligence (Selfridge and Neisser,
1960). When we consider all living subsystems as primarily concerned with maintaining the same shape through organizing processes
of input and output, it becomes apparent then that the notion of identity (Erikson, 1964) is another special case.

Whenever we seek theoretical solutions, we operate in the broad
area of homeomorphism. All we can know we learn by transferring
a pattern from a context in which it is familiar to a context in which
it is unfamiliar. The discoveries of mankind are based upon analogies
previously unsuspected, or metaphors previously not applied to the
situation under investigation.

The propositions I want to advance here rest upon a very simple
notion; namely, that we can, in relation to living systems, usefully
substitute the term instruction (Shands, 1968b) for familiar terms
such as stimulus, input, or even cause. Any significant input carries
information, which means by definition that in 'makes a difference',
and in accordance with the principle of homeostasis-homeomorphism,
the system must, if it is to maintain its shape within tolerable limits,
act to reestablish the regularity disturbed by the input of the information. Food 'instructs' the chewing apparatus to chew and the diges-
tive apparatus to churn and mix and to secrete its characteristic
juices. Each phase of digestion ends when the processed substrate
no longer issues appropriate instructions. The fact that we generally
construe such sequences attributing agency (and consciousness) to
the other party is alternative (and complementary) to this view.

Adopting this different convention, traditional distinctions disappear.
When we use the term instruction in this very broad sense, we understand behavior as a continuous ongoing process, continuously shaped
and reshaped by myriad instructions. As the organism lives and learns,
it deals with instructions in more predictive terms, so that as it becomes more sophisticated in both phylogenetic and ontogenetic context, the organism is characterized by an enhanced ability to anticipate instructions. Shaping characteristically also involves retrospective instructions in positive or negative feedback. Sequences of
behavior are retrospectively facilitated or inhibited by contingencies
of reinforcement, and the retrospective assessment operates as a
predictive influence on the next exhibition of the behavior in question.

I have elsewhere explored the reasons for suggesting forcibly that
what we ordinarily call 'conscious' behavior boils down to behavior
susceptible to description, and thus to the basic idea of verbal behavior (Shands, 1968a). Here I want simply to point out that starting
from the top level of the behavioral armamentarium of the human being and proceeding to lower levels, instead of starting at the bottom
and proceeding toward the more sophisticated levels, appears to be
the procedure of choice in the formation of theories as well as (in
Freud's prescription) the rule for the application of a psychothera-

peutic point of view.

Human affairs feature the idiosyncratic use of symbolic method using verbal tokens. But when we examine a host of recent findings in genetics, immunology, and virology, we find unsuspected analogues to the process of abstraction, hitherto considered simply a function of symbolic process. Abstraction rests upon the biological capacity for a shape to be used to instruct a living system to reproduce the same shape, a basic pattern widespread in nature. When we understand that one of the possible consequences of this method is endless replication, we find a model for at least some forms of neurosis and cancer.

The immediate impact of our cancer study was to obliterate many distinctions often made between the 'imaginary' and the 'real'. We found, to what now seems my naive astonishment, that the disturbances of 'real' trauma were very similar to those of 'neurotic' trauma. The disturbance to the informational economy involved centers around the input of novelty (Shands, 1967), and in turn the novel can be circularly defined as the unexpected or unexpectable.

Taking the next step, we can then say that 'personality' has an important family resemblance to a program (Shands, 1963), as the term is used in computer technology, and to grammar as this term is used in relation to symbolic-linguistic systems. In all three cases we deal with what might be called, perhaps tautologically, structures of instructions. In all three cases the entity is primarily one having a shape differentiating it from its surround. I would suggest here that the appropriate term for that surround is context rather than environment: when we say an organism lives in an environment, we suggest that the two are fundamentally different, but when we say that something exists in a context, we more easily think of system and subsystem, mutually or transactionally interdependent. Using this model, we see that when the context is 'natural', the system responds to 'natural' instructions; when in a human context, instructions may be as well 'artificial', 'symbolic', or 'conscious'.

Personalities, programs, and grammars are internally structured in ways usually so regular as to have a high degree of redundancy. The subsystem 'expects' (Cantril, 1950) a continuous series of instructions, and in the normal case each such instruction sets off a train of inner programmed instructions affecting the subsystem. Learning, in the broadest sense, is a process of establishing a stable system of inner communication related to the instructions received from the larger system. We can speak of the internal processing of information and the setting up of stable sets of internal instructions as discipline. After a period of learning, a disciplined subsystem predictively relates itself to its context, and the stability of its own internal discipline predictively discounts a wide range of novelty in the relation of system and subsystem.

In the human context, processing instructions at more and more general levels allows the subsystem to become so disciplined that it can tolerate amounts of novelty that are unbearable (traumatic) to less sophisticated systems. Many transient relationships - as between parent and child, perceptor and novice - buffer the latter during

a developmental period: these relationships "temper the wind to the
[naked] lamb". Premature rupture of such a relationship may ex-
pose the unsophisticated member to traumatic injury.

Human beings have to develop programs oriented both 1) to the
social context, and 2) to the nonhuman and inanimate context. This
amounts to a dual adaptation. Both system and sybsystem in either
context are continuously involved in sending and receiving instructions, and in obeying, ignoring, or defying instructions received.
Much of learning involves experimenting with the limits of tolerance.
Through modern science and technology, human beings have achieved
an astonishing capacity for instructing the inanimate context to 'obey'
- in mines, factories, smelters, and the other manifestations of
man's grasp of scientific law. The obvious, corresponding failure to
maintain appropriate discipline in social systems stand in sharp contrast to this remarkable success; a measure of the failure is that,
as human beings, we obviously do not know what kinds of discipline
are socially appropriate, and each cultural subsystem tends to set
up its territorial coaims in opposition to other sybsystems.

When we consider the vicissitudes of growing and learning in a
developmental context, we understand the different outcomes of
programs of instructions more comprehensively. The obsessive-
compulsive person is one in whom symbolic instructions have attached exceptional ('magical') potency; he is over-disciplined in
many obvious ways. When we study such a person, however, we
find him under-disciplined in his capacity to follow human instructions. His counterpart, the delinquent, is inadequately responsive
to symbolic instructions, but delinquent behavior is too ready an
obedience to instructions conveyed by the context of the moment.

During the second world war, Bartlett (1947) investigated highly
skilled activities. 'Skill' is a term used primarily in relation to
muscular activities; it is appropriate here because 'highly skilled'
is a term close to 'disciplined' in its connotations. The skilled person
demonstrates a high degree of integration in relating instructions
received from the context and from inside himself. Every skilled
movement integrates the demands of the context with the movement
sequence from which the response to the outer demands takes origin.
Bartlett points out that there are two thresholds of significance with
relation to highly skilled work. The lower threshold is that of indif-
ference, the upper that of tolerance; certain instructions are too weak
to be known, and certain tasks remain beyond the capacity of even the
skilled person.

These two thresholds change in temporal sequence; repeated learning, with drill and repetition, results in changing the level of both
thresholds. The skilled person ignores many cues distracting to the
unskilled person, while at the same time he is acutely sensitive to
nuances he has come to understand as significant. The skilled performer is more efficient and more tolerant of performance, hus-
banding his resources by performing only the essential activity. With
practice, the skilled performer is able to carry on for much longer
periods of time. In the opposite direction, prolonged activity eventuates in evidence of impairment and of fatigue. These tend to be as-

sociated with changes in the two thresholds: the tired person is less sensitive both to significant cues and to his own deteriorating performance. When tired, he has to work harder than when fresh, for the same result.

This general description covers a variety of skilled performances. Skills include speaking and writing, as well as directing an aircraft or motor car; the physiological activity of the body fits the scheme as well. Cannon points to the importance of realizing that the infant 'learns' homeostasis through training autonomic activity, and contemporary investigators more and more present immunological theories in terms of prior 'instruction' by an attack of the pathogenic agent or through the 'laboratory' of vaccination. We can consider evolutionary progress in species as the manifestation of learning 'by the species', through the selection of mutations aiding skillful adaptation to the environment.

Application of these ideas to problems of disease requires that we first consider the analogies that dictate our theories. Descartes' pervasive influence has mostly led us to understand the animal body as a machine, responsive to instructions of a causal nature. This notion is easy to follow when we consider that a machine has to be turned on in some manner, from a previous state of passive inactivity. When we then turn the machine off, we do not have to consider issuing "Stop!" instructions - it is included in the loss of power supply. The animal organism, on the other hand, is categorically different, since it runs (necessarily and unavoidably) without pause from conception to death. To turn off some ongoing pattern of behavior in the living organism often requires a specific "Stop!" instruction. We have paid far too little attention to this problem, although (cf. obsessions and compulsions) it is obviously of importance when we take it into account.

A recently clarified case in point is the problem of obesity. A number of studies now present strongly suggestive evidence that obesity is not so much caused, as by too large an appetite or by disorders of metabolism, as it is a function of a disordered susceptibility to the cessation instruction. The fat person, to say it simply, does not know when to quit eating; it is not that he is hungry so much as it is that he is responsive to the food's implicit instruction. "Eat Me", like Alice confronted by the little cake in Wonderland.

In various kinds of learning we can ignore the problem of the cessation instruction simply because human beings are limitedly docile. They tend to issue the cessation instruction to themselves. In many deviant conditions, however, we find that this is no longer the case. In a psychosomatic context, I have mentioned the problem of obesity. In a psychiatric context, we find the cessation problem uppermost in phobias, "crystallized conflicts" (Shands, 1968b), and obsessional and compulsive disorders. At the immunological level, allergic disorders are primarily acute inflammations that do not follow the ordinary path of cessation through resolution; hay fever, for instance, is a protracted rhinitis and conjunctivitis. We find a striking parallel in myth in the story of the sorcerer's apprentice who learned how to turn on the broom but could not turn it off, and in the addictions we find a very similar pattern. In all these we can understand an organization with a usually predictable shape becoming deranged by a loss of the terminal boundary. The boundary that limits the extent of the organized process is ruptured, and the process becomes perseverative, like a broken record.

The principal characteristic of neoplastic tissue is that it responds to instructions saying "Grow!" without being then obedient to the ordinary instructions that say "Now stop!" This lack of terminal obedience is often associated with the activity of filterable viruses, and when we turn our attention to these part-organisms, we find the pattern typical. An active virus enters a cell and diverts the physiological precesses of that cell to its own use, thereby initially establishing something of an analogy to the cuckoo that lays its eggs in the nest of another bird after pushing the appropriate eggs out of the nest. The special feature of the virus molecule's activity is that under favorable conditions, it tends to replicate itself endlessly. It requires an active process of cutoff to suspend the activity of the virus; the virologist speak of 'repression' in this connection, with 'derepression' when some traumatic event affects the capacity of the cell to resist takeover by the virus (Lwoff, 1966).

The repressed virus becomes a part of a situation, imbedded in that situation in a manner making it impossible to differentiate part from whole. The part retains its potential autonomy, and it appears again in an autonomous state when derepressed. Then the liberated virion is freed to scan its surround to find a suitable host for the subsequent takeover. Whitehead (1925), in his "philosophy of organism", points out that the part is an aspect of the environment for the whole. In the case of the virus, the part takes command of the whole.

The aspect of this transaction to which I want to call special attention is that a virion can be considered an instruction. In its basic activity, it is like any 'to whom it may concern' instruction, moving freely until it encounters its appropriate second party. In the ordinary bodily economy, as Wiener has noted, hormones (chemical messengers), have such a function, as does the aversive message of the skunk's odor. Through the circulating humoral instruction, the pituitary gland as a central source of master messages controls the activity of endocrine glands throughout the body.

The message carried by the virus has one major difference from the message carried by the hormone; namely, that since its goal is to replicate itself, it is potentially infinite in its activity. No humoral message can so transcend its goal; the destiny of the humoral message is to terminate at its target origin. When we see this difference, we grasp that the virus in its own peculiar character is analogous to the symbolic message, rather than to the chemical message. The message carried by the symbol, or by the symbolic system as a whole, is highly similar to that carried by the virus, in that the symbolic system has as a primary goal the replication of itself in other hosts. Since the symbolic message as pure shape (Schrödinger, 1951) is never used up, it is potentially infinite in its dissemination; its only limitation is in the number of potential hosts.

Internalizing a symbolic system is like internalizing a virus: no
matter how inapparent the difference, the host is never again the
same. Under appropriate circumstances of susceptibility, the host
can become the victim if the internalized instruction; I see disaster
of this sort as the core problem of neurosis in the symbolic context,
as the consequence with a derepressed virus may be a spreading
infection.

The extraordinary homeomorphism then evident is that the relation
of cell and virus reveals the basic structure of abstraction. In both
instances, the part comes to gain control of the whole in functioning
as an instruction oriented toward its own replication. For this reason,
the part operates autonomously and without natural termination. The
feedback system comes to be positive, rather than negative, and
success breeds further success - while we must always then remember that from the other point of view, failure breeds further failure.
What is success from the point of view of the part is failure from the
point of view of the whole.

The point of central significance is that we have been fundamentally
in error in likening living systems to inanimate objects and physical
systems. The inanimate system cannot learn, whereas the living system has to learn if it is to come to the full deployment of its potential
for adaptation. The developmental history is as crucial an aspect of
the living system as are its component molecues. We must always
bear in mind that there are many different explanatory ideas about
disorder of any kind in a living system. In relatively simple situations,
a cause-and-effect explanation may yield significant insight for effective methods of understanding, but in many others, linear formulation is misleading.

An organism progressively learns to dispense with preceptorial
buffering as it internalizes preceptorial methods in a gradual increment of discipline. The process described by Cannon at the level
of automatic learning is homeomorphic with processes of cognitive
learning. Disorder is to be understood in terms of integrative function, with the clear implication that integration is learned progressively. In the course of learning, temporary crises occur in which
the input of novelty may be for the moment partially disabling; in
many of these instances the need for buffering by a preceptor reappears temporarily. When the crisis is successfully weathered, the
result is an increment of integrative capacity. If the crisis is inadequately met, if temporary buffering is not available, there may
be a further worsening of the adaptive state because trauma impairs
adaptive mechanisms, through positive feedback.

Viruses are like ideological patterns existing for extended periods
in some kind of fragile equilibrium, inducing a morbid state when
trauma allows rerelease of the dangerous pattern and its spread
among previously uninvolved aspects of the system. Hoffer (1951)
points out in his studies of the mass movements of the twentieth
century that alien ideologies tend to affect the frustrated and the
disadvantaged. We scarcely need remind ourselves of the relevance
of his predictive comments in the present state of affairs in our universities, our country, and in the world. It need scarcely be noted,

either, that when we say 'alien ideology' we speak in relativistic terms, since the nature of human cultures is such that any imported ideology tends to be alien. Since the incident at the Tower of Babel, man's condition has been that of enmity toward his conspecific fellow of a different persuasion.

The thought I want to present, then, can be restated in terms of the subject matter of this monograph. It is that the disorder of physiological function seen in, say, hay fever, is analogous to the disorder of cognitive function seen in obsessions and in phobic states. At a different pair of levels of function, the disorder of loss of terminal control is that seen in neoplastic illness and that metaphorically evident in the myth of the sorcerer's apprentice who could turn on but not turn off. In the broadest context, the process is that of abstraction, the use of a part to instruct the whole; and inherent in abstraction are the potentialities of neurosis. When we see the extensive homeomorphisms from level to level in this model, then the interrelation of emotional and neoplastic disorder appears theoretically inescapable; we have already seen in many different contexts that the empirical relation is readily observable.

REFERENCES

Bartlett, F. C.
  1947   "Measurement of Human Skill", Brit. Med. J. I, 835-877.
Bentley, A. F.
  1950   "Kennetic Inquiry", Science 112, 175-183.
Bernard, C.
  1865   An Introduction to the Study of Experimental Medicine
          (New York: Macmillan, 1927).
Cannon, W. B.
  1932   The Wisdom of the Body (New York: W. W. Norton).
Cantril, H.
  1950   The "Why" of Man's Experience (New York: Macmillan).
Erikson, E.
  1964   Insight and Responsibility (New York: W. W. Norton).
Hoffer, E.
  1951   The True Believer (New York: Harper and Row).
Lwoff, A.
  1966   "Interaction among Virus, Cell and Organism", Science
          152, 1216-1220.
Richter, C. P.
  1957   "On the Phenomenon of Sudden Death in Animals and Man",
          Psychosom. Med. 19, 191-198.
Schrödinger, Erwin
  1945   What Is Life? (Cambridge, England: Cambridge University Press).
  1951   Science and Humanism (Cambridge, England: Cambridge
          University Press).
Selfridge, O. P., and U. Neisser
  1960   "Pattern Recognition by Machine", Sci. Amer. 203, 60.

158

Shands, H. C.
    1963   "Conservation of the Self", Arch. of Gen. Psychiat. 9,
            311-323.
    1966   "The Informational Impact of Cancer on the Structure of
            the Human Personality", N. Y. Acad. Sci. 125: 883-889.
    1967   "Novelty as Object", Arch. Gen. Psychiat. 17, 1.
    1968a   Psychoanalysis and the Twentieth Century Revolution in
            Communication", in: Modern Psychoanalysis, ed. by
            Judd Marmor (New York: Basic Books).
    1968b   "Crystallized Conflict", delivered at Speech Communi-
            cation Center, Univ. Wis. at Milwaukee (Feb., to be
            published).
    1968c   "Coping with Novelty" (unpublished).
Shands, H. C., and J. E. Finesinger
    1948   "Lymphocytes in the Psychoneuroses", Amer. J. Psychiat.
            105, 277-285.
Shands, H. C., J. E. Finesinger, S. Cobb and R. Abrams
    1951   "Psychological Mechanisms in Patients with Cancer",
            Cancer 4, 1159-1170.
Shands, H. C. and D. Menzer
    1953   "Eosinophil Variation in the Course of Insulin Coma Ther-
            apy", Amer. J. Psychiat. 109, 757-766.
Shannon, C. E.
    1948   "A Mathematical Theory of Communication", Bell System
            Tech. J. 27, 379-423.
Sherrington, Charles S.
    1906   The Integrative Action of the Nervous System (New Haven,
            Conn. : Yale Univ. Press. 1948).
Spitz, R. A. with W. G. Cobliner
    1965   The First Year of Life: A Psychoanalytic Study of Normal
            and Deviant Development of Object Relations, Chapter XIV,
            267-284.
Thompson, D'Arcy
    1961   On Growth and Form (Abridged edit., Cambridge, England:
            Cambridge University Press).
von Bertalanffy, L.
    1950   "The Theory of Open Systems in Physics and Biology",
            Science 111, 23-28.
Whitehead, A. N.
    1925   Science and the Modern World (New York: Mentor Books,
            1960).
Wiener, N.
    1948   Cybernetics (New York: John Wiley).

DISCUSSION OF THE PAPER

Dr. Salk: I found this to be a very fascinating discussion, and had the
impulse to want to break in at a number of points along the way. Dr.
Lwoff spent about six months at our institute this past year, and he
is a most extraordinary scientist, a highly intuitive person - I used

the word poet two days ago – and he is one of the rare people who can describe the field in which he has worked in the terms in which you have interpreted them.

He is basically an artist and his work is magnificent, and, as you all know, he shared the Nobel prize with two other remarkable people about two years ago. He is fundamentally a molecular biologist, but he sees the Gestalt of what he is doing, and it is for this reason that he made so significant a contribution. He spent time trying to understand the shut-off mechanism, at the molecular level. If you look at the organization, or the order in a cell that becomes neoplastic, it is equally clear that the regulatory mechanism has somehow been jammed in the on-position rather than the off-position. Molecular biologists are applying themselves to try to understand precisely the structural nature of the process that is involved. And they are trying to define precisely the chemical elements responsible for neoplasia.

Now, earlier you talked about linguistics, and said that language was uniquely human. Other forms of communication between animals are merely communication. Human language is a specialized form of communication. You then jumped to the molecular level, and I was glad that you did that, because there are parallels in that both express forms of communication. The code needs to be translated, and what we tend to do with abstraction is to code them, and then they have to be decoded again.

We have a strange institute because Roman Jakobson, the linguist at Harvard and MIT, has spent several months of each of the last several years with us, working with Dr. Bronowski, who gave a lecture the other day on magic and science. What has been going through my mind during ths conference, in part, has been about the nature of the evolution of thought processes in attempting to explain natural phenomena. There was a time when magic was a way in which we could explain things. Now we use science as a way of explaining things. Perhaps I can tie the two periods together by using the phrase that Bronowski used when he talked about the difference being between black magic and white magic.

I suppose I could characterize some of the discussions that I have been listening to as gray magic. An attempt is made to take an observable fact and offer an explanation that is almost magical in its quality. What we are really trying to do is to understand nature. What are nature's explanations of the phenomena that we observe? And that, perhaps, is the difference in the approach that I hear from the two different sets of minds that are both addressing themselves to this very interesting and complicated problem.

Dr. Shands: It seems to me that the most important problem that we are now confronting is whether or not the frame of reference in science that has existed triumphantly for over two hundred years is now appropriate to the requirements of this era.

It is my own opinion that traditional science is obsolete. What is succeeding it is a much broader field, concerned primarily with communication and organization, of which science forms a special case.

Dr. Abse: What I was going to talk about has become distracted by

the dialogue between Dr. Salk and Dr. Shands, I certainly do not agree
with you, Harley, that we depart from science. However, I feel that
your discussion is relevant.

Many years ago, actually in 1885, there was a book called The Life
of Speech, by Wegener, who was a German linguist. It is a very remarkable book, in that he shows that language evolves in the child
through a process on the one hand of orderly emandation, (I cannot
go into all the aspects of this), but on the other hand, what is very
important for the evolution of discursive language is the metaphor.
And in the work, as you know, of Suzanne Langer, this business of
symbolic transformation acquires a great deal of importance. In
fact, it is through metaphor - the evolution of live and dead metaphor
- that discursive language evolves, and it is fundamentally posited
upon physical impressions that we have to use for semantic movement
in order to encompass novelties. And in this way, we acquire a basis
for an orderly view of the universe.

When somebody has a psychosomatic disorder, in general, there
is regression in one part of the mental apparatus. I think that this
part, however, gets dissociated from another part. There is still
orderliness. There is orderliness in one sector, there is organization
in one sector, but there is another sector that is disorderly, in which
there is regression; there is regression in the symbolic transformation, so that you get back to the fundamental physical processes, I
think that what we are dealing with is a certain loss of shape in one
aspect of the ego, the body ego part of the total mental ego.

Dr. Shands: When one says 'organization', it presupposes that there
are many different lower-level organizations, any one or any number
of which can be in good working order, or in fair working order, except that something is interfering with the total integration. It would
seem to me that it is entirely logical that if something catastrophically
disturbing happens at the symbolic level, in terms of the discovery
of some terrible event or the receipt of some dreadful news, it is
quite likely that the whole organization will be temporarily disorganized while preparing itself for reconstitution.

VII

THE CHALLENGE OF INNOVATION

Biological evolution is nature's method of ensuring a persistent input
of innovation. New species emerge constantly, but the process is
very slow. Those who show a mutation are highly vulnerable, and the
vast majority perish early without leaving any trace. Cultural evolution begins at the point where biological evolution eventuates in the
formation of a group so organized as to be able to shelter the young
during periods of vulnerability, and the difference from the state of
nature allows a much increased rapidity of innovational change.

The process of cultural evolution replicates the pattern of biological
evolution in large part in traditional societies, which reject change
with great intolerance. Traditional human societies show as well as
a marked tendency to resist increasing their own numbers, with
practices that seem to a welfare-oriented society cruel and heartless.
Abandonment of the aged, infanticide, exposure of female infants and
of infants impaired for any reason are all familiar in the practices
of primitive groups living in marginal states of adaptation.

The paradox often found in less innovative societies than our own
is that the discoverer or inventor is often highly praised in retro-
spect, just as is the revolutionary who succeeded. But both the revolutionary and the innovator have been feared and suspected by their
contemporaries. The massive change taking place in Western society
since the beginning of the scientific age is the consensual value now
given to innovation in the scientific-technological sphere. This change
is a radical one; its ramifications constitute the major challenge to
the human race at the present time. The spread of the positive appraisal of innovation to the economic sphere has led us now to a worldwide consensus among economists that prosperity is dependent upon
chronic progressive growth, extrapolated endlessly into the future.
As a part of the same enthusiastic praise of growth, many countries
have laws which foster and accelerate the growth of their own populations - with the partial rationalization at least that population growth
fosters economic growth.

The problem of augmented innovation is worldwide at the present
time, and its consequences and implications are to be found in every
daily newspaper. To take a spot example, an issue of the Los Angeles
Sunday Times for March 8, 1970 presents three news reports which
indicate the global status of the problem of innovation and the logical
consequences thereof. One such article reports that the current
growth of the Japanese economy is "without precedent or parallel".
The figures present a rate, compounded yearly, of 9% in the nineteen-
fifties, of over 10% in the early sixties, and of at least 13% in the

later sixties. Japan is said to be encouraging this rate of acceleration by investing an unprecedently large portion of its national product in research and development.

The second article suggests that the remote and hitherto inaccessible Pacific islands of Micronesia are on the verge of a tourist boom. An enthusiastic tour director was able to recruit only a hundred visitors to these 'unspoiled' islands in 1969, but he confidently expects that by the middle of the decade there will be at least ten thousand such tourists a year, together with the jet airports and many-storied hotels that have arisen in Hawaii, Acapulco, along the Costa Brava, and in all the other places being 'developed'. The article suggests another instance of "the jet's capability of mass destruction of the world's sleepy, peaceful paradises".

In the third article, it is noted that both Russian and American travellers accuse each other's countries in the same terms, complaining of "interminable waiting, pollution, poverty, poor snow removal and crime". In the article, special note is made of Lake Baikal in Siberia, the deepest lake in the world, where Soviet paper pulp mills are polluting the previously pure lake in the name of progress. Parenthetically, it can be noted that the need for paper pulp is not least in the gigantic Sunday editions of papers of the magnitude of the New York Times and the Los Angeles Times. Further, the author points out that a peninsula on the Black Sea graced by a unique stand of enormous pines is being bulldozed to provide space for a row of huge hotels and a board walk in the manner of Atlantic City or Miami Beach. The author points out that Leningrad has now developed the same black pall of industrial pollution which characterizes the industrial cities of the United States.

These reports, seen in the same newspaper without any special search having to be made, indicate how worldwide is the principal movement of our time. This movement rests upon growth of all kinds – of industrial growth at exponential rates, of a massive growth of a population increasingly demanding luxury and services of unprecedented extent, of transportation across vast distances at high rates, with the demand for 'unspoiled' areas leading to a persistent invasion and spoiling of such areas, of a movement of the same trend across political and ideological boundaries. The tourist boom threatens Micronesia, while the requirements for oil threaten the Alaskan tundra.

Traditional attitudes still conceal from us what is happening. Forward-looking, liberal members of the American society have always tended to deplore the fact that new ideas and new techniques have been so much resisted by the conservative, and especially that many inventors and discoverers have been disregarded or even punished for their contributions. In these days, this complaint is still frequently heard, even though resistance to change has in dramatic trends undergone rapid reduction all over the world. The most remarkable of developments is the conviction, based upon the familiar miracles of science and technology, that whatever problems we encounter will necessarily be solved by new discoveries piled upon the new discoveries which have led us to the present situation.

The same orientation which underlies research and development prescribes that the proper activity of the investigator is prediction. That is to say, one tries to foresee what new events will occur - and we find ourselves back with another version of innovation. Therefore it seems perhaps more useful to look if not backward at least to our own context and to try to find there an understanding of how we arrived at the point at which we find ourselves. To put the problem in the form of a highly abstract question - what are the methods of innovation?

The man who sees the problem in terms of the glowing future of technology sees a continuing floor of innovative improvements, while he who sees disaster finds his prediction growing closer in an accelerated way with each new crop of distressing statistics having to do with losses, pollutions, and population increases. The common feature is an acceptance of the scheme of innovative change in an incremental way, at exponential rates. The pattern of patterns is a meta--problem, and the 'locus' at which the problem is operative can be said to be 'deutero-locus'. The context in which this meta-problem is set is the whole world; we are clearly now 'involved in mankind' in an unprecedented way.

Recent expansion in understanding points again and again to the basic nature of human methods of communication as the characteristic innovative feature of our era. We have always spoken of the specific human characteristic of using language, and we have always contrasted levels of abstraction in intellectual and philosophical context. What is truly novel in this time is the instrumentation of abstraction to an unprecedented degree in design, in manufacture, and in the use of new methods. These innovations occur both in the metal and in forms of organization: they include the development of computers as well as of managerial techniques, the proliferation of schools of business, of highly advanced kinds of research in science and industry.

Throughout business, government, the military, the space program, science and technology we see the unification of variants of abstract method. Where we have always known that the generic human characteristic is that of speech, we now see the meta-development of general forms of universal language used in computers for whatever purpose is required. The dream of many scholars through the centuries has been that of developing a universal language, but, except for the esoteric language of mathematics, no such universal language has appeared - until recently. Now we see the transcending of the narrowly chauvinistic forms of 'natural languages' by the universal languages devised to fit computers. Computers have the enormous advantage, compared with the human being, that there is no emotional involvement in 'my' language as over against 'yours'. The computer, as a well-designed machine, is totally indifferent to the significance of the data it processes or to which language it uses. Numbers of dead soldiers or numbers of dill pickles or numbers of eye-blinks - it is all the same to the machine. The decision as to Fortran or Cobol is easy to make on the basis of efficiency without nationalism.

As we begin to grasp the meta-significance of these meta-methods, we find ourselves back to an expanded kind of understanding of the

basic human problem of the relation of 'message' and 'medium'. We
have naively always taken it for granted that the universe presented
to us in development in one's own social system, in the particular
variant of early intimate training, is the 'real' universe. This conviction has never been shaken by the numbers of the available deviant
who for one reason or another see a different universe - we have been
able to reject their evidence on the basis of its 'craziness'. There
is no culture of insanity, and the single deviant is of no significance
in an orderly statistical treatment of the problem. The problem of
discordance between the world-views of different groups of people
has been avoided in the past on the basis of lack of contact between
widely separated groups of people.

Now it becomes ever clearer how much the kinds of formulation
used in different groups affects the forms which result as we examine
the ideologies-in-action represented, for example, on the battlefields
of Southeast Asia, where these doctrinal conflicts take a daily toll in
blood neatly shown in a box on page one, with comparative numbers
(Enemy dead: 100 vs. American dead: 10) entered into the computer
for the various kinds of record-keeping that are so large a part of
modern technology in war or business or science. The Babel of
tongues related to the multiplicity of ideologies gives repeated reinforcement to those who seek clarity and precision in prediction
through the use of detached and objective kinds of formulation - but
at the same time the vividness of report from the battlefield gives
to the naive television viewer a totally new sense of horror as improvements in color technology make the blood ever more life-like.

In this revolution of innovation, it may be important to note that
power remains primarily in the hands of those who live at detached
levels, as for instance the generals in the Pentagon and the politicians
in the cabinet and the White House. These officials are able to maintain a considerable distance from dramatic events at the level where
they are daily experienced by the mass of the world's rapidly increasing population. One such dramatic development - and again one
worldwide in its occurrence - is a totally different view taken by
those who because of age and number and lack of power live closest
to the problems that are so rapidly multiplying. Only in the groups of
such dissidents does one finds a drastic sense of urgency in the
dangers which the human race is now facing. Those insulated by age,
power, and luxury have many kinds of denial available to them.

To a psychiatrist, many of the observables are not unfamiliar -
except that these observables are more familiar in the clinic than
in the larger society. If one tries to make a 'diagnosis', one finds
a convenient label in the 'gap' or separation between the consensus
of the established and the consensus of the concerned. In the former
instance, the belief is universal that more of the same will relieve
the problem - it is just that we have not quite got the technology yet.
On the other side, the belief is urgently held by many that it is the
technology itself that is the disease. It is perhaps not too great a
distortion of a medical term to speak of this divided spirit as 'schizophrenic' - in the Biblical words quoted by Lincoln, it is at least
possible that a house divided against itself is in danger.

If I may use the term, let me suggest a 'diagnosis', with the hope that in the following pages I will be able to present some account of the 'pathogenesis' of the contemporary disorder. It is entirely clear, to continue the metaphor, that prescription of treatment is totally beyond my competence. The special claim supporting the temerity required to make a discriptive comment is simply that of a prolonged preoccupation with the problems of human communication. The diagnosis can be made that the ideology of innovation has been institutionalized throughout the world at the levels at which power is now held. Because innovation is so much more powerful in highly specialized areas, the tendency to intensify innovation without taking any account of its ramifying implications leads to progressive isolation of the desired goals from the unanticipated complications. But the technological implications of specialization rapidly leap out into general areas of concern - as did the techniques emerging as application of the intellectual preoccupation with atomic fission.

In the discussion below, the thread followed is the notion that ideologies are meta-patterns found in all kinds of linguistic systems. The detached and intellectually 'neutral' forms of objectivity which have so powerfully influenced the course of modern science and technology are fully as much rooted in an ideology as are ancient religious practices or those of newly emerging political systems of the far left and far right. Ideology is a word having two roots meaning 'the same' in the former case and 'word' in the latter. 'Word' in this sense implies a preoccupation with communication, and many learned disciplines in which experts discuss their problems with each other are known as '-ologies', e.g., biology, physiology. Ideology is similar in its meaning to 'spirit of the discipline' or 'spirit of the language' in a somewhat different sense. The connotation is that of essence, and the suggestion is that of an unchanging doctrine or dogma that underlies a wealth of phenomenal manifestations.

When we examine scientific thought, we find that the basic problem is inherently paradoxical since its ideology is that of continuous innovation. The 'essence' of science is change, whereas the essence of most religious ideologies is permanence and persistence. One Old Testament description of God is "The Same, yesterday, today, and tomorrow". We begin then with an internal paradox, and the only way in which we can retain the notion of an ideology is to see that it refers in this case to an attitude, widely shared among scientists, that the appropriate way in which to approach any unknown is in an attitude of curiosity, with technical approaches which purport to give to the investigator some eventual control through prediction and through anticipatory activity with reference to the problem in focus.

If one holds the paradoxically conservative American values now resting upon the radical ideal of continuous endless growth, the spread of the American influence through the world promises that every country can aspire to attaining the American standard of living. On the other hand, if one sees a major threat in the idea of endless growth, one can say that the ideology of innovation is spreading epidemically, in the etymological sense in which the term means 'through the people'. The epidemic spread has not been stopped by the Iron

Curtain, and both the antagonistic capitalist and communist countries
compete to spur their own economies to greater and greater heights
of achievement.

The problem appearing at the 'meta-level' of concern is that of how
this exponentialization of innovation shall be valued. It is only in the
very recent past that we have begun to follow out the implications of
the feed-back involved, because it is only in the post-war period that
things have begun moving so fast. The evidence indicates strongly that
the pace reflects not only rapidity but acceleration. What attitudes
shall we take? What changes in attitude, if any, are required to move
in industry and politics? The basic strategy involved in the scientific
attitude is reasonable in the extreme: the implied direction is to solve
soluble questions, leaving those which seem insoluble to some future
data at which all who share the scientific ideology believe that techniques of mastery will have emerged. At any given time, however,
it is implicitly prescribed that we deal with what we can manage. The
Nobel prize winning physicist Wigner points out explicitly that physics
has had its astonishing success by restricting its objectives to the
attempt to understand regularities in the behavior of objects.

The situation in which we find ourselves now is that of having solved
an enormous number of soluble problems while remaining helpless to
a very great extent in relation to the traditionally insoluble problems.
We have developed techniques of production, of transportation, of
communication which progressively revolutionize the world, allowing
a man to fly around the world if he wishes in a few hours - or even
to reach the moon and walk upon it. Meanwhile, back on earth, there
are increasing evidences of the lack of success with traditionally insoluble problems such as those of human relations in the small sense
and international relations in the wider sense. Specialists make possible the development of immense power in limited areas in many in-
dustries, but the problem of developing a general method of approaching the general problems which follow the major specializations is
still far from any kind of solution.

If I may again refer to the psychiatric context from which the preoccupation developed here emerges, it may be instructive to comment
upon the kind of thinking demonstrated by highly disturbed or 'psychotic' patients. If one listens carefully to what such patients say, it
is often notable that their logic is not at all in error. What is at fault
is the basic assumption upon which their behavior is based. If a
'schizophrenic' person assumes that every single other person he
encounters looks at him with intense criticism and hostility, and
that he has no means whatever of countering this universal imaginary
aggression, then much of his otherwise unaccountable behavior begins to appear quite 'reasonable'. In similar form, what we find
nearly universal in the contemporary American scene is the basic
assumption that all problems are susceptible to solution in the scientific mode, through the further development of objective and rational
means of approach.

This near-universal acceptance of an ideology of research and
development in the basic search for endless innovation is all the
more interesting when we examine the history of human society and

of animal processes. Animals are clearly quite incapable of reason - but animal species have a very high rate of stability and species-preservation. Traditional human societies lived more or less at peace with the other aspects of their worlds, as we know from the reports of millions of buffaloes on the great plains inhabited for hundreds of years by the Indians, and the billions of passenger pigeons that so astonished early visitors to the American continent. Rational Western man, using objective methods, has so conquered this country and so changed the conditions of immense areas of its once bountiful lands that much of it is rapidly approaching the status of the once-luxuriant valley of the Euphrates (the site of the Garden of Eden, some think) and the once verdant hills of Lebanon on which the cedars were so much admired.

Western man has been most proud of the development of rational and objective method in the scientific tradition. The sociologist Max Weber points out that although many other social systems have shown marked capacity for invention, no other part of the world has systematically developed the implications of invention rationally. The Chinese invented gunpowder for firecrackers, while Western man colonized the world through its rational application to problems of warfare. The Chinese invented print, but it was not until Gutenberg developed the printing press that the conversion of a world to the ideal of literacy was accomplished. An obscure German physicist showed that atoms could be broken with dramatic effect, but it took the managerial efficiency of a Manhattan project to develop new fissionable materials and to apply the invention to destruction and to peaceful uses.

The strategy of rationality is that of specialization, with a reduction of a large problem to many different manageable parts, and the systematic exploitation of whatever is learned in progressive theoretical integration. Specialization is segregation; the modern epoch shows us the quite different evaluative estimation of these two terms in the further and further breakdown of learning into small segments and the pressure for integration in a society that once quite ignored the problem. Again we see logical consequences of closely related forms of understanding going in divergent directions. As we become more able to describe the fine structure of the atomic nucleus, we see at the same time a worldwide movement in the young idealizing the removal of artificial boundaries between people. These divergent movements present the threat of destruction and the germ of salvation - the point of interest is that both are novel, both present patterns so innovative that they are unprecedented in the history of the world. Many seek 'law and order' these days - but the fascinating problem is that legal practice rests upon precedent, and the problems appearing are unprecedented.

Is it possible that innovation is both slave and master, both bringer of luxury and harbinger of death? If we continue as we are going, shall we run out of the world's store of raw material? Or shall we, in a glorious achievement of hitherto unimaginable technology, arrive at atomic fusion in time to supply us with endless power and to vaporize our waste materials in a vast recycling made possible by bringing the sun to earth? And if we do succeed in importing the sun, is it possible that there may be some unbelievably powerful possibility of pollution that we have not imagined because we could not envision a world renewed so fantastically through the harnessing of fusion?

No one can accurately foresee the future, but it is possible through the application of the methods which underlie innovation to make limited predictions on the basis of known probabilities. The initial probability is set by theory in the communicational context: the divergent paths are those of negative feedback resulting in a fading-away or the establishment of stable organizations, and positive feedback which results in progressive instability of organization. Where one part of a total organization, in this case, the specifically social aspect, remains conservative and even grows more conservative in the same time and context that the technological organization grows more and more radically innovative, the probability is high that further and further discrepancy between the two will occur.

The most fascinating of facets of this process is its theory, particularly its meta-theory. What we see emanates from the possibility of abstraction found only in the human species and specifically encouraged by human education. The higher the educational level, the more emphasis is placed upon abstract method. Abstraction rests upon the human capacity to separate pattern from material context, as Aristotle already knew in his duality of causa formalis and causa materialis. The most innovative of developments in the past century has been the emergence of epistemological understanding which allows us an incrementation of power through the processing of pattern – most grossly in the use of computers, but far more importantly in habits of thought.

Human beings have traditionally mistrusted fantasy and magic even while fascinated by their practice. In this time, we have learned how to control fantasy and to harness magic so that now the imaginative scientist or engineer is able to carry out most of his work in the imagination, especially when that imagination is coupled with a servile computer which obligingly models any conceivable reality on command. Through these means we no longer have to go through tedious processes of experiment in a vast number of areas. We have learned how to imagine productively, by-passing many of the tedious calculations and constructions once necessary.

The challenge is whether, using some such method in the largest context, we will be able to devise methods and model potential realities so that we can continue to grow and invent while taking care not to blow ourselves up or grind to a halt submerged in solid waste, in air-borne pollutants, in water so foul it sometimes burns or becomes almost solid in masses of algae, or in radio-active fallout.

The focal point of origin, from which this development had spread, is clearly the United States. The French journalist Servan-Schreiber has recently discussed the question in a book entitled The American Challenge in which he points out the rapidity with which American business is taking over in the European scene, specifically because of American methods of management. In a particular case, he underscores the difference between the concrete and the abstract orientation by noting that an American businessman contrasted himself with a European colleague, saying that where the European concerned himself with the production of his factory, the American took primary note of the profit margin. Profit margin is another way of saying 'communicability', since it is only those products that can be sold that matter, only those that enter into the stream of distribution. Thinking in terms of product is more concrete than in terms of profit. For understanding innovation in the human context we need to understand communication. The term taken widely can be seen to refer to the many different systems of distribution. We tend to think of distribution in terms of goods and money, but the current distribution of people through unprecedented means of transportation is more and more important in the affairs of the world. At the roots of human organization in primitive cultures, kinship systems have the function of organizing the distribution of women between subgroupings of a tribe or people. In the human brain, the dramatic feature in the fantastic numbers of connections between billions of cells - again a problem of internal communication.

The central human characteristic is that of language. Under the influence of evolutionary biology, the prevailing opinion of many workers in this field several decades ago was that the derivation of human language from animal vocalization had been a relatively simple evolution. This opinion has now been comprehensively falsified, from a number of points of view. Neurophysiological and neurological evidence establishes that the significant central connections for linguistic function (cortical) are totally different from those for vocalization in animals (in the brain stem), and that it is therefore clear that the functions are discontinuous.

Language in the human sense is more closely analogous to the learned skills of mankind than to the genetically mediated vocalizations of lower animals: language itself rests upon a technology. Linguistic structure is potentiality governing emerging linguistic forms. The structure is never visible; it is demonstrable only through manifestation in overt speech or writing. Such a structuring is analogous in some ways to a program once the program is fed into a computer. It can be recovered by making a study of the variations in the output, just as a virus is most easily identified by the disease which results after the virus takes over, as when one finds himself with a 'cold sore' during the course of a febrile illness as the herpes virus emerges from repression.

Language goes through processes of disappearance and reappearance in thinking. The human being learns to think many problems out in various kinds of shorthand or in terms of highly compressed images (as in dreams or fantasy) which are not specifically formulated in words, although they are capable of being formulated so. Under conditions of demand, it is possible to reveal these images or fantasies through description; psychoanalytic therapy depends upon a consistent effort to verbalize the previously rapidly transient series of internal constructs. The most interesting observable is that when the random 'associations' are verbalized, they appear in strict grammatical accordance with linguistic structure.

In Chomsky's discussion of philosophical grammar he underscores

the unavoidability of some such concept as 'mind' - but, if we look in
a different tradition, it can as easily be said that the tendency for the
overt linguistic phenomenon to follow grammatical rules is a manifestation of the 'spirit of the language'. Ancient philosophical discussions distinguish between the 'appearance' and the 'reality', with
the notion that the unseen structuring part of the process is 'real',
while the overt is 'mere' appearance. Such a usage would say that
the overt disease, say smallpox. is 'appearance' while the hidden
covert agent, the virus, is 'real'. It would seem far more satisfactory to formulate both as equally 'real', with the relation that of
a transaction. The deep structure is related to the superficial structure as 'structuring' and 'structured'. Again we find the parallel relation of 'signifying' and 'signified' in the structural linguistic formulation of Saussure.

Chomsky makes much of the innovative potentiality of language,
referring in Language and Mind to the work of a Spanish writer of the
sixteenth century who emphasizes the relation of intelligence to the
idea of genesis. In the work of Vico the repetitive emphasis is upon
the same theme. Vico points to the birth connotations of the word
'nation' and the genetic implication of the Latin for people, gens. The
suggestion is that to human beings, innovation and genesis are the
most fascinating and emotionally meaningful possibilities - even in
those instances in which we see clearly how threatening (i. e. , how
negatively associated with emotion) the new can be.

The metaphorical resemblance between the genetic code and the
linguistic code is clear in the repetitive use of the metaphor by the
molecular biologists. The reverse possibility is that the human attribute of language emerges from the same mechanisms as those which
make genetic messages possible. Language does not so much resemble
the whole genetic method as it does that aspect of the genetic method
highly developed in the viruses. A virus is a part of a whole which
instructs the whole to 'replicate the part' rather than, as in the case
of the full genetic message, 'replicate the whole'. The similarity to
the linguistic message is clear. The linguistic message is an instruction to reconstitute or to replicate aspects of the whole. As in
the case of the virus, the efficacy of the message requires a highly
prepared recipient.

In this dialectic of part and whole, the specific outcome is that the
part comes to control the whole. In a social system, one member as
leader is given the authority to direct the activities of all the members
of that culture insofar as their membership inclines them to obey
that part of the situation endowed with that instructive potency. The
history of much of the human race is the effort to gain and to employ
the control of others which we call 'power'. But the essence of the
linguistic relation is power, and the application of linguistic method
is technology has now brought us to the culmination of man's power.

It is possible that our most sophisticated form of structure, in the
linguistic methods universal among man but enormously differently
developed in different cultures, different times, different individuals,
may be at base most closely related to the transmission of information
and instruction from generation to generation in the genetic process?

If so, then it would not be too difficult to imagine that specialized development of certain potentialities might underlie the different kinds of results of different kinds of development. The occurrence of neo-plasia in many different kinds of animal has now been intensively studied by the molecular biologists. Their results can be interpreted as indicating a relation of the ideology of innovation to the specialized development of language similar to that of the relation of neoplasia to the specialized genetic processes of the virus.

For human beings, novelty is not only incessantly generated, it is also derived from re-examining the familiar and the old-fashioned. What 'was believed is discarded and then revived. Chomsky and Lenneberg have restated and renewed some old notions having to do with language. These new-old ideas emphasize the creative (i. e. , innovative)potential of 'natural languages'. They suggest that training human beings to speak inculcates the possibility of innovation in spite of a lack of specific training.

The rules of grammar are generative in a significant way. Through detailed study, it is possible to derive many different equivalents - transformations - of certain basic notions. Wiener once pointed out that if one wishes to pick up a pencil, he can do it in any number of ways, even with one's teeth or one's toes if necessary; the goal takes precedence over the technique. In the same way, it is possible to present a message in any number of roughly equivalent variants in different choices of words in different kinds of legitimate sequence sentences.

Chomsky notes repeatedly that the observable in the human use of language is that of a quality of complexity different from any other kind of communication-system we know. The degree of complexity in the computer increases consistently, and presumably will continue to increase as circuits become more complex and more connectable - but there is no question whatever that the computer has no close similarity to the human thinker with reference to this meta-problem of the quality of complexity. The specific capacity of the human being is to generate information as he experiments, formally and informally, with novel analyses and novel combinations of the various facets of his experience and the various kinds of artefacts and machines that he can construct. In The Savage Mind, the French anthropologist Lévi-Strauss suggests that the primitive may seen as a bricoleur, that is, as a kind of handyman who uses whatever is available to mend, to construct, or to carry out plans of action. It is this capacity to imagine the innovative use of materials of all different kinds which is the human attribute. From the "bricolage" kind of inventiveness the challenge of innovation, positive and negative, appears as the dominant theme of our time.

In a situation where it is now obvious that the technology of abstraction has evolved beyond the wildest dreams of all our forefathers, recent developments in molecular biology allow us to postulate homologes between linguistic and genetic processing of information that are quite striking. Genetic patterning is expressed in a specific context, that of the arrangement of amino-acids in the DNA molecule. But the carrier of the message is not the material but the arrangement.

The same amino-acid molecules arranged differently convey different instructions. The leap to linguistic kinds of communication is simply that significant form is emancipated from a dependency upon <u>any</u> specific material context at all, although it remains dependent on <u>some</u> material substrate.

The focal problem of neoplasia, that is, of the growth of tumors and cancers in varying degrees of immaturity, is an innovativeness unrestrained by the usual messages which communicate the instruction to stop growth at some point. The elucidation of some of the problems of neoplasia in the work of contemporary oncologists and molecular biologists is fascinating. Filterable viruses are markedly simplified bits of DNA that can act alternatively as 'organisms' and as 'crystals'. They are strict parasites, living (when they show the signs of life) at the expense of cellular organization through invasion and control of bacteria or cells in organs. In isolated form, they may persist for long periods of time stored on a shelf in a bottle, but when given the appropriate context, they come to life again and reproduce themselves. Many experts believe that many or all the phenomena of neoplasia can be traced to the activity of viruses.

Viruses show a similarity in their behavior to a language. The stored, isolated pattern is meaningless, while the pattern in circulation may be very powerful in exerting control. Under ordinary circumstances, the language is implicit in human behavior while it may not be at all apparent - we say it in terms of 'conscious' and 'unconscious'. Through the pattern of reproduction, every virus is continuous with all its predecessor and successor molecules, even though that similarity may be concealed in parts of the life-cycle of the virus by the way in which it is incorporated into the chromosomes of a cell. On the other hand, each molecule of virus is highly similar to, if not identical with, all others in its species. Thus we find, at the lowest level of life, the patterns we know in the figures of speech: <u>metonymy</u>, characterized by contiguity, and <u>metaphor</u>, characterized by similarity of form.

Progressive simplification which we see as a development through the evolution of languages results in the markedly simplified form of English - a form well suited to scientific and technological development because of its loss of most of the apparatus of declension and conjugation, and because of the simplification of gender. Significance in English is of all languages the most dependent upon sequence, just as significance in biological codes is inherent in sequence.

If we follow the pattern of a conflagration or of an epidemic we see that the original focus remains for a long time the site of an inconspicuous process of initiation, slowly increasing in its intensity and spread. A similar kind of prolonged latency is postulated in many forms of neoplasia. At the end of a variable critical period, with the opportunity presenting, the message spreads - whether that 'message' be the temperature reaching the point of ignition, or of virulence which allows the disease to spread epidemically, or of the tissue growth which starts the process of metastasis, there is an inherent metaphorical similarity.

I suggest, as the crucial point at issue, that there may be not only the metaphorical element of similarity of pattern but also the metonymical element of contiguity in processes across this wide spectrum. The important idea is that deep structure, in the linguistic sense, may have an actual biological basis in deep structure in the molecular biological sense. Since the disease which characterizes the invasion of a virus into a living body is so different from the viral instruction, it is persuasive to believe that the phenomena of the modern revolution in innovation may traceable to the very different message inherent in the ideology of language. Such a notion at the very least introduces regularity into the otherwise extraordinarily ambiguous problem of the quasi-autonomous life of language noted in detail by Lenneberg and Chomsky.

Both these students of language point out that a feature difficult to explain in any system which supposes that basic language is learned in any comprehensive sense is that the speaker shows a remarkable facility in formulating the same meaning in any number of different ways, and in inventing new ways of presenting old ideas. Thus, the speaker of a language is constantly innovating on old themes, but in doing so he finds ever-renewed ways of combining, all according to accepted grammatical rules the speaker has never even thought of. The point is that he is always following a meta-message in a deep structural patterning he has never been taught and has no idea about - at least until he becomes very sophisticated in reflexive kinds of consideration of the human condition.

The metaphorical similarity which then springs to the attention of the psychiatrist is that precisely the same ind of statement can be made about the myriad of neurotic and psychotic syndromes - collections of symptoms - which can be observed in the office or in the madhouse. No patient is identical with any other patient - but every patient shows signs and symptoms shown by many other patients. Thus there is a similarity between the psychiatric syndrome and the spoken sentence. At the basis of both there is obviously some kind of inherent patterning - and what more likely than that patterning should participate in the same processes as those which characterize heredity? This is not to say in any crude sense that 'mental disease' is hereditary, any more than it is to say that language is hereditary. The fact is unavoidable that the potentiality of patterning has to be evoked in some substrate, but it would appear that that substrate can be any aspect of human condition, from speech to tumor to industry to ideological revolution.

The ancient question man asks himself is, "What shall I do to be saved?" and the answer is not available. The possibility exists, however, in an attractive fashion, that making a diagnosis may well be, in the larger as well as in the smaller context, the first step toward finding some kind of solution. Perhaps the most important additional fact to be taken into consideration is that this disease of innovation, if that is a useful figure of speech, is worldwide, affecting every human being on the globe. It may therefore be somewhat easier to persuade all human beings that they are all con-specifics, and that whatever remedy is or is not to be found must be species-wide. All men are now, perhaps in extremis, clearly brothers; all are involved in mankind.

It is fascinating to find in the comments made by Lwoff in his Nobel lecture a presentation of the essentially dialectical process characteristic of language, with reference to a basic philosophical problem. He notes, that, for the philosopher, "order is the entirety of repetitions manifested, in the form of types or of laws, by perceived objects. Order is an intelligible relation. For the biologist, order is a sequence in space and time. However, according to Plato, all things arise out of their opposites. Order was born of the original disorder, and the long evolution responsible for the present biological order necessarily had to engender disorder. "

This quotation gives us a view of a rather dire possibility that a progressive increase in orderliness necessarily engenders disorderliness. The variant formulation which seems applicable in the industrial context is that the progressive emphasis upon innovation, which is to say, upon information and order, necessarily brings in its train the reciprocal emphasis upon randomness, disorderliness - which we tend to speak of in other words as pollution. There is little doubt that wordwide disorderliness at the social level is operative now, in the many uprisings, revolutions, 'wars and rumors of wars' everywhere apparent - perhaps the disorderliness is only the reciprocal of innovation in the context of science and technology.

PART FOUR

PSYCHOSOCIAL IMPLICATIONS OF SEMIOTIC THEORY

VIII

SOCIATRY: SOCIAL PSYCHIATRY AND THE PHYSICIAN'S CALLING
(*)

The innovations introduced by contemporary psychiatry into American
medicine have occasioned alarm among conservative physicians. In
turn, the more radical innovations introduced into psychiatry by social
psychiatrists and their more recent associates, the community psychiatrists, have occasioned alarm among conservative psychiatrists.
We are forced to the conclusion that the accelerating changes in medical care, and especially in psychiatric care, are evidences of a social
revolution. The discussion that follows is an attempt to understand,
in a perhaps characteristically psychiatric mode, the developmental
implications of this movement, and to examine the physician's role
in this novel context.

The term 'disease' has at least two major implications. In that
more commonly understood, the process called a disease is a specific
syndrome, typically with some etiologic explanation, consistent to a
considerable extent from one patient to the other. In a wider rendering,
'disease', from the root dys-, implying a negative quality, connotes
distress, uneasiness, or displeasure. The modern problem can be
stated in oversimplified fashion by noting that the scientifically trained
American physician tends to regard himself as a specialist concerned
with the entities included in the first definition whereas the patient,
particularly the untutored patient, tends to regard the physician as a
consultant to whom to bring all sorts of problems of distress.

The development of modern psychiatry is a specialist's response
to the gap between these two definitions. To the patient complaining
of frigidity or impotence, unexplained anxiety, or unrealistic feelings
of worthlessness, the psychiatrist is now in a position to offer at least
the setting in which these problems can be discussed with the maintenance of some dignity and respect for the legitimate basis of the complaint.

The physician, offering care for disease, found himself confronted
with dis-ease. In a second step, the psychiatrist, offering care for
some kinds of dis-ease, has increasingly found himself having to deal
with many kinds of behavioral aberration. With the advent of community psychiatry, the profession (either by choice or by selection
and direction) is charged with responsibility for a large number of
disorders of behavior, including delinquency and addiction, and for
disorders of deficiency, especially mental retardation.

It is often some help simply to underscore a change in fact by adopting a change in name. In this respect there seems at this time a good
deal of justification for changing the designation of the discipline:

modern psychiatry is increasingly something better called 'sociatry'.
The modern 'patient' is not the individual but the group. We see this
trend in the development of family psychiatry and family therapy, in
the proliferation of group therapy of many different sorts, and in the
contemporary trend that offers to the 'sick' community a caring institution, thus providing essentially for the treatment of a group by
a group.

Along with these developments there is increasingly a shift in the
very definition of our goals in the once specifically medical area.
The traditional physician is oriented toward an individual patient, and
the tradition is still strong in many a physician's self-identification.
The public health specialist was originally regarded with some distrust by the conservative physicians of his time of origin. It was especially galling to the traditionally oriented physician that the practice of public health medicine often required overtly coercive measures
and infringements on 'individual freedom', e. g., the disposal of
garbage and excreta as the individual prefers. Compulsory inocula-
tions ran (and sometimes still do) into outraged protests from religious groups interpreting their scriptures as proscribing the introduction of foreign matter into the human body. The list is long.

Preventive Psychiatry

With the shift toward public health, there comes an increasing emphasis on the preventive aspects of medical care. "An ounce of pre-
vention is worth a pound of cure"; but we find that, as we introduce
preventive measures, we come increasingly into conflict with the
structure of society in its conservative, self-preservative orientation.

When we begin to apply the public-health concept more widely in a
psychiatric framework, we are confronted with this problem in an
exaggerated way. 'Psychiatric illness' is never the problem of a
disease in a person; in every single instance, as one investigates
the problem it becomes a function of social process, either in the
closest group-of-two relations of parent and child, spouse and spouse,
or employer and employee, or in wider groupings identified by a belief system, a geographic location, a social class, or an economic
level.

To illustrate the dilemma in a specific instance, let us consider
the matter of the level of cognitive competence. There is increasing
consensus that obvious mental retardation is the responsibility of
the psychiatrist. There is broad agreement that finding an I. Q. of
50 is diagnostic of mental retardation, often in these days referred
to as a disease. If we regard this result as a measure of difficulty
in learning, then non-learning comes to be, in this case, diagnostic
of a condition requiring or qualifying for care by an expert physician,
or even for hospitalization.

When we examine the same I. Q. result in a different context, we
find quite a different picture. Bruner and his associates (1) report
that, unless schooling is continuous and effective, cognitive growth
ceases at the age of nine. Assuming that an I. Q. can be measured

accurately (an assumption about which there might well be widespread doubt), the unschooled child of 18 could be found to have the intellectual development of a nine-year-old and therefore an I. Q. of 50. Is such a deficient human being sick? If so, is he an appropriate patient for the psychiatrist? If not, why is the mentally retarded child so easily assigned to the psychiatrist? The problem becomes one of definition. We are obviously no longer concerned with 'mental illness', whatever that confusing term may be understood as meaning, but with a failure of the responsibility of the social system for the education of its members.

If one defines the appropriate field as sociatry rather than as psychiatry, some of the difficulty disappears; but it is not the case that the problem is much easier. The orientation of 'sociatrists' is toward 'sick groups'; but it is obviously much more difficult to try to define a sick group than a sick person, since by the principle of cultural relativity what is general in a large enough group is by definition normal. When we turn this definition around, we find that the 'sick person' in a psychiatric sense is more precisely the deviant person, whether his deviance is in any one of the traditional areas of thought, mood, or behavior. If, as this line of reasoning suggests, the problem is very largely social, in that problems repeatedly can be reduced to differences among groups, and to deviance within the group, one might then think it probable that the sociologist should be the appropriate specialist to be assigned the care of the patient or of the patient group.

The sociological tradition dominant in this country, however, is that of research in the tradition of the survey. Trained groups of interviewers sample opinions and validate hypotheses through statistical correlations. In this tradition, therapeutic activity is not considered - it is often disdained. The goals of survey research are highly similar to those of the academic research tradition. This is to say that the research is often useful, and frequently impeccably designed; but it is not involved in action or intervention.

The dilemma, then, perhaps becomes more clear: we have experts who have no therapeutic orientation or zeal on the one side, and physicians not expert in the relevant specialized knowledge on the other. If therapeutically inclined, how can we utilize what knowledge we have to approach the treatment of groups?

The answer would seem to be that a completely new kind of therapeutic institution must emerge. It is unfortunate in many ways that the beginning of such an institution should carry the label 'community mental health center' since it is obvious that the need is different from any simple definition of health. The preventive techniques that can obviate the 'sickness' of no schooling, for instance, are certainly in some sense oriented toward the production of social competence; and social competence is 'healthy'. But does that mean that psychiatrists are to become school teachers, or school teachers psychiatrists? Obviously not, but the importance of an intimate interrelationship between teacher and psychiatric consultant would appear, at the very least, a first step.

But there is a further problem. Once a 'disease' is identified in

a school child, what are the public health implications? If it is clear
that the child's 'disease' is in some degree, say, due to inadequate
mothering, or to disordered conditions of life at home, what are the
preventive indications? From Spitz's (2) work in institutions charged
with the care of orphans and the abandoned we know that the very
conditions of institutional life make for serious 'sickness' in them-
sleves, no matter how dedicated or self-sacrificing the attendants
at such an institution may be.

It would seem in this case that we would have to face clearly and
directly the obvious requirement: if the conditions of life in a mother-
child relation are such that the child is very likely to be affected
with some ultimately grave disorder, then the social responsibility
is to prevent further child-bearing by that mother, at the very least.
But here we immediately run into the ancient prohibitions that pre-
cluded interference by the social system into familial matters. Direct
intervention is authoritarian; non-intervention makes us accomplices
of a kind of 'Typhoid Mary'. The solution to this grisly dilemma is
far away, obviously. But it seems of considerable importance to
underscore the fact that it is with respect to this kind of decision on
the part of the social system as a whole that the psychiatrist, even
in his present state of ignorance, could offer advice.

Social Psychiatry

Much of the confusion thus visible in psychiatry appears to be at
least partially resolved by a change in the very definition of psychiatry
over the last two or three decades. The movement was noted, in his
perceptive fashion, by Edward Sapir, (3) the father of modern anthropological linguistics, who suggested:

> ... psychiatry is moving away from its historical position as a
> medical discipline unable to make good to that of a discipline which
> is medical only by tradition and courtesy and is compelled, with
> or without permission, to attack fundamental problems of psy-
> chology and sociology as far as they affect the well-being of the
> individual. The locus, then, of psychiatry turns out to be not the
> human orgaism at all in any fruitful sense of the word but the
> more intangible, and yet more intelligible, world of human re-
> lationships and ideas that such relationships bring forth.

Social psychiatry progressively denies Freud's idea that neurosis
is an 'intrapsychic' disorder. The human being is in a social environment in almost as obligate a fashion as the fish in water. He more
and more appears primarily as a communicant, and the unique character of the 'individual' is his particular combination of memberships.
'Psychiatric illness' becomes in this rendering the result of inadequate
integration into relational systems. Psychiatric treatment becomes
a matter of helping patients learn methods to cope better with associates and relatives or, conversely, in custodial practice, of providing
simplified, highly structured environments demanding little or no

adaptive capacity from the inmates.

Other readily available studies indicate that to maintain social competence requires a continued exercise of one's capacities; it is said that Robinson Crusoe quite forgot how to talk in his long period of isolation. Studies show that, even at the sensory level, deprivation when extreme and continued leaves the subject suffering from a kind of disuse atrophy of his sensory potentialities for extended periods. Ethologists demonstrate in many different species that it is not only the kind of teaching that is important, but also the timing; critical periods allow learning that is thereafter never again possible. Dubos (4) has inquired into the early conditions of life in deprived children of Latin America in work that indicates that early nutritional deprivation is irreversible.

These many straws in the wind, although not yet conclusive, suggest strongly that the typical American faith in curative measures may be unfounded; and it behooves us in planning for future developments to take this possibility more firmly into consideration. The evidence suggests that preventive measures in altogether unfamiliar and staggering amounts are required.

Integration and Specialization

The achievements of modern American medicine emerge from a technologic genius based upon a widespread acceptance of scientific method, with its closely associated tendency toward narrow specialization. In the contemporary epoch, we are becoming aware, with a sense of alarm, that the various kinds of specialization we practice are threatening the life of the culture. All of a sudden, from every point, these developments force themselves upon the awareness of a people long oblivious. The reduction of infant mortality, the obliteration of epidemic disease, and the prolongation of life give us the problems of population explosion and the increasing accumulation of feeble and impaired human beings. The paper mills that provide us with the raw material of business and government pollute our rivers and threaten our drinking water; the means of keeping warm and maintaining artificial illumination pollute the air with noxious fumes. In these terms, perhaps the 'sickness' of our times is most impressively a lack of integration of the various specializations. Perhaps the inheritors of the world will be only the artificial human descendants, computers who do not need to drink the water or breathe the air!

Integration is basically a problem in communication; when we operate in an integrated fashion, we have systems in which every part is in relation to every other part in a mutually sustaining fashion. Disease in the limited sense is often the result of the failure of some portion of the bodily system to play its function in an effective manner. No matter how efficient or pspecialized an organ may be, it can live only as part of the system.

The specific <u>human</u> specialization is to those symbolic methods of communication that enable us to talk to others and to be conscious of

ourselves. These methods allow human beings to develop the notion
of individuality - which is in its own right a matter of specialization.
In the many animal species in which the blind unconscious methods
of nature can be observed, an integrative process constantly acts to
preserve the whole system in balance, no matter what the cost to
the individual. Human specialization all too grequently results in im-
balance and disintegration.

Specialization tends to feed on itself, to demonstrate 'positive feedback', in the current phraseology. There is a marked and continuing
acceleration of the processes of conscious thought and its primary
derivative instrment, the digital computer. The process is threatening
in that it tends to assume that whatever is not quantifiable is useless
or in error.

The support of specialized research programs since the Second
World War has progressively reduced motivations for nonquantitative
investigation by making rewards for the quantitative variety dispro-
portionate. The current shift toward support of service programs
may be a kind of unconscious social reaction to the gragmentation of
intellectual analysis previously so dominant. A hopeful idea is that
in some sense, no matter how bumbling, sociatric methods are those
of integrative evolution rather than of narrow analytic inquiry.

Soul and Mind

Analytical methods formulate problems in terms of linear sequences
and causal agents. It is in this tradition that the ancient formulation
of a 'mind' that controls a 'body' is to be understood. When one thus
concretely uses terms applied to an organ, it is easy to think of
'diseases of the mind' in a manner quite analogous to the use of
'diseases of the heart' or of the kidney, lungs, or other organs or
organ systems. When one takes a different basic position, assuming
instead that emotional disorders are primarily disorders related to
the human condition, one gets a quite different view of the psychiatric
discipline.

It is instructive to look briefly at the origin of the term 'psyche',
the root from which psychiatry takes its name. Personification is the
rule when we find that Psyche was a legendary princess said to have
been the chosen of a mysterious lover who not only refused to give
his name but even refused to let Psyche see him. Driven by curiosity
(note here another 'agentification' in the use of curiosity as a 'driving
force') and unsatisfied by the 'mindless' gratifications of the sexual
act, Psyche lit a lamp to look at her lover and found that he was Eros,
the god of love himself. But in the process she spilled hot oil on him,
thereby radically altering a previously blissful relation of ignorance.
Psyche is thus connotatively associated with curiosity.

In another connotative context, the word psyche literally means
'breath'. Psyche, the spirit, is thus identified with breath. We use the
same root idea from a different language of origin when we say 'inspiration' to refer both to artistic creativity and to respiratory function, and when we say 'expire' to mean both breathing out and dying.

In the context of the modern interest in linguistics, perhaps the most specific connotation is the realization that the medium of human relatedness, speech, is only shaped breath.

The spirit or the mind resembles breath in that it is both essential and invisible. We tend to pay no attention to air unless it is restricted, and similarly we take sanity for tranted until it is impaired. In the Middle Ages, the deaf-mute was thought to be without a human soul - because without human language. These considerations lead us toward the notion that the psychotherapist is a specialist in human communication techniques. He works in the medium of spoken language to improve the patient's grasp of communication technique and to help him participate more fully in the consensual expectations of his group.

The Human Limitation

Traditional science shares with ancient philosophy a preoccupation in which the establishment of timeless relations of invariance set out in mathematical symbols has been the ideal. Perhaps the clearest example of the partial accomplishment of this goal is the capacity of astronomers to describe with great exactitude the movements of the heavenly bodies as extrapolated backward and forward for centuries or millennia.

When believing in the perfection of the distant goal, including the perfect, idealized version of human life in heaven, man could retain the goal of perfect rendering in theory. Even so revolutionary a scientist as Planck displayed his nineteenth century bias in declaring, in his scientific autobiography, that his faith in the use of reason to find the 'real world' was unchanged. The hope of attaining so metaphysically idealized a goal has, however, been formally abandoned by physical theorists and mathematicians in the twentieth century. This event is most significantly conditioned by the realization that man cannot avoid himself in the pursuit of knowledge. As Bertrand Russell (5) points out, it becomes obvious that, when we observe events in any 'external world', we are actually only observing events in ourselves. Much evidence now points to the uncertainty of any kind of knowledge - a dramatic instance being the development of storage mechanisms in the modern television studio that make it impossible to tell the difference between the live and the taped program.

We are therefore thrown back upon ourselves, faced in a most important way with the demonstration that communication techniques make events in a putative 'external world' only probable at best. We can only increase the probability of accuracy, never establish it as certainty. The more observers who agree, the more likely in general it is that a given sensation or observation is reliable - but the universal demonstration is that whole social systems have believed implicitly what other social systems regard as error or even as nonsense.

The modern idea of hypothesis-testing advanced by Popper (6) and

widely accepted is that such hypotheses are subject to falsification
but not to verification - that is, a thousand positive demonstrations
·indicate that the chances are a thousand to one that the idea is correct,
but the 1001st experiment with a negative result will cancel the whole
former series. In this way we get a somewhat different view of the
delusions and illusions of psychiatric patients: if a single negation is
enough to throw doubt on a hypothesis, then a single delusion is enough
to throw doubt upon the certainty of 'reality' as normally accepted;
and we are forced again to realize how much all our certainties are
based upon consensus and social reinforcement.

Social Context

As we understand communication process more nearly adequately,
we increasingly come to grasp the importance of the social importance
of the social context in which learning occurs. In this century the
Gestalt psychologists have called attention to the importance of the
background as it presents the figure, and Freud's great contribution
has been to call attention to the unconscious background of human
conscious data-processing. When we study difficulties in learning,
we realize that the infant learns in the context of the mother-child
relationship; the student, in the context of the preceptor-novice relationship. To learn easily, the student has to be sheltered by a
'favorable environment' of social support.

When we apply these ideas to psychiatry, we understand that the
most important factor for success or failure of 'treatment' is the
quality of the therapist-patient relationship. We can suspect that the
content of the discussion between patient and therapist may be for
many purposes totally irrelevant. What is important is the sense of
mutual involvement, hopefully in pursuit of a goal shared with feeling
by both participants. In a new kind of ideal, the ultimate result of a
satisfactory psychotherapeutic relationship may be similar to that
of a satisfactory parental relationship, namely, mutual independence
of the one from the other with the maintenance of mutual feelings of
respect and regard.

To attain this goal seems to require the maintenance of 1) a therapeutic attitude similar to that in which a physician encourages events
beneficial to the patient's recovery, and 2) an educational attitude
similar to that of the teacher fostering events beneficial to the
student's learning. The psychiatrist is involved in therapeutic education, with emphasis first upon a useful relationship and second
upon teaching the patient patterns for understanding his own behavior
and that of others.

Psychotherapeutic technique rests upon the assumption that one
cannot directly discover the significant factors, but that these emerge
only in re-enactment of relationships with others in the 'transference'
relationship established with the therapist. When we learn this in
psychotherapy, it becomes much easier to apply it to the context of
teaching and to see that, in general, the teacher who establishes a
positive transference relationship with the student is that teacher

who is most easily able to facilitate the learning of the specific subject matter of the course. The relation becomes a general facilitator of learning. This fact is well known in religious circles, and the influence of early childhood upon later attitudes and specific performance is quite clear to amny religious educators.

The sometimes heart-breaking implication that must be faced as we redefine psychiatry in an educational context is that "The moving finger writes, and, having writ, moves on - and all your tears cannot cancel half a line." The implication is that emotional and social disorder can never be fully reversed.

This conclusion points to a radical re-orientation of our thinking along lines familiar in the context of public health. The appropriate technique is that of hygiene, especially in the attempt to provide a 'favorable human environment' for the largest possible number of future citizens.

This idea does not make the task of psychiatry any the less, but perhaps even somewhat greater. In any given generation, the emphasis is to be placed upon training. But, since the children of any generation are the direct responsibility of their parents, any hygienic, public health approach must begin by identifying problems in the parental relation and taking measures to affect these problems.

When one begins to think of the therapeutic education of thousands of disadvantaged children, one realizes that the professional investment must be fantastic - in the same category, for instance, as that of the effort to put men on the moon! But putting men on the moon is primarily an exercise in concrete instrumentation and technical mastery of the inanimate environment; it requires little fundamental change in social orientation.

The revolutionary social movement of this time is one that is changing the nature of medical care through alterations in the concepts of social responsibility. The use of money in large quantities is hastening change in a continuous fashion. Social responsibility for the care of a wide variety of problems of disease and distress is being insistently offered to physicians, with the clear if unspoken implication that, if the challenge is not accepted by the physician, it will be imposed upon him, probably in ways that will be far less palatable to him than the compromise he can make with his own traditional attitudes.

The Physician's Calling

Max Weber (7) makes much of the notion of a 'calling' in his discussion of Western religious thought. A 'calling' is a strong feeling of personal commitment to a social role defined by a culture; it is a characteristic manifestation of this institutional role that "many are called but few are chosen". The social system has evolved many procedures to narrow the access to the physician's role.

When we compare social role and therapeutic efficacy, it is important to remember that the powerful armamentarium of the modern physician is of very recent development. Up to the beginning of the twentieth century there were mostly drugs of sedative or analgesic potency, with a few natural remedies such as cinchona bark and the foxglove. The scientifically trained and oriented physician is an invention almost as new as the computer. Previously, throughout civilized nations (and even now in many nations), the dominant variant in medical practice was folk medicine. Indeed, it is only necessary to examine the 'nature foods' faddists and the vast sales of books commending the values of black-strap molasses and wheat germ to realize that the scientific physician has a limited appeal even in this country. Rational considerations (characteristic, and uniquely characteristic, of Western thinking, Weber notes) have no effect upon wide areas of medical practice. In contemporary China, and even in the more advanced Soviet Union, primitive techniques (e.g., acupuncture) and magical agents retain full popularity as therapeutic procedures.

Human beings develop in their social systems various 'offices' having a general similarity. There is the political leader, the king or president; the religious leader, the priest; and the physician. Originally, in many societies, these three offices were held by a single person. The increasing specialization of complex social systems has tended to separate the three so that each such office is now generally filled by an occupant whose role-definition is clearly differentiated from those of the other two.

The physician's profession appears to be a 'calling' generally similar to the 'vocation' of minister or monk. We find the recurrent emphasis of communication technique in the derivation of these terms. 'Calling' is a term derived from the vocal call; vocation also implies the notion of speech; and a profession is that in which a trained person professes or prophesies. The impression is confirmed that it is the public presentations of such general roles that characterize and define the occupants; they are specially trained in certain methods of communication. It is relatively easy to come to an understanding of the offices held by the politician and the religious leader; but, if we accept the idea that the physician has always (until very recently, and now in specially limited areas only) been ineffective as a curer of disease, what, then, is his duty? In this connection, Freud's definition of the psychoanalyst as a 'secular spiritual guide' suggests some of the functions of the religious spiritual guide without the supernatural connotations.

The function traditionally given to the physician is that of taking responsibility for personal health. It includes the making of a diagnosis, the prescription of some treatment regimen, and the establishing of a prognosis. The typical non-specific effect displayed is the mysterious but highly significant 'lifting of the spirit' and relief of anxiety when the physician enters the sick room, no matter what the demonstrable efficacy of the physician's armamentarium is. The suggestion is strong that it is this function from which the current movement in medicine stems, and that it is to the psychiatrist in the community context that this responsibility is being almost forcibly extended.

The predictable response to this novel assignment of responsibility to psychiatrists is an increasing widening of the definition of therapy, and an increasing awareness of the necessity to work with a variety of other professionals and specialists toward the common aim of therapeutic education. The new definition insistently threatens the narrow 'territoriality' of traditional medical practice as we find ourselves confronted with what McLuhan (8) calls the 'implosion' of incessant communication within and among social systems of the modern world. The emerging role of the psychiatrist appears to have both novel and general potentialities, but the fact that the tradition can be traced to earliest events in human history reiterates the basic conservatism of human social systems.

To one psychiatrist, at least, it comes as something of a relief to find reason for suspecting that modern social psychiatric developments are not radically novel, but rather are a contemporary manifestation of the response of professionally trained persons to an imperfectly articulated requirement of the social system. This gives a reassuring sense of the continuity of the vocation or the calling of the physician no matter what his technical armamentarium in the way of skills and pharmacologic agents.

NOTES

(*) Reprinted by special permission: in: Mental Hygiene 53 (1969), 393-402.
(1) J. S. Bruner, et al., Studies in Cognitive Growth (New York: Wiley, 1966).
(2) R. A. Spitz, "Infantile Depression and the General Adaptation Syndrome", in: P. H. Hoch and J. Zublin (eds.): Depression (New York: Grune and Stratton, 1954).
(3) E. Sapir, Journal of Abnormal and Social Psychology 27 (1932), 229.
(4) R. Dubos, "Environmental Determinants of Human Life", in: D. C. Glass, Environmental Influences (New York: Rockefeller University Press, 1968), 138-154.
(5) B. Russell, quoted by G. G. Simpson, Science 139 (1963), 81.
(6) K. R. Popper, The Logic of Scientific Discovery (London: Hutchinson, 1959).
(7) M. Weber, The Protestant Ethic and the Spirit of Capitalism (New York: Charles Scribner's Sons, 1904).
(8) M. McLuhan, Understanding Media (New York: McGraw Hill, 1965).

IX

THE NOTION OF STRUCTURE IN COMMUNICATION AND COMMUNITY

Retrospectively, it now appears obvious that psychotherapy in the 'classical' psychoanalytic style requires, as Freud said, a 'reasonable education' and a 'good character'. By these criteria, a vast number of the uneducated, the disadvantaged, the addicted, the sexually deviant are 'not suitable' for psychoanalytic therapy. When we then realize that the bulk of 'mental illness' is to be found precisely in the 'unsuitable' group, we are forced to reconsider the widely accepted notion (at least in the United States) that psychoanalysis is the primary theoretical system adapted to 'mental illness'. This paradox, namely that the system claiming generality is related to a highly specialized practice among the hyper-advantaged, has been widely ignored.

Community psychiatry orients itself to precisely that group excluded (or, perhaps, in Goffman's term, 'excolluded') by the application of Freud's own criteria. To say then, as Bandler has recently done, that psychoanalysis must be the basis of theory in community psychiatry seems to me simply unbelievable. The statement is tantamount to saying that the operations of the secondary educational system must be based on practices derived from Groton or Exeter. No doubt private school education is effective - as is the psychoanalytic procedure in selected instances. The relevance of so esoteric a system to the 'population at risk' for the bulk of mental illness according to most statistics is problematic.

The problems that emerge in the other direction, when one begins, as a middle-class professional with a relatively enormous amount of education, to address himself to the general population in situ in the local community, are fantastically great. How is it possible to communicate with the community, when 'the community' is mostly defined in terms of ghetto populations, welfare recipients, educationally disadvantaged, addicts, and all the host of other 'problem-carriers' from whom highly educated middle-class persons have been systematically separated throughout their lives? The 'stock in trade' of the middle-class professional is theory, and the following discussion has to do with possibilities emerging when one takes a new theoretical look at the community-communication system.

Communication and community are words showing an obvious 'family resemblance'. They are members of the munis family, and two other members of the same family are municipality and immunity. The derivation suggests some interesting relations: munis is a word meaning 'duty' or 'obligation'. In ancient times, a municipality was a city under the jurisdiction of Rome but having the duty of regulating itself. The terms with the prefix from cum, meaning 'with', imply a sharing of obligation or responsibility. Immunity suggests a freedom from the possibility of infection. In the municipal context, the custom of giving a distinguished visitor a 'key to the city' is tantamount to giving him the freedom of the city, or allowing him the immunity ordinarily enjoyed by the citizen. We find then a curious paradox, one of a number I want to comment upon; in this case immunity or freedom is attained through having been structured by an infecting agent in the medical context, or through having been indoctrinated in the customs of the city in the process of acquiring or growing into citizenship. When we review the whole series, what appears as most emphatic is the notion of discipline or regulation, with the freedom attained a freedom within, the product of a rigorous indoctrination. Prsuing the derivation process one step further, it is of some interest that indoctrination is cognate with doctor, so that in the medical context we are doubly reminded of the basic meaning of duty or obligation. With this background, it becomes clearer that community and communication have to do with common discipline or shared obligation. We see this in such usages as the 'community of scientists' who work within the same 'discipline'. When we change focus then to processes of communication, it becomes clear that any kind of communication depends upon the prior development of a common body of knowledge, a shared group of techniques, a mutual structuring. In ordinary human life, the methods by means of which these obligations and structurings are imposed is so subtle and gradual that we never ordinarily think of how much discipline is involved in learning one's own 'native language' - but the difficulties are instantly apparent when one tries to learn some other language.

When we examine the assumptions upon which community psychiatry rests, we find these considerations of immediate importance and relevance, because the notion of community in this usage implicitly assumes that in this time and place we are striving to produce a comprehensively integrated community the members of which share a common discipline, a common set of assumptions. This is an ancient American dream, built into the ideal of the 'melting pot', a great common locus in which the cultural diversity of immigrants gives way to some general uniformity in an integrated mass. Presumably, when this shall have occurred, we will at the same time have obliterated mental illness and done ourselves out of a job. I propose below to examine some of the reasons why I am not currently worried about joblessness, at least from this cause.

When we realize something of the incredibly complex structuring processes involved in linguistic communication and in the performance of the obligations of citizenship, it becomes clear that the term 'freedom' so commonly encountered these days gives a misleading impression. It is far more precise to say that the goal of a civil rights program is that of providing immunity to all members of a community. It is perfectly clear to any observer of judicial process, for example, that the differential immunity provided by solvency and a middle-class status is astonishing. For all practical purposes, jails and prisons are filled with the uneducated poor. Outstanding exceptions in the case of flamboyant financiers falling afoul of securities and tax laws occur, but these are, statistically speaking, so rare as to be of no practical importance.

When we say, 'uneducated' and 'poor', we place the emphasis in the appropriate order, since the educated and often self-chosen poor know how to avail themselves of the resources of society. Education and vaccination - both providing the means of predictive structuring - both also provide immunity. The difference is important, however, in that education requires far more active participation on the part of the student than does vaccination on the part of the person being immunized.

Predictive Structuring

When we examine the means by which human beings achieve any kind of knowledge of any kind of behavior, we find that the unavoidable starting point is that of a regularity in the observable. When we describe, we can grasp only that which is regular, and regular means 'predictable' in that what we describe as occurring now is what we expect to have occurred in the past and to occur again in the future. Taking the pattern into an abstract status in description apparently takes it out of time, but in fact it is easy to see that it sets the problem into a future-oriented kind of context. Education, learning about regularities, can then fairly easily be seen as a predictive structuring which is based upon the assumption that what is to be is what has been. Vaccination similarly is a predictive structuring which assumes that the pathogen to be encountered is consistent with the contemporary set of pathogens. In Piaget's system he speaks of an accomodative process which, by forcing the organism to take account of a present problem, prepares that organism for a future problem. It is easy then to see that all forms of learning and describing have the built-in limitation of a special vulnerability to the novel. In the most dramatic way, the pandemic and lethal proportions of the measles epidemic engendered in an unprepared South Seas population by contact with Europeans is a dramatic instance of the vulnerability implied in a lack of predictive structuring.

Since psychiatry in the United States has tended to emphasize its biological relations, in a specifically medical context, it is of interest that the pursuit of understanding through analogy has been more widely developed in the opposite direction. By this, I mean that immunologists, virologists, and oncologists have been actively using linguistic and societal models for the past decade or two, while the equally appropriate application of immunological findings to the psychiatric universe has been largely ignored. If we try to establish a level of generality allowing applications to be made across the disciplinary boundaries, we can begin with the notion of organization applied to such diverse entities as cultures, languages, biological organisms, and games.

'Objects' are 'entitized' through processes of regulation emphasizing consistent patterning within some defined boundary. A most interesting comment is made by Peyton Rous, the cancer researcher, when he says, "Every tumor is made up of cells that have been so singularly changed as no longer to obey the fundamental law whereby the cellular constituents of an organism exist in harmony and act together to maintain it." In a very similar kind of statement, André Lwoff says, "An organism is an integrated system of interdependent structures and functions. An organism is constituted of cells, and a cell consists of molecules which must work in harmony. Each molecule must know what the others are doing. Each one must be capable of receiving messages and must be sufficiently disciplined to obey." Later in the same article, he underscores the parallelism further in saying, "An organism is a molecular society, and biological order is a kind of social order. Social order is opposed to revolution, which is an abrupt change of order, and to anarchy, which is the absence of order."

In our society, the notion of a 'melting pot' suggests that cultural diversity can be cancelled through mixing. This is a misleading notion beased upon an inorganic metaphor, comparing a social system to a group of metals which when raised to an appropriate temperature flow together into an amalgam or an alloy. It is notable that the 'operator' in this concept is the verbal metaphor - we are far more affected by the linguistic operations we employ than we would like to believe.

In sharp contrast, contemporary understanding strongly suggests that instead of using physical science models to understand social process, we do much better to use social science models to understand biological as well as social process. Thus, Jerne speaks of an "immunologically competent" organism as analogous to a "purged xenotypic dictionary", meaning a dictionary in which all alien elements have been 'purged' or excluded. When we pursue the notion in learning how organisms establish an identity, we find that they do so by a process which can only be called that of radical segregation. The dramatic 'rejection' processes which have made it impossible to maintain life for very long in many patients with a heart transplant are examples of a universal process which is so powerful that it forces an individual to commit a biological form of suicide when an implanted alien tissue is essential to life.

The problem of integration thus assumes a somewhat different aspect when we examine it from the standpoint of biological regulation rather than from that of social idealization. We can look further in the biological context to find instances of integrated organisms which do in fact include portions once alien to each other. Again here we find the immunologists following the lead of social theorists, in this case the myth-makers of long ago. The mythical dragon fought by Bellerophon with the help of his winged horse Pegasus was called Chimera, a beast in front a fire-breathing lion, whose body was that of a goat, and in the rear a serpent. Immunologists call organisms made up of diverse elements 'chimeras'.

When we pursue the goal of establishing full integration within a society composed of diverse elements, we are concerned with producing a generation of what might be called cultural chimeras. The

immediate consequence of this process may well be part of the contemporary phenomenon of the 'generation gap', since it is clear that
integrational process is far more advanced in the young than in their
elders. The conflict that occurs is one between the sequence of generations and the contemporary process - between what structuralist
theorists speak of as the 'diachronic' and the 'synchronic' contexts.
If we succeed in effecting the production of a generation of chimeras,
we will necessarily at the same time succeed in effecting a massive
alienation of this generation from its predecessor. Groups of parents
will be analogous to the lion, goat, and serpent origins of the legendary beast.

This kind of fact is one which regularly occurs in cultural context
and never occurs in the non-human world of physical science. It is
largely for this reason that we can be enormously successful in
technological progress while remaining confused and fumbling in the
cultural context. The human condition, to put it another way, is a
condition of necessary paradox, but the primary goal of 'objective'
human intellectual effort since the beginning of recorded history has
been the pursuit of clarity and the avoidance of paradox.

When we compare the divergent aspects of human intellectual success through the ages, we find two major divisions, the logical-intel-
lectual-rational on the one hand, and the poetic-emotional-irrational
on the other. Since these two are both characteristically and traditionally human, it is of considerable interest to find that the sharp dichotomy between them reappears in every epoch. We might say that the
indication for integration is perhaps most urgent here - but the most
powerful of attitudes in the established 'objective' hierarchy remains
that of rejection and suppression of the irrational. We find even in
psychiatry, obviously the home of the irrational, that the establishment insists upon a rational rendering of social process. The effort
is obviously as interesting and as ineffective as that of King Canute!

When we have clearly in mind the biological requirements for the
establishment of identity, we can turn back to history to examine
some analogues of the mutual rejection of different kinds of entities.
When we look around us, we find Nigeria recently split in a fratricidal conflict of civil war proportions; Kenya is the scene of extreme
tension between Kikuyu and Luo. China and Russia, the great fraternal
Communist powers, often seem to be on the verge of a major war.
Egypt and Israel are both inhabited by Semitic peoples, and in Yugo-
slavia and in Ireland there are ancient fratricidal antagonisms which
divide a people with common blood through their differing religious
affiliations. Returning once again to biblical myth, we realize how
much wisdom is compressed into the story of Babel - where God
himself became afraid of a united people and first adopted the strategy of "divide and conquer".

Turning attention to a somewhat different aspect of the same general
problem, we can see what happens in human organizations when the
internal integration fails for some reason or another. In biblical
terms, a house divided against itself cannot stand. If we, following
again the lead given us to look back at ancient mythological formulations which compress so much of human wisdom into storied form,
take as example the history of the house established by Cadmus, the

194

great grandfather of Oedipus, we find an astonishing series of happenings.

Cadmus established Thebes in the process of searching for his sister Europa, abducted by a divine bull. He fought and killed a dragon and was told from on high to remove the dragon's teeth and sow them. From the teeth there sprang up a race of fearsome giants whom Cadmus divided by throwing a stone into their midst. Those hit thought themselves attacked by their neighbors, and they fell into a mass fight out of which only a few emerged alive to help Cadmus found the city.

In psychiatry, we are familiar with the great grandson, Oedipus. Because of the central position of the Oedipal myth in psychoanalysis, it is easy to forget the tribulations of his relatives, but it may be informative to note them briefly. Oedipus killed his father and married his mother; from this union there were born four children: Polynices, Eteocles, Antigone, and Ismene. When the dreadful sin was discovered, the wife-mother Jocasta committed suicide while Oedipus blinded himself and abandoned his throne. The throne fell into contention between the two sons; in their ultimate attempt to settle the succession, they fought so fiercely that they killed each other. To protect his own ligitimacy, Creon the regent, brother to Jocasta and thus uncle to Oedipus and to his children as well, refused ritual burial to the remains of Polynices. When Antigone defied Creon to bury her brother, she was condemned to death by him - and when she was buried alive in a cave to execute the sentence, she was accompanied in death through the suicide of her lover Haemon, Creon's son. Here in a compressed summary of the occurrences in one of the root myths of Western civilization, we find multiple suicides, fratricide, patricide, and filicide. By implication, we read that few families exist that do not suffer from internal division. It is clear that the display of aggression in human affairs is not of recent origin, nor is it entirely generated by the television!

Paradox: The Human Condition

Much of the complex paradoxical nature of the human condition can be summed up in saying that human beings are generally the same in that they are members of the same species, whereas they are specifically different because they live in separate groupings. Since the basis of these groups is symbolic and linguistic, in terms of cultural systems and languages used, the diversity becomes ever greater when the groups remain separated. We implicitly recognize this fact when we speak of 'dialectical' differences between human groups. The double meaning of dialect is clear when we note that two members of a given group use the same dialect, but the dialectic relationship is one of thesis and antithesis. The circularity of process is clearly shown in the derivation of dialect and dialectic, from dialektos, the Greek word for 'conversation', a 'turning together'. Two colinguists confirm their relation to each other by speaking a language different from that of other human beings. We find in every human paradox this same contrast of sameness through mutual differentness: we are like each other because we are similarly different! The basic immunological relation is that of rejection of the alien by the 'self'. The same kind of lethal antagonism is apparent at the social level in terms of conflicting symbolic meanings or conflicting roles within the same cultural context.

Training the participants in any group is basically a matter of training them to use the same dialect, where 'dialect' is taken generally to suggest the assumption of similar attitudes as well as the use of a given set of words and grammatical rules. When the members of such a group are assimilated to each other so that they share a structure, then they are free to roam within a territory the limits of which are included in the agreement which (explicitly or implcitly) establishes the cultural game in which all are players. The paradox we find is that freedom within the game is based upon a disciplined acceptance of the rules; we are only free within a structure, never outside of some structure. To way it another way, if we want to play a given game, it requires that we find similarly regulated others with whom to play.

Whenever groups that were previously separated come into contact with each other, the immediate consequence that can be anticipated is antagonism, just as we anticipate that the immediate consequence of encounter with an alien antigen is an antibody response with the strong possibility of rejection of the alien. To avoid future possibilities of rejection an early structuring to tolerance is requisite. The ability to tolerate the alien is a function of the chimera state, as noted above - and the chimera is, by definition, 'abnormal'.

Traditions of Segregation

The traditional solution to the problem of lack of tolerance is that of separation of groups from each other. When the world was large and the human race small, separation was the general rule because of difficulties of communication between groups and because of the slowness of transportation across distances. The same general principle covered separation or segregation within a social system through class distinctions - as well as through the more specific kinds of occupational disciplines. In all traditional social systems, the restrictions on communication across class barriers have been stringent - perhaps most dramatically so in the case of East Indian 'Untouchables'. The urgent problems of our time are all implicit in the widespread acceptance of a new theoretical system without adequate practical and technical methods of implementation.

To trace this problem to some of its roots is fairly easy. We live in a country in which stated ideals have always been strikingly different from actual conditions. This has been made possible by the fact that the processes of separation and segregation have so effectively barred communication across class lines that it was quite possible for an elite group to congratulate itself upon its achievements without noticing that these achievements were of local occurrence.

In ancient Greece and in the emerging United States the most elo-
quent proponents of freedom and democracy were slave owners capable of writing immortal words about all men being created free and
equal. If so, what about the slaves of Washington, Jefferson, and
Patrick Henry? Obviously, these men gave no considered thought
to the further implications of their radical doctrines. They were
writing in a localized, limited community of peers in which it was
taken for granted that 'all men' is a phrase which limits itself to a
certain highly selected subgroup of the species Homo sapiens.

Similarly, the aristocrats of Greece cultivated their intellectual
processes to a remarkable degree by discourse among themselves,
using the Socratic method from which notions like that of the dialectic naturally emerge - but they were enabled to do so because they
lived supported by a large machinery of slave labor in the midst of
affluence bestowed upon them through inheritance. To these aristocrats democracy was an ideal applied to groups such as their own.
How can men accept democracy and slavery at one and the same time?
The answer is a simple matter of definition. 'All mankind' includes
those defined as human using a definition limited to a particular region in space time.

The major barrier to communication has been the simple separation
of groups from each other, in a variety of methods many of which
have been purely accidental in their operations. When the world was
composed of many relatively small groups communication between
which was difficult, an automatic 'quarantine' was in effect. That this
quarantine was not entirely accidental is shown by massive constructions such as the Great Wall of China and the policy of island nations
such as Japan and England to restrict access to their shores.

Within social systems, the traditional practice since the beginning
of recorded history has been that of segregation by class. In every
group we know, the major differentiation has been made between the
member and the outsider, whether that outsider is called a pagan, a
barbarian, an outlaw, a goy, a heathen, an untouchable, a commoner.
Universal acceptance was long paid to the notion that the 'blood royal'
was something so special that it could only be preserved by rigid ex-
clusion of the lower-class, even the noble class, from participation
in reproductive practice. In ancient Egypt, it may be remembered,
ritual incest was institutionalized, with royal brother and sister
regularly producing inbred offspring to preserve the segregated sanctity of the 'blood'.

We come to the paradox that it has long been the custom for groups
of men to use the generic term 'man' in a highly restricted sense.
To the Chinese, neither Japanese nor Westerners (foreign devils)
are 'human' nay more than an Untouchable is human to a Brahmin.
In a famous report, a group of explorers encountered Eskimos in the
frozen wastes of the Arctic only to find the Eskimos refused to accept
the newcomers as men, because it was a basic article of faith that
the only human group known was the Eskimo group in question. It is
a universal characteristic of man that he should refuse to accept his
bother of another group as 'human'. It is then quite clear how one
can say "all men ..." - slaves are obviously non-men, and the
Supreme Court, it may be remembered, affirmed this doctrine

scarcely more than a century ago, in the Dred Scott decision of in-
famous memory.

If we return then to the notion of freedom and immunity, we find
the interesting and paradoxical notion that what has suddenly disrupted the traditional structuring of our nation and especially of
our cities is a simple application of the radical notion of freedom
throughout the people. We can say, to continue the metaphor, that the
minority groups in question have been infected with a virus latent in
this country since the publication of the Declaration of Independence
at least. Curiously enough, many of the sentiments passionately dear
to civil rights enthusiasts are similar to those espoused traditionally by the proponents of states' rights - except that where the state
is established through geographical definition, the minority group is
established through some kind of ethnic definition. The astonishing
internal contradiction is clearly shown in the behavior of the Daugh-
ters of the American Revolution some years ago in passionately
espousing the radical doctrines of the Declaration of Independence
while denying to a black singer the use of the very hall in which
'freedom' is most celebrated.

When we add some of these incompatibles together to get a logical
product or sum, we find the hypothetical notion that the radical idea
of equality has now spread through a society from a focus in an elite.
Since the parts of the social system which have traditionally been
suppressed are now those most obviously infected, the answer comes
through clearly that it is possible that the lack of immunity observed
is a function of the lack of predictive structuring - which is to say,
that the complications of freedom are that it shows many signs now
of being unrestrained by structure. This conclusion would point to
two opposite possibilities: the one, that excessive repression or re-
repression is in store, a notion widely entertained: the other, that
the only way in which to avoid this catastrophe is through an intensive
educational effort of maximum, and unprecedented, extent.

Remedies

I have suggested above that we find ourselves in an unprecedented
condition - and by the very nature of the human capacity for learning,
we are helpless in the face of the novel, the irregular, the unstruc-
tured. What we are now committed to doing is not only a task never
accomplished in the history of the world, but one which, as noted in
the findings of immunologists and molecular biologists, having some
gravely threatening aspects when we use models taken from molecular
'social systems'. The interesting question that emerges is whether
or not there are in the same kinds of universe perhaps promising or
hopeful patterns.

If we continue to try to advance understanding through the use of
ancient wisdom, we can apply to the present situation the myth of
Pandora and her box. Again referring to the derivation of the word,
we find that Pandora means 'all golden' or, as the dictionary puts it,
'having all gifts'. There is a striking similarity here to our affluent
society in which there may be enough for all to have all gifts were it

.only to be possible to regulate distribution so that a more uniform level could pertain. But, strictly like Pandora, we find ourselves in a state in which all the troubles of the world are pouring out to afflict us just at the point where we thought to be able to relax and enjoy the affluence of a technological-industrial mastery.

If we take Pandora's example seriously, we can anticipate that Hope will appear only after a long and trying period of troubles. I would suggest that the very best hope of all lies again in an understanding of the difference between the biological universe and that of culture. If we go back to the basic understanding that we have of human life, we find the most pervasive fact that of the con-specific nature of all human beings. We are all members one of another, all 'involved in mankind'. The immense differences which separate human beings into mutually destructive groupings are based upon cultural diversity rather than upon biological diversity.

We can take the second step when we find the abundant evidence, curiously appearing only very recently, which indicates that linguistic usage is, at the basic level, a species-specific potentiality spread throughout the whole group. At more superficial levels, the systems of verbal tokens that we use, and the variant grammatical systems of rules, are all of artificial and historical significance. Each such system proceeds through cultural evolving in which the 'selection' process is not that of individual survival but that of consensual selection, a process obviously subject to immensely expanded degrees of freedom when compared with the exigencies of survival and reproduction.

The Hope then to be found at the bottom of the box is that human beings will so learn to grasp their own diversity in terms of a historical understanding of human development that cultural patterns will no longer engender lethal antagonisms between the subgroupings of the human race that I have called 'co-linguists'. It is the process of identification with a basically artificial set of norms, rituals and standards that separate human groups from each other into warring sects. Theoretically, given the appropriate investment of time, effort, money, and passion - in perhaps reverse order - it should be possible to train a generation to massive tolerance. Unfortunately, it would appear that at the same time, it would be imperative to train such a generation into hitherto unprecedented levels of mutual responsibility - especially in terms of limiting populations no longer subjected to the vagaries of poverty, disease and war. We must also remember at all times that any kind of approximation of such a condition in a whole generation would be necessarily productive of nearly complete alienation from the previous generation of less universally-oriented parents. The final paradox of this series would then seem to be that we can only look forward to saving the world at the expense of losing our children!

The general conclusion I would then propose, if we consider the relation of community and communication, is that we must pour resources into education to a far greater extent than that to which we have poured money into public health - but the complications we can expect are obviously far greater, and the necessity to concentrate resources in hitherto inconceivable amounts is obviously unavoidable.

We have to come somehow to an understanding that, just as affluence has made the American adventure in Southeast Asia possible to us but not even thinkable to our poorer national fellows, if the possibility of vaccinating the human species against genosuicide is to be attained through education, it will have to rest upon unprecedentedly radical conceptions of both the nature and extent of education.

It is not too difficult to estimate the kind of education likely to be most effective over the long run; there are already many studies pointing to the general goal. In order to effect a general structuring of human expectation and human behavior, it is now obvious that the beginning of education will have to be put back a number of years into late infancy.

To make it possible for the child to continue to live in his own family, it will be necessary to educate that family at the same time - with special emphasis upon the education of the mother. The problems are immediately evident, in that we have now only the most remote possibilities of recruiting the essential emotional and financial adjuvants to this plan of action. To implement the idea would require a comprehensive re-orientation of the whole educational system of this country and probably of the whole world, with the implied investment indicated of a nearly astronomical figure. Less of an effort seems scarcely likely to have an appreciable effect.

X

MORALITY AND COMMUNICATIONAL PROCESS (*)

Culture is a name applied to certain kinds of structuring of human
behavior. Language is another. Still a third is morality. Moral codes,
linguistic codes, cultural rituals demonstrate the <u>consensually</u> structured in the human addition to the <u>genetically</u> and <u>environmentally</u>
structured forms of animal behavior. Because of the vastly increased
human range of variation made possible by the cooperation implicit
in culture and language, the intraspecific potentiality of competitive-
ness is greatly enhanced. Morality and ethics characteristically restrain forms of consensually disapproved behavior within one's own
group while often at the same time promoting similar behavior in
relation to 'alien' human groups.

Consensually ratified structures allow innovation, and recently,
innovative methods of enhancing innovation. This reflexively accelerated process brings us now to the point at which all human happiness,
not to mention all human life, is jeopardized by the unexpected results of uncontrolled innovation. The same linguistic codes which
allow cooperation allow competition; at the same time that creativity
is enhanced, entropic decay is accelerated somewhere else in a
system which is obviously now finite, to our shocked astonishment.
Innovation has therefore more than a passing resemblance to its
analogue, <u>neoplasia.</u>

It is possible that the most pressing need in the whole world seen
as a single system is some universally accepted morality of termination prescribing points of cessation of growth and innovation.

Man, Language, and Culture

There is good reason for believing that the relation between man and
language is at least reciprocal and transactional in the most extreme
sense. An unspoken language is useless, an man wihtout language is
'autistic' or 'insane'. When we look to the most intense feelings of
which human beings are capable, we find them precisely in the area
of ideologies, and thousands of men yearly lay down their lives for
fheir beliefs. Lest it be thought that belief is old-fashioned, it is
only necessary to remember the vigor with which Arabs and Israelis
kill each other, the tension between Russian and Chinese Communists,
the three hundred thousand casualties in the contemporary Viet Nam
disaster - and so on and on. In each case, a central consideration
is the belief system, whether Communist or anti-Communist, Stalin-
ist or Maoist, Hebraic or Moslem.

The principal characteristic of a human group is a belief system

(*) In press: presented at University of Iowa (1970)

formulated in an ideology and institutionalized in a culture. But these
fancy words conceal the fact that what we are talking about is a group
of human beings cemented in consensus. What the consensus osten-
sibly refers to is irrelevant; it is enough that consensus reigns. But
if consensus reigns, then the belief is more important than any given
member. As a rather consistent rule, it is the sacrifice of some or
many members to the belief which consolidates the belief and justifies
martyrdom. In the early history of human cultures, it is a regular
finding that certain members of the group - even the king - are ritually
sacrificed, often gruesomely, to celebrate the belief system. To my
mind, this indicates a paradoxically consistent <u>relativity</u> in the design
of human groups which has been greatly disregarded.

The widespread disregard of the importance of consensus is to be
understood as the reluctance or the inability of human groups to grasp
the basic paradox of generic consistency and phenomenal diversity.
It is not until a language has grown quite sophisticated that its scholars
begin to try to describe its rules in a grammar, and it remains the
case that the alien language is much easier to 'see' than is one's own
language. The same is true of all kinds of constrictive and restrictive
rules operating implicitly in every human group. It is here that we see
the relevance of the questions of morality and ethics.

It is often obvious that the behavior of our neigbor or that of the
bordering country or cultural group is reprehensible. All of us are,
always and unavoidably, in the position of Solomon, to whom it was
necessary for Nathan to say "Thou art the man" with reference to his
sin with Bathsheba, and in that of Oedipus, to whom it was necessary
for Teresias to convey the same message. In both instances, the power
of the consensus can be seen in the ensuing behavior of the rules; Solomon, more restrained and more routinely offending, was satisfied
to repent, while Oedipus, appalled at the consensually abhorrent crime
of incest, was moved to blind himself even as his wife-mother Jocasta
killed herself.

These mythological examples attest to a truth daily evident in our
court rooms. The defendant is not guilty until said to be guilty; 'guilt'
is not an absolute <u>moral</u> judgment, it is a relativistic <u>consensual</u>
judgment. The man reliably reported to have killed his fellow is only
a murderer when he has been officially described as such. In this
culture, we ask, "Is he guilty?" meaning "Did he do it?" But in this
usage we are falsifying our own legal system. The problem is that
killing may be a fact, but murder is a judgmental description.

But we can move a little deeper in noting that it is the public display
and the internalization of external judgments which often provide the
crucial cue for both <u>feelings</u> of guilt and the self-retributive acts often
notable. A financier of the stature of the 'Match King' can parlay his
wealth year after year into a fantastic display with enormous admiration from those whom he was cheating, only to react with suicide
when exposed. Those defendants who show great feelings of guilt in
court are, more often than not, people who have been quite free from
apparent guilt feelings during all the time that they were performing
the acts for which they are being tried. It is the public fact of discovery which is the relevant reciprocal of such feelings, as we have

all noted in surprising a child happily stealing cookies or beating a
pet until the adult comes, saying, "Aren't you ashamed of yourself?"

To cite animal analogues of some of these feelings, we find the
method by means of which one member of a species 'turns off' the
aggressive attack of another. Versions differ, but most involve the
exposing of a 'soft underbelly' to the thereby unrestricted threat of
the other. The paradoxical fact is that where resistance often furthers
conflict, a "soft answer terneth away wrath", in the animal as well
as in the solomonian version.

In affairs of morality and ethical questions, we find the background
of relevance that of relativity and consensus: a culture is primarily
defined in its own terms. A culture is analogous to a dictionary - each
word (or member) is defined in terms of other words (or members)
which only have value in a system including all. This means, in turn,
that objectivity is a myth, and perhaps a most dangerous and even
lethal myth. In human affairs, there is no such thing as objectivity,
and therefore no such thing as a universal system of morality or ethics.

External and Internal

To pursue these notions, it may be useful to comment on the manner
in which evolution has selected sensory equipment used by higher
animals. In the wild, or in the conditions of environments not specifically changed to suit certain requirements, the environment is the
source of threat. It is important to be able to expect danger as far
away as possible. Selective process emphasizes the evolution of
'distance receptors'. In mammals, the emphasis upon reception has
remained close to the ground, so to speak, and the mammal uses his
more remote distance receptors to allow him to bring his most significantly developed modality, olfaction, into action.

In the primate series, learning how to put distance between self and
danger by climbing trees was a factor in the selection of grasping
upper extremities and the distance-receptor functions of seeing and
hearing. Birds able to fly away from remote dangers had no need
for the selective insistence upon developing coping methods, but primates show a progressive elaboration of neocortex in the cerebral
hemispheres. The development through this method emphasizes the
external danger even while, in the case of the primate, also emphasizing coping by the retreat up trees. Along with the external implications of this kind of defensive method, primates also have 'creatively' worked out elaborate methods of communicating making it
possible for the group to be regarded as a primitive kind of 'cultural'
group. Patterns of primate relatedness are quite complex, requiring,
as in the case of man, a prolonged and intimate period of dependence
followed by a prolonged period of peer-group experimentation. In
the step to man, methods of communication change to the specifically
linguistic.

The primate depends upon the tolerance of all his fellows and upon
his own capacity to learn the primate game, but the human being has
a far more complex task in learning linguistic potentialities in the

idiosyncratic mode of the group into which he happens to come, whether by birth or by adoption. The human difference is that, instead of a primary dependence upon his most highly developed distance-receptor modalities which are oriented to the outside world, he has to learn human relatedness on the basis of feeling, and feeling can only be taught 'at one's mother's knee', in close personal contact. The human being 'obeys' those moral instructions he learns from his fellows in a sharing. If successful he 'feels like' his relevant others. Conversely, the group so established is seriously threatened when any member shows deviant behavior. If such a deviant persists, he threatens the group with recruitment of others in a revolving, i. e., revolutionary, process. The internal danger long outlives the standard forms of 'external' threat (weather, food, etc.).

We have then the problem that the internalization process has to take place using sensory modalities oriented to the outside. It is a miracle of adaptation that the process often occurs smoothly, but the method is clearly demonstrated in some of the deviations encountered. Religion requires a consensually validated 'object' which commands universal allegiance (in 'feeling') in ritual observance.

The main point, of course, is that the deity thus objectified is a projection of the consensus. The deity does not 'represent' anything other than the belief system of the faithful. To go beyond this stage into one in which cultural practice is freed to further experimentation was the achievement of the genius of Moses who 'disobjectified' the deity in objectifying the law. It is no accident that under the less charismatic leadership of Aaron, the people reverted to the visible and the tangible deity in constructing a golden calf, nor an accident that Moses' first official act in finally returning with the Tables of the Law was that of destroying the idol in the most extreme detail.

Communication and Morality

Morality refers to a system of internalized standards as a projection of the consensus. Where the deity is presented as external, the trend in the associated culture is often that of inculcating feelings of shame. In Spartan culture, the young were specifically trained to lie and steal as long as they could get away with it; the culture hero of the Spartan lad was the boy who stole a fox and was so much a creature of his training that he allowed himself to be killed as the fox ate away at his body while the thief steadfastly denied his act. It is not the act but the consensual value applied to the act, which is relevant to the problem.

As peoples become more sophisticated, we find them moving into more complex forms of religious thought. Note two kinds of events in the history of Christendom. The recognition of the equation of 'Word' and 'God' is fundamental to the Christian ethos. This recognition moves Moses's invention of monotheism and the abstract deity into a stage at which man can hope to become God by participation - the transformation from human to divine is specifically called 'translation' in certain parts of the Bible. The paradoxical denial of the systematically illegitimate transformation of the concrete and the abstract into each other is the hidden message of Christian theology. We are told that "in my flesh shall I see God", in spite of the thousands of years which may have elapsed since the bodily form has been observable. Here we see the advantage of the abstract over the Egyptian ideal in which bodily form will be reconstituted ultimately only to the extent that it has been preserved so far; because of the expense of embalming, resurrection in Egypt was only for aristocracy. The Christian theory 'proletariatizes' religion by abstraction. No matter that the body may have been burned or that it may be dismembered - its form remains an idea (analogous to a Platonic idea) and the idea continues to be susceptible to reformulation according to the manner in which Christ as God's idea became flesh to redeem the whole world - and most dramatically, as the initial congregations show, the proletariat.

The 'price' of the transition from a concrete to an abstract deity is the internalization of that deity. If the deity is so universal and so diffuse, so susceptible to infinite manifestation, then there is no hiding place from him. For this reason, the notion of an internalized deity is associated with the feeling of guilt, as the person seeks to turn his 'soft underbelly' to the internal agent rather than to the external one. Since the deity is internalized, it becomes potentially insatiable - and, as Weber has suggested, the insatiability of the deity is the principal feature of the Calvinist theme in the Reformation, with the paradoxical notion of predestination.

The Reformation itself is a step in this process of internalization-externalization. In the centuries following the beginning of the Christian era, the Church tended to become more and more consolidated and institutionalized. As it did, it more and more concretized its operations into the ancient forms of idols and icons, with externalization reaching its apogee in the selling of indulgences in which a purely external commodity, money, could be exchanged for freedom from guilt, thus constituting a major regression in the sense of a developing abstractness. Protestantism is a reversion to ancient principles of symbolism neglected and forgotten by an established church. The protestant movement rejected the mediation of the priest in favor of an internal justification - while at the same time arranging matters so that the 'individual' was subjected to so consistent a pressure from the group that he was instantly made aware through group pressure when he seemed to have strayed from the stringent self-control idealized in the Calvinist discipline.

Consensus and Morality

What I am trying to suggest is that every system of morality is at base a consensual matter continuously ratified, in successive generations, by the relevant group. The continuing consensus is the primary characteristic of the persistent group; it is its 'cement', and unless the structure can be appropriately maintained and supported, that group must undergo serious revolutionary change in its search for a new and supportable consensus. We need only look at the rev-

olution in morality in our own days to know how much it is possible
to shift traditional attitudes in a very brief period of time when the
consensus for whatever reasons happens to move in that direction.
Let us look for the moment at two contexts in which unbelievable
change has occurred in direct contradiction to the established norms
of the culture. In the Christian context, it is assumed that the Bible
is the 'Word of God', revealed to the faithful by special acts of revelation. Since this is true, the word is to fundamentalists literally
true, no matter how absurd God is sometimes made to appear in the
process. But we know from the long history of the Catholic Chruch
that it is possible to change the unchangeable, to modify the absolute
- we have seen it happen in both directions lately in the promulgation
of the doctrine of the assumption of the Virgin as 'absolute truth',
and in the radical modifications of basic practices of the mass and
the loosening of the clerical testraints in Vatican II. The divine is
readily modifiable by consensus, no matter how much prior emphasis
has been put upon its 'external' status.

In a second context we find that the question of sexual self-restraint
has traditionally been so central to protestantism that when Americans
use the word 'morality' they generally mean 'sexual morality'. In less
than a generation, the loosening of sexual restraint has been extreme,
at least in the 'leading sectors' of our society. Where virginity was
formerly enshrined in honor and universally celebrated at least in
public, it has now become obsolete, and marriage is an ultimate
rather than a preliminary relation of sexual contact. Along with this
occurrence, we find a rejection of the 'sturdy' values of American
society. It is now rather ridiculous to be patriotic, and in widespread
behavior, shop-lifting is regarded as a casual activity enjoyed by
many. The 'eternal verities' are not really very durable - it just requires that the conditions allow their loosening up.

Language Games and Cultural Games

Let us take a frivolous metaphor and apply it to the questions exam-
ined here. If we assume with Wittgenstein that language is to be
understood as a game, then we can say as well that culture is a game
played by the members of the relevant group. What characterizes
the game in this usage is its internal rules. No game is of interest
to another game, although there may be many proficient at more
than one game. The game may be purely abstract, and in most instances it makes no difference whether the significant objects used
are old or newly constructed. All that matters is that the players
all accept the values consensually. Whenever a player refuses to
accept the rules, he threatens the existence of the game, and he
must be coerced or rejected if he is not to spoil the game for the
others. Very early in childhood and consistently throughout a culture
such as ours, the ideal is impressed upon the novice that not only
must he play the object game, he must also play the meta-game which
we call 'playing the game'. The ethical implication is that playing
the game is good while refusing to play another game is bad. The

clever player soon learns that the meta-goal not often consciously
pointed out is to play the game in such a way as to win, whether or
not one follows the rules - but it is apparent to such a clever fellow
that if he seems to be following the rules he is much more likely to
enjoy the success that he will have. For this reason, there is a
widespread conspiracy among the mutually successful to gloss over
many of the private maneuvers through which the game is apparently
played straight while actually being manipulated from some or other
direction. In the Olympic Games, for a very good example, it is
clear that the ideal of 'amateurism' is often bypassed, sometimes
with obviousness and sometimes with an elaborate camouflage.
The clever player learns, soon enough in his life for him to be able
to exploit the knowledge adequately, that the supposed 'real' meanings
and value are only those publicly supported. In order for the public
support to be continued and for the social system as a whole to be
maintained, it is highly desirable for all the powerful people who
know the meta-game to give major support to the sincere believers
who present and promote the system at the 'object' level. It is for
this reason that all politicians tend to be so conspicuously religious,
no matter how many curious practices turn up in their life histories
some decades after they have died.

The Capital Game

The cultural game appears to have a single principal characteristic,
that of passing various significant tokens around between the members.
The purpose of kinship systems, according to Lévi-Strauss, is that
of ensuring the appropriate distribution of women among the members
of the contrasting groups concerned. The purpose of commerce in a
complex society is that of passing around the various kinds of tokens
representing value, that is, money. The basic business of a human
cultural system is that of passing around the words which constitute
the language.

In relatively simple societies, the passage of various things among
the members has a tangible quality, just as religious systems participate in a tangibility through the use of idols and human sacrifice.
As abstract competence increases, the same kind of transfer of
meaning to abstract tokens takes place in commerce as in religion.
Just as the deity no longer has to be presented in concrete form, so
does money come more and more to be represented by abstractions,
by numbers on pieces of paper or by numbers coded into magnetic
tapes in computers. Paper money begins as promises to pay, ratified by experience and resting upon the experienced honesty of the
parties to the given transaction. As civilization becomes more complex, more and more the government takes over the mamagement of
the tokens, and more and more the system works on an as-if basis
which in turn rests upon consensually ratified notions spread through
the whole society, and in the modern world spread through world
monetary systems.

This system allows a new and comprehensive redistribution of

power according to the manipulation of the symbolic tokens. The game
becomes one in which know-how becomes more important than tradition and inheritance. It is of considerable interest that competence
in manipulating others or in exploiting monetary symbolic tokens
often characterizes managerial ability in many not particularly 'intelligent' by standards established in schools.

It has been traditional in established societies to look down upon
those who have not gained their privileges through inheritance. In
old countries like Spain and England, power remains concentrated
in the hands of those who still represent the landed gentry, in spite
of the socialist tinge of the British political system. It is primarily
in the United States that we see the proliferation of a new mode of
dealing with symbols, a trend which comes to fruition in the exploits
of the contemporary capitalist and which is closely associated with
the perfecting of machines which remove the drudgery from all routine kinds of thinking and calculating. Capitalism is an ideology which
specifically exploits the way in which command of monetary tokens
implies command of the whole game. The principle in question is the
ancient pars pro toto, the part for the whole. All those in an industrial organization realize that power rests in the ability to make certain decisions about the distribution of the sums which represent
money. We see the similarity of pattern between the animal's behavior and the control of that behavior, between the computer's behavior and the control implicit in the program, and the industrial
organization and the controls implied in the assignment of money to
this or that purpose.

Through the investigation of various possible sets of instructing
situations, and through the conjoint exploration of various sets of
appropriate actions, the human being is enabled to live in a simulated
world, one in which the principal activity is that of planning. What
we find in modern techniques of computer simulation and practically
all the important commerce of the world is handled through the
manipulation of numbers, whether those numbers are written on
paper money or on various kinds of checks or other banking instruments. Because of the fact that in this context money becomes truly
'imaginary', it becomes possible to pile signification upon signification so that movement takes place at exponential levels, with ever-
expanding ceilings. The astronomers speak of an expanding universe,
but modern capitalism has invented an expanding supply of money
which has continued to build itself upon itself for a very long time,
with only occasional gross failures of confidence and resulting panics
and depression.

The Ethics of Capitalism

Some of the ethical questions implicit in capitalist practices can be
explored using the notion of 'negentropy'. Schrödinger describes
life as a process of drawing negentropy from various kinds of organic
substances to add to support the living organism. Negentropy means
just 'orderliness'. Anabolic activity breaks down food, 'analyzing'

it into its components and releasing the energy locked up in holding
the components together in organized form. This energy is changed
from potential to actual in the metabolic process, and some of it is
then rebound as the feeding organism changes some of the ingested
components into its own characteristic tissues, again storing
negentropy in organization.

The specific human achievement is that of transferring the notion
of organization from a concrete context into an abstract context, just
as we noted above that Moses managed to take the notion of God into
an abstract context. The move from the one to the other level has a
specific connotation of major importance. In the physiological system, the food which enters the body 'issues instructions' in a totally
automatic fashion, and the bodily mechanisms respond in a similarly
automatic fashion. When we move to the level of abstract instructions, however, we find a quite different situation, in that the responding organization has to have been informed as a part of its preparation. Only after learning, which is to say after having been informed, does the instruction carry its appropriate meaning to the
organization responding at an abstract level. The response observed
incorporates within it an interpretation, and it is frequently possible
through observation of the eventual patterns of activity to extrapolate
backward to the original situation and find the pattern of the instructions.

When the coding of money into numbers is made effective, it becomes
possible to issue an endless series of instructions through the use of
words supplemented by numbers which represent money. One says
to a merchant, "I will buy that ... " and adds to his verbal instruction
some kind of promise to pay, whether in the form of a check, a credit
card, or actual paper money. It has become illegal to convey actual
gold in commercial transactions in this country, a curious commentary on the solely symbolic value of money. It shakes the foundations
of the whole elaborate system of consensus if any one person refuses
to play the game, whether that person be a seller demanding 'real
money' or a buyer insisting upon using his concrete resources. The
game is so important to all that any refusal to play threatens the
whole system. In the present state of revolutionary activity, what is
most interesting is the activity of young middle-class 'drop-outs' in
refusing to play the game, thereby throwing uncertainty into the whole
system.

At the abstract level, money, or rather the series of numbers in
the appropriate books, basically represents orderliness or organization. As the commanding instruction in such a social system, the
money thus stored represents power in a most important way. The
one who controls and issues the instructions comes to be invested
with the power implicit in it. Because of the aura of money, it is a
matter of interest that those possessing great wealth are often able
to display a meanness in its use which has connotations quite different from those one might expect. Thus the old man Rockefeller was
able to convert his malignant image of a ruthless tyrant into that of
a benign old man handing out dimes at all occasions.

The ethical problems which appear are those inherent in the form of exponential games, in that success leads to further success, and failure tends to be succeeded by further failure. The basic tendency of concrete natural events to find an equilibrium state is contradicted by the meta-process of further and further accentuation of the process under way, whether it leads to more wealth or more poverty. We know from the laws of conservation which govern all events in the universe that there is never any change in total quantity of matter or energy (or, since Einstein, matter-energy). What changes is the distribution. We know that if we concern ourselves with a certain smaller system, its internal dynamic situation is such that an accumulation of negentropy or organization or orderliness in one part of the system tends to be compensated by decreased negentropy elsewhere. In human affairs, we find the further complication that the borrowing of orderliness can take place in the form of promises and credit - in other words, by displacing the transaction into the future.

Morality and Dissociation

In the traditional kind of kinship system in primitive tribes, the structural system worked out in a quite unconscious fashion adequately manages the problem of distribution with reference to women. By the working of this system it is possible for related cooperating-contrasting groups to remain stably consistent generation after generation. In an unsophisticated culture, the prevailing mode of the distribution of linguistic tokens, and the power implicit in the use of these tokens, is tolerably possible to maintain generation after generation. Such a tribal group has no money in the abstract sense.

As soon as the various kinds of abstract potentialities are encountered, however, the system begins to change, with a progressively greater disturbance in distribution as abstraction becomes more widespread. The point can be made that the hidden implication of abstraction is precisely disequilibrium. With increasing sophistication in establishing the kinds of social system which depend increasingly upon abstraction, with the leader using the services of the scribe in a still menial capacity, it becomes possible for the accumulation of resources to be expanded while still orienting the storage system to the concrete goal of larger and larger areas of land.

The further development of abstraction entails a greater awareness on the part of the scribe group of their own potentialities of attaining power. In a curious kind of paradox, many Jewish families learned, through the difficult period in which Jews were denied the luxury of land ownership, that it was possible to recruit increasing power by the manipulation of abstractions. The history of banking is that of the increasing awareness of how consensus can be used instead of goods, services, or treasure. The distribution system then progressively becomes one in which the primary relation is abstraction-to-abstraction, with the underlying process always that of the implicit consensus, ratified and reinforced without the conscious awareness of any of the members of the enforcing group. Where they were concerned with consensus, they thought themselves concerned with 'truth'.

Still, as long as it was possible for separate groups to develop their own systems in relative isolation from each other, it was of little importance that internal distribution became so lopsided. At the least, internal competitive striving tends to keep some degree of equilibrium in such a system, as we see when we follow out the imperative kinds of internecine striving between members of royal and princely houses. Conflict repetitively ensures distribution, thus unconsciously but effectively preventing the hegemony of one over all the remainder of the nations, churches, or financial houses.

What has now happened is an indication of the extraordinary novelty of the present world situation. The processes to which we are subject can be traced in large measure to the efficiency of scientific method in skewing the distribution of symbolic meaning. By differential success in instructing inanimate nature to yield up her secrets, by differential success in discriminating between persons on the basis of inherent intellectual potential and the possibility of educational experience, the gap between statuses of persons in our kind of social system has become progressively greater. In the very recent past, we have witnessed another astonishing phenomenon in that the scribe-expert in symbolic technology has evolved into the scientist-technician-financier expert who not only knows how to invent and develop but also how to exploit the potentialities. The most astonishing of such stories was reported in the press recently, in the case of a man who, by developing and marketing computer 'soft-ware', has run up a personal fortune of more than a billion dollars in less than a decade. This man shows such expertness in the grasp of symbolic technology that he accumulates numbers in exponential quantity (10^7 dollars), through writing programs which are nothing more than strings of symbolic instructions. Along the way, he demonstrates also a competence in publicizing his achievement, in manipulating the financial resources of the 'capital market', and so on. In the most important sense, one can say this billion dollars is 'all in his head'.

The reality of this situation is actually very close to that implied in the Biblical comment that the word became flesh and lived among us. The fact is in the case of the billionaire that the symbolic instructions have turned into 'material wealth' - but the metamorphosis must be understood as one in which the word has become instructions. 'Money' in this sense is totally illusery - it has the same connotations as 'power'. The metamorphosis involved is that of supplying an irresistible neutral adjuvant to instructions. "By the power vested in me as ..." becomes essentially similar to "by the money I am able to invest, I command ...".

Returning now to the problem of distribution, we find the crisis of the contemporary world in the considerations of systemic negentropy mentioned above. As long as the system seems infinitely capable of yielding up more and more negentropy, it is then possible to ignore the problem of relative distribution. As soon as the bottom of the barrel is in sight, then questions of distribution become much

more urgent and forceful. When distribution can be seen to be increasingly skewed, then the seeds of total disruption of the system
would seem to have not only been sowed but to have begun to grow
with rapidity.

Terminal Morality

We have learned in an economy of scarcity - which is to say in fact,
a social system in which abstraction is inadequately understood -
that the principal points of focus have to be upon initiatory instructions.
How do you begin to train an educated man? How can scientific research and development be used to control the environment? How
to institute the processes necessary to utilize fission to wipe out
cities? How to initiate fusion through an innovative use of fission?
How to grow, how to expand, how to save, how to invest?
    When one sees the extent to which abstract technology now makes
it possible to control and coerce, the question shifts sharply to:
How is it possible to stop? The problem is that of the Sorcerer's
Apprentice, who 'turned on' but could not 'turn off'. It is also and
precisely the question of the control of neoplasia, the setting of
limits upon the terminal growth of tissue. Now we see the same kind
of need for terminal instruction, in education, in finance, in weapon-
ry, in the growth of the economy, in the growth of the military industrial establishment. In almost every context, we find the ancient faith
in the ultimate belevolence of growth now turned into a despair at the
cancerous expansion of potentiality, with its attendant total alteration
of the basic distribution of tokens throughout the system.
    Let me close, abruptly, because the subsequent steps in this ar-
gument are not yet clear to me. The principal point at which it is
possible to find increasing despair is that the idea presented is antithetical to all, not merely to one or another version of the social
theories of this world. No matter whether democratic or communist
or socialist or theocratic, all social systems in this period look to
persistent 'development' and limitless 'growth' as the ultimate ideal.
In my current state of pessimism, this is tantamount to the idealization of cancer as a way of life. But at the same time, the ideal of
growth in income, prestige, and power is one to which every single
effective middle-aged human being of my acquaintance is committed.
We have to change, if this speculation has validity, the entire moral
system underlying distribution in the whole world.
    Curiously enough, this is an idea not too distant from that of some
of the dissenting usually'youthful members of this society. We have
seen near total change in other kinds of morality - perhaps it is not
too late to wonder whether a total change in economic distribution
might be effected by the recruitment of a massive consensus oriented
toward a terminal rather than an initiatory morality.

PART FIVE

LANGUAGE, MENTATION, AND REALITY

XI

LANGUAGE: MEDIUM OR OPERATOR? (*)

"They were learning to draw", the Dormouse went
on ... " and they drew all manner of things - everything that begins with an M ... such as mouse traps,
and memory, and muchness - you know we say things
are 'much of muchness' - did you ever see such a
thing as a drawing of a muchness?"

Lewis Carroll

If one examines the operations in which psychiatrists are specifically
concerned, he finds them all mainly concerned with language. We
make diagnoses through interviewing patients; we report evaluations
in various kinds of legal procedures; we attempt to persuade or to
give insight in pshychotherapy; even when we use drugs, we give
careful instructions and repeatedly elicit descriptions of changes
under the influence of the drugs. Psychiatry qualifies in this sense
as applied linguistics. Nevertheless, one finds only the briefest and
most cursory examination of linguistic theory in most psychiatric
textbooks and in most learned discussions in psychiatry.

This fact demonstrates the curious ability of language to conceal
itself. Human beings are so intimately and so intensively trained to
use language in the patterns of the relevant groups that it becomes
'second nature' to ignore the complications incident upon the linguistic nature of the human condition. A favorite metaphor used to express the function of language is that of a glass or lens, with the
implication that the goal of learning is so to polish this metaphorical
transparency that we 'see clearly'. When this is done, of course what
we see is what is there. But the bulk of evidence suggests strongly
that this is not true. What we see is what language presents to us,
and what is presented is at least highly selected and at most remarkably deformed.

When we use a microscope, we begin by spending a good deal of
time trying to understand how the instrument allows us to see more
clearly, and as well how the instrument introduces artifacts into
whatever we can examine with its use. We use language so 'intuitively'
that it is far more difficult to begin to try to understand what happens.
In recent decades, there have begun to appear many studies that
suggest revolutionary implications for epistemology as we approach
human knowing through the study of linguistic-symbolic method. The
great names in this field include a variety of linguists, philosophers,
psychologists, and psychiatrists. A very partial list may be given:

(*) Reprinted by special permission: in: Language Sciences II
(1970), 11-15.

Cassirer, Langer, Sapir, Whorf, Vygotsky, McLuhan, Duncan, Saussure, Lévi-Strauss, Wittgenstein.

The purpose of the present discussion is to suggest that at the very center of contemporary understanding, especially in the West and particularly in the scientific universe, we find language exerting enormous influence through its basic form. We assume, with the greatest self-conficence, that we know the basic structure of 'reality'. But when we examine the many ways in which the same ideas recur, we find them all characterized by linearity - and linearity is the basic underlying structure of language. More and more in recent decades, process has appeared as a circular structure - which means, at the very least, that there is always and unavoidably a translation process whenever we attempt to formulate description - and the postulation of a 'natural law' is nothing more than the establishment of a highly reliable description.

By its very form language seems to point beyond itself to something other than itself. Thus, from the beginning of philosophical discourse, we find the notion of 'representation'. We say, "a word represents an object", quite forgetting as we do that there are a large number of words to which no possible 'object' can be related. What is the 'object' represented by 'a' or 'upon' or 'five?' In a similar way, we say, bemused by the words themselves, that 'actions' are 'represented' in the motor cortex. Evidence accumulated by such men as Lashley demonstrates the lack of a specific cerebral localization for 'engrams' or 'actions'. When we realize that ablation of large parts of the brain is possible without abolishing the actions supposedly 'represented' in the ablated cortex, we realize that there must be something seriously wrong with these traditional conceptions.

Increasingly in recent years it has become evident that much of traditional thought of all kinds does not 'use' language in any simple sense. The fact is rather that language imposes its form upon human thought in such a way that we are hard put to it to decide which is master, which slave. Linguistic-symbolic systems take over in social context, often, as in the case of a new religion, coming to dominate the social system in a brief period of time. St. John the Divine underscores this fact when he says that the Word is God. In a more mundane comparison, I have suggested in this time that we can learn much from the model of the filterable virus. Such a virus, a nearly pure 'program' of biological instructions, invades a cell and turns its machinery into a factory for replicating the virus.

It is of primary importance to understand these power-implications of language itself. In a matter very close to our own primary concern in a scientific society, the linearity necessarily characteristic of linguistic utterance has imposed upon generations of scientists and philosophers an idealization of linearity. We habitually use cause-and-effect, subject-and-predicate, subject-and-object, stimulus-and-response models that bear little relation to complex processes as we know them in contemporary investigation. For one very clear example, it is evident that neurones are not 'caused' to fire in any simple sense; they are rather responding to a complex group of factors, including inputs from hundreds or thousands of summating, doubly-valued, contacts with other cells, the humoral setting, the relation of present input to past firing - i.e., to dynamic balances not reducible to simplistic 'causal' analysis.

The most interesting aspect of this persuasion by modelling is to be found in the 'representation' theory of speech. Just as a cause produces an effect, so does a word produce an object. But the simplest observation of human beings in action shows us how completely wide of the mark such a theory is, in spite of its unthinking acceptance by generations of savants. With the help of some notions borrowed from the most stimulating of contemporary philosophers, I would like to present below a theory that appears as a theory nowhere else, to my knowledge, although the theory is clearly demonstrated in the passages at the beginning and at the end of this essay. The whole quotation is from Alice in Wonderland, separated into two segments to illustrate somewhat different aspects of the ambiguity intrinsic to linguistic practice. The first principle of this theory is that language is by its very nature ambiguous; all attempts to 'make our ideas clear' through the proper use of language are doomed to failure because language can never be linear in its social action, no matter how linear it looks on paper or seems in speech. Rather, language is always primarily subject to interpretation, mutually and circularly, as anyone knows who has been involved in a court case or in a friendly dispute about just what was said last night at the party.

Despairing, after many years of intensive search, of discovering a satisfactory theory from either traditional philosophy or traditional science, I chose a model from contemporary art. This notion is a collage theory, from the practice of such contemporaries as Picasso, Cornell, Rauschenberg, and Nevelson, all of whom construct aesthetically satisfying artifacts by organizing junk. Old boxes, bottles, broken-down machinery, bed clothes, alarm clocks, all the contents of attics and rummage sales have been used to produce collages highly valued both by critics and in the marketplace. Rauschenberg has taken the process a step further in his use of the collage technique to meld a variety of photographic images through silk-screen techniques into paintings and lithographs of remarkable novelty.

All such collages and collage-like constructions demonstrate the superiority of the whole over its parts. It is no one of the parts, nor all of the parts taken separately, nor the sequence of construction, but rather the organization of the whole that is the significant consideration in terms of aesthetic worth. Such organization is characteristic of the whole and of the whole alone. If one 'analyzes' such a whole, he is left with a bunch of junk. Similarly, if one analyzes the brain into cells and enzymes, he is left with a rapidly deteriorating mess bearing no relation to the thinking in which that brain may have once been involved. It is the 'essence' of abstraction that the whole is far more than the sum of its parts. We daily exemplify this basic possibility by routinely abstracting pattern from chance observation of accidental juxapositions, such as the triangle abstracted from three rocks randomly placed on a beach.

What I call a collage has what Wittgenstein calls a 'family resemblance' to what he calls a 'game'. It is of more than passing interest that the book in which Wittgenstein presents the work of his mature

years is a 'non-book'. It has many of the qualities of free-associational material. After considering one aspect of situations, he
jumps without apparent linkage to an entirely different aspect. He
presents to the reader an enormous challenge, similar to that presented to the therapist by the patient's wandering comments. The
problem is one of integration with the goal of so organizing the apparently random material as to get out of it certain important abstract
structural notions.

Let me follow out some of Wittgenstein's notions using his own central word, 'game'. He points out that there are card-games, board-
games, ball-games, and language-games. To his list I would add
the metaphorical use of 'playing the game', the criminal intent involved in 'con games', the use of the word 'game' to refer to the goal
of the hunter. Morgenstern and Von Neumann present a mathematical
theory of games. We use the term very broadly in asking. "What is
the name of the game?" and less broadly in occupational context by
asking "What's your game?" When we try to find the one single characteristic that makes all of these different kinds of situation fit into a
single class, the reflexive and circular answer is that the only single
thing in common is the name itself.

More deeply, we find that meaning swings from one to another usage
through connotative jumps. From one to another to another of the
series, we see each time a relation in common - but this may be
entirely different from one to another of the terms far along the series.
If we take the game that hunters engage in we find that its goal is the
class we call game. In a similar double meaning, to which I shall
return below, if we make a category of 'all those things which I greet
with a similar attitude' we find a set in the mathematical sense defined
by a psychological set. It is in this kind of peculiar inguistic operation
that we see that 'subject' and 'object' can be described using the same
word. How can this be? We can go back to Freud's quoting of Abel to
note that many primitive words have directly antithetical meaning, as
though we were to say both "yes" and "no" with a single word.

Such connotative relations are included by Wittgenstein under the
term 'family resemblances'. Hunting and hunted can both be 'game',
as husband and wife can be either lovers or antagonists. No two uses
of the same word can ever be precisely similar; every such use is
modified by connotations. Taking this idea into a somewhat different
context, it is clear that 'family resemblance' defines a set in the
mathematical sense: the class includes all those items with something in common. When we trace derivations in a dictionary, as it is
often fascinating to do, we find words changing their meaning over the
years, but always with some observable relation joining the prior
meaning with the current meaning - sometimes with many different
steps. Family resemblances occur in two major contexts: they are
relations in the synchronic context, which is, say, in a context of
timelessness- but there are also significant relations in the diachronic
context, namely, in historical sequence. In many instances, we find
our understanding of the use made of words in the contemporary scene
greatly expanded by the history of that word's derivation - a fact that
accounts for the livelihood of the lexicographer.

Note one other easy observable: we say that a word is the same
from one day to the next, and we generally think we say 'the same'
word today that we said yesterday. But in the very simplest instance,
any word said today is not the same as the word we said yesterday it
is merely another example in the class to which the word belongs.
Thus we find ourselves not only with ambiguous words but with ambiguous classes. How is it possible for a word said in a baritone
voice to be identical with the word said in a soprano voice? If we
think of the differences in two such voices saying "yes" we get some
idea of the difference between 'the same' word in different contexts.

But, this is far from being the end of the problem. Let us try
another tack in seeing something about the combination of words.
For instance, take John Smith. What does John Smith mean? An impossible question; John Smith is a name, with a function of identifying
or designating, but it is devoid of meaning. We can instantly introduce
meaning by saying "John is a Smith." This becomes a proposition.
Let us ring a few changes: We can say, "John has a smith", meaning
that John has hired a blacksmith to shoe his horses; or we can say,
"Smith has a john", meaning that someone designated by the name of
Smith has a toilet. These are all very different statements, each of
which has a meaning, no matter that the meaning may be absurd.

What is the difference? In propositions we put words, otherwise
meaningless or useful for pointing or designating, into an organization.
We then come to the simple notion that meaning is a function of organization. Three stones on a beach are just there - but three stones
seen all together are 'triangle' when we grasp their common relation.
Similarly, we have to put words together to produce meaning. John
Smith becomes meaningful with the simple addition of two words of
relation, the word designating inclusion, is, and the word designating a class, a. "John is a Smith" places John in a universe of
meaning as it includes him among a group of relatives (all of whom
have at least "Smith" as a family resemblance).

It is impossible to grasp meaning from either John or is or a or
Smith when these words are separately considered. The proposition
gains meaning as a function of retrospective integration. When a
highly imaginative artist takes a piece of a newspaper, a few pieces
of glass, an old bottle or two, some metal scraps and some driftwood
and puts them all together with glue, he may produce a combination
that is meaningful. Its 'beauty' or its validity or its meaning is a function of the integration of all the pieces with each other - and it is
quite impossible to give any kind of critical appraisal of the whole
until after it is done. Then, in a process of retrospective integration,
we arrive at a meaning, an evaluation, a price.

This is the reason for calling the notion a collage theory: a sentence is a collage constructed by the sequential placing of a series
of tokens that refer to groups each of which is a set of relations. To
say it the other way, every sentence can be seen to be the mutual
intersection of all the sets designated by the words constitutive of
that sentence. Only after the sentence has been said does it become
possible to go back over its sequence and find the meaning. That we
do this habitually and almost instantaneously remains a marvel.

Words are markers or tokens that loosely designate categories or sets. A set is all those instances in which a pattern is manifested in linguistic operations, and the pattern is an <u>aspect of the situation.</u> Even the noun refers not to an object but to an <u>aspect</u> of a <u>class</u>: what is most often the referent is the aspect constituted by a <u>shape</u>. "Table", to use a favorite example of the philosopher, is a combination of a top and legs: the top may be an inch or hundreds of feet in length, square, rectangular, triangular, marble, mahogany, or whatever; there may be three legs or even two in the case of tables made to lean against a wall, or there may be hundreds of legs in the extended centipedal tables used at banquets. Where is the 'object'?

Philosophers are fond also of referring loftily to 'sense data'. When we examine the background of sense data, however, the neurophysiologist tells us that all such data are relations in series of events beginning in some peripheral locus and transmitted in code to central loci where mixing and integrative interpretation takes place. It is of special interest that there are no methods of differentiating one kind of message from another in neural transmission. The initial differentiation is made on the relation of source (as the nose or the ear) to destination (as the olfactory or the auditory cortex).

Even in these processes we see astonishing developments. For example, in the work done by Paul D. MacLean on the 'limbic system', it becomes clear that what was once the site of a major processing of inputs from the olfactory organs has become, in phylogenetic sequence, an area much concerned with 'emotional' data processing. (1) It is not uncommon to hear an expert say of a situation that he gets some kind of hunch through some kind of 'smelling' when it is quite obvious that no olfaction is concerned. An old physician said he could 'smell typhoid', and we hear of men 'smelling danger'. The suggestion emerges that the transformation of function in this most central of cerebral data-processing areas may well be analogous to the process of 'translation' or at least of 'metamorphosis' in the linguistic or symbolic sense with the persistence of intuitive components that in lower animals are directly related to olfaction.

In another most interesting notion, the physiologist Gregory points out, in discussing visual data-processing, that the image falling upon the retina is in a strict sense a symbol. We do not 'see objects', we rather participate in a process in which an input of visual information ultimately allows interpretation yielding a 'world-view' or a Weltanschauung. Gregory emphasizes that the eventual result of a visual input is always a function as well of touch and of the training through which both touch and vision have been educated. Thus here again we see the notion of a composite, yielding meaning as a function of integration. Wiener suggests, on the basis of considerations similar to these, that if it were possible to put in coded nerve impulses from some other source which could be processed in the visual cortex, the patient might 'see' with no eyes at all.

When we observe we are involved in series of relations. We look from this angle and that, we smell, taste, touch, grasp - we act to establish the kinds of relations from which sensory data emerge. Each such observable, whether a smell or a hardness or a shape or

(1) Personal communication.

a pain, is a characteristic established on the basis of some <u>poten-</u>
<u>tiality of relatedness</u> implicit in a sensory organ, its neuromuscular
apparatus of movement, and its relations to neural structures and
functions - and these in turn are only themselves evident when working together. The important considerations, as von Bonin puts it is
describing the function of the cerebral cortex, is that "patterns of
relations are all that can be called 'mind'."

What then is an 'object'? Why, exactly the same thing as a sentence
when the description is sufficiently abstract: an object is a <u>retrospec-</u>
<u>tive rationalization of a series of experienced relations.</u> It is an or-
ganization of data, retrospectively integrated into some whole through
the naming process; the named whole is then used for extrapolative
purposes as we try to predict what kinds of relations we shall encounter later. The point of greatest interest is that the whole process,
occasionally susceptible to precision and specification, is rooted in
the utmost ambiguity. It is no wonder that those most 'intellectual'
in their operations are most likely to be those fascinated by 'word
games', especially by puns and witticisms ringing the changes on
linguistic ambiguity.

In a medical context, we find all these statements applicable to the
method of making a clinical diagnosis through the elicitation of many
possible aspects of disease states, which are ultimately retrospectively integrated to give a diagnosis that serves to guide treatment
and further investigation. Feinstein has reviewed in great detail the
manner in which the clinician uses Venn diagrams in his reasoning,
even though he may not realize that he is doing so. He estimates probabilities by a process of repetitive integration as further observation
yields more and more information about signs and symptoms, i. e.,
about aspects of disease. The modern discipline of semiotics - the
study of 'patterned communication in all modalities' - can be traced
specifically back to the work of John Locke, a philosopher who was
a physician in his gainful occupation.

The point of central emphasis is that the human condition cannot be
separated from linguistic practice, and language is by its very nature
ambiguous, requiring interpretation and integration at every step of
the complex process of thinking. We all know somehow that it is quite
impossible to separate feeling from thinking or from willing. We
mostly operate in terms of rapid decisions we make quite without reflection except in those instances in which the situation is different
from what we expect. When we think or feel or examine and report,
we are unavoidably involved in the verbal, specifically human, condition.

Let me close with the remainder of an appropriate quotation:

"Once upon a time there were three little sisters", the Dormouse
began in a great hurry; "and their names were Elsie, Lacie, and
Tillie; and they lived at the bottom of a well -"

"What did they live on?" asked Alice, who always took a great
interest in questions of eating and drinking.

"They lived on treacle", said the Dormouse, after thinking a
minute or two.

222

"They couldn't have done that, you know", Alice gently remarked;
"they'd have been ill."

"So they were", said the Dormouse; "very ill."

[Alice] repeated her question, "Why did they live at the bottom
of a well?"

The Dormouse again took a minute or two to think about it, and
then said, "It was a treacle well." ... "And so these three little
sisters - they were learning to draw, you know -"

"What did they draw;" said Alice ...

"Treacle", said the Dormouse ...

Alice did not wish to offend the Dormouse again, so she began
very cautiously, "But I don't understand. Where did they draw the
treacle from?"

"You can draw water out of a water well", said the Hatter, "so
I should think you could draw treacle out of a treacle well, eh,
stupid?"

"But they were in the well," Alice said ...

"Of course they were", said the Dormouse - "well in."

"They were learning to draw", the Dormouse went on ... "and
they drew all manner of things - everything that begins with an M."

"Why with an M?" said Alice.

"Why not?" said the March Hare ...

REFERENCES

Alvarez, Luis
    1969   "Recent developments in Particle Physics", Science 165,
            1071.
Bonin, Gerhardt von
    1950   Essay on the Cerebral Cortex (Springfield, Ill. : Thomas).
Buchler, Justus, (ed.)
    1940   The Philosophy of Peirce: Selected Writings (New York:
            Harcourt).
Feinstein, A. R.
    1963   "Boolean Algebra and Clinical Taxonomy", New England
            Journal of Medicine 269, 923-938.
Gregory, R. L.
    1967   "Origin of Eyes and Brains", Nature 213, 369-372.
Pribram, Karl H.
    1969   "The Neurophysiology of Remembering", Scientific Ame-
            rican 220, 73-86.
Wittgenstein, Ludwig
    1953   Philosophical Investigations (New York: Macmillan).

XII

WHY THE MIND IS NOT IN THE HEAD (*)

In beginning his Philosophical Investigations, Ludwig Wittgenstein
(1953) quotes a passage from St. Augustine's Confessions, which
seems to give two implicit theories of language. The first sentence
states: "When they [my elders] named some object and accordingly
moved toward something, I saw this and I grasped that the thing was
called by the sound they uttered when they meant to point it out. " This
rather simple 'see it and say it' theory is contradicted or at least
greatly expanded by the next sentence, which reads: "Their intention
was shown by their bodily movements, as it were the natural language
of all peoples; the expression of the face, the play of the eyes, the
movement of other parts of the body, and the tone of the voice which
expresses our state of mind in seeking, having, rejecting or avoiding
something [emphasis added] (1).
    The first sentence gives an implicit 'noun' theory of language, the
second a 'verb' theory. In discussing these notions I want to point to
a number of bodies of evidence which suggest that not only is the
'verb' theory far more easily supported by the available evidence,
but in a considerable extension, that all forms of mentation involve
the whole body. Mentation resembles the circulation of the blood in
that there is an incessant flow of significant patterns throughout the
entire system. The notion is by no means new. In a one-hundred-
year-old book recently made available to Western readers Ivan
Sechenov (1863) states that:

> The infinite diversity of external manifestations of cerebral ac-
> tivity can be reduced ultimately to a single phenomenon - muscu-
> lar movement ... To help the reader reconcile himself to this
> thought I shall remind him of the framework which has been cre-
> ated by the popular mind and includes all manifestations of cer-
> ebral activity: This framework is "word" and "action". Under
> "action" the popular mind undoubtedly visualizes every external
> mechanical activity of man which can be accomplished exclusively
> with the aid of muscles, while "word" as the reader will readily
> appreciate, implies a certain combination of sounds produced in
> the larynx and in the mouth cavity also by means of muscular
> movement. (2)

To bring Sechenov's statement into the context of this essay, it is
only necessary to point out that the process he describes is a circular
one: the input of information from the muscular actions into the brain
is fully as important as the output in the opposite direction. The con-

temporary situation is described by another Russian interested in
movement. Bernstein says of the cybernetic view of mentation: "It
is now beyond any doubt that the most general and prevalent form of
organization in live organisms is not the reflex arc but the reflex
ring. " (3)

Overwhelming evidence suggests that mentation involves the whole
body in ways which progressively change with progressive competence.
Like any other skill, however, thinking (as Bartlett notes, 1958)
requires exercise and protracted effort leading to a disciplined system. (4) Thinking exists only in time, just as motor skill exists in
time - the miniaturization effect in thinking allows us to ignore the
exercise-discipline limitation. In another direction, thinking uses
language, first as overtly exhibited and more and more as implicit.
Many of the traditional illusions having to do with thinking take origin
in an inadequate grasp of the structuring effect of linguistic usage.

The theory of mentation we have inherited suffers from a fallacy
of misplaced concreteness (Whitehead, 1960) that fallacy which assumes that process has a spatial location (5). The concreteness evident in this kind of formulation has a poetic quality of appeal which,
added to the simplification, makes the whole attractive to those seeking understanding. Shakespeare asks "Where is fancy bred?" and
Emily Dickinson puts the same kind of problem in concrete imagery
by asking, "Will there really be a 'Morning'? Is there such a thing
as 'Day'? ... Oh, some Wise Man from the skies! Please to tell a
little Pilgrim where the place called 'Morning' lies!"

Thinking or mentation is a process involving sequential passage
of patterns through a large number of combinations and permutations.
Although it is essential that the process occur in some material setting, it becomes more and more apparent that many parts of the
process can occur in a wide variety of artificial settings. In man
the evidence indicates clearly that the whole human body is necessarily
involved in mentation. With adequate learning, overt movements in
the periphery can be minimized - in ways abstractly similar to those
in which communication processes in contemporary machines are
effected through progressive miniaturization of components. But the
essential feature is that the process primarily occurs sequentially
in time, and not in some static spatial localization.

Mentation in the broad sense is similar in its principles of operation
to abstraction. In both instances it is the pattern which matters. The
pattern is manifested in one or another of a myriad of possible substances and locations - the material context is irrelevant but essential.
The pattern of movement establishes the basis of thought and communication. In its most private sense thinking is a process of communication to oneself. Human thinking is based upon a developed method
of inner speech, much reduced in its overt manifestation by the shorthand techniques easily available to associates as intimate as 'I' and
'me'. (6)

Western conceptualization has traditionally used a dichotomizing
technique for describing. The basic reason is more closely related
to the structure of language than to the structure of reality - whatever
that may be. Reality is grasped only in communicational techniques,

observational and descriptive, and reported only in linguistic-symbolic forms. When we compare sentence structure with physiological relations, we see that sentences are necessarily discursively linear, whereas physiological systems operate in circular feedback relations. In thinking of the pituitary as a master gland or of centers of control in the central nervous system, we are adopting linear patterns, suitable to the language, which implicitly ignore the fact that the pituitary gland is controlled by the level of circulating hormones emanating from its 'target organs', while the central nervous system depends at all times upon the reflux inflow of data from the periphery.

When we separate a directing 'mind' from a responding 'body', we are perpetuating an ancient myth that the executive controls the system of which he is a central official. Even in the most autocratic of regimes the executive has to depend upon the consent of the governed, even if that consent is implicit and unconscious. A conspicuously inadequate executive tends to be overthrown even in a strongly authoritarian setting, as we find in English history in the cases of Richard II and Henry VI. The executive is supported by the kind of structure in which he finds himself, so that a great deal more tolerance for incompetence is found in highly structured settings, but this fact is far from absolute.

It is not unusual for parents to learn new dialects from their children. It is unusual, however, to learn from an inanimate 'child', but this is one of the features of the contemporary scene as we learn from metallic 'brain-children' who think, in limited ways, better than their parents. We can describe human mentation in computer dialect by saying that the human computer processes data only on line, in real time. The reason for this is easy to find in the extraordinary vulnerability of neural function. Any serious interference with the free supply of either fuel or oxidizer not only stops neural function but rapidly begins to injure the neural structure. Those parts of the nervous system most involved in complex kinds of thinking are those most vulnerable to this traumatic interference.

When we speak of 'storage' in the nervous system, we are talking about a very active process. Data are recirculated in reverberating circuits, patterned into different forms of interconnectedness between cells, somehow encoded in changes in molecular configurations, but however encoded they are maintained in a constantly active, living process. One fascinating indication of the electronic nature of some of the neural events is the notion that in some parts of the nervous system the storage function is attained through the formation of a 'standing wave', incessantly renewed.

The time span of neural 'reality' is measured in seconds or fractions of seconds. In a curiously contradictory fashion, neutral existence is coterminous with the specious present presented as illusion by classical philosophers oriented to invariance and to eternity. From an understanding of the physiological fragility of neural integrity it becomes clear that all we can think we think now. Storage in the nervous system is active storage; each cell in which some part of the storage process is carried out has to remain in a state of physiological balance if it is to perform its function.

Because of this extreme lability and the temporary nature of neural physiological process, the invention of writing gives human beings storage methods far beyond the capacity of any other animal - and, indeed, far beyond the capacity of the illiterate human being. When philosophers early began to understand the power implicit in written records, they tended to celebrate this technique in a worshipful attitude. From the fact of durability beyond the life of any single human being it is easy to extrapolate to the notion of eternity. From the fact of durability of the message written down in some form it is easy to extrapolate to the ideal of invariance. From the fact that records are kept in safety in specific buildings it is easy to suppose that storage in the mind is equally static, equally resident within the bony walls of the cranium. These eternal verities turn out to be nonsense, however, to be replaced by a much more astonished wonder that so transient and so pervasive a function as the data processing of thought could take place so rapidly in so complex a fashion.

Animals think, if thinking can be construed as predictive problem-solving. Some of the feats of animal knowing are astonishing, as for example the technique by means of which bats flying in the dark unerringly find enough tiny flying insects to keep themselves adequately fed. The human advantages in thinking depend upon the capacity to speak and upon its derivatives in written language. While there is good evidence that a human being, once trained in linguistic method, can think without having to go through detailed sequential verbalization, there is no doubt that unless the human being is trained to talk in the language of his peers, he will not be able to think in human terms.

What we call a 'word' is a shaped respiratory event, entirely dependent upon a skilled exhibition of muscular coordination as the respiratory muscles expel air which is shaped as it passes through a series of organs which are themselves altered through muscular action. Learning to talk is learning a complex motor skill shared in a common patterning of grammatical structure. The importance of the skill aspect can be easily observed in watching a young child learn to cope with words: he begins by saying them aloud, continues by mouthing them, and ends by 'thinking' them in implicit form. But an expert speaker and reader of English often finds himself repeating this sequence in trying to grasp the significance of a French or German sentence; to understand, he has to go back to saying the words aloud to himself during the learning process. When he does go from speaking to writing, he is superimposing a subsequent manual skill upon an antecedent respiratory patterning. Learning difficult new subject matter (especially in mathematics) requires going through the act of writing the symbols down.

When we think of seeing as a function of eye and brain, or hearing as a function of ear and brain, or touching as a function of sensory endings in the skin and cerebral connections, we ignore the facts of our own experience. In every case it is not only the activity of the special sensory organ which is involved alone; just as essential is the activity of muscular mechanisms which arrange for continuous movement in the relation of sensitive surface and system of interest. Only in the course of relative motion can sensing occur; the muscular movement which establishes the background of sensation tends to be unconscious in a most important sense of the term. Much of the training undergone in the course of developing sensory skills is training to regulate the muscular skill component so that it can be taken for granted.

Frederic Bartlett emphasizes throughout his book Remembering that perception is a transactional relation involving the special sense organ, as one party, and the "whole body responding", as the other party. (7) Bernstein comments that all peripheral receptors are equipped with "efferent innovation and a muscular system on which depend functions of optimal adjustment (in a very broad sense), and also the countless phenomena of search, guidance, haptic tracking, etc. " (8) Arnold Gesell and his associates comment upon the for- mation of an "eye-hand system", noting that vision is the cue for the hands emancipated in man from a supportive function, while the hands direct the eyes in a manner in which "it is idle to differentiate between cause and effect". (9) They note that the human advantage is implicit in the increase of brain tissue, which allows human beings to exceed all other species in ocular and manual skills.

Jean Piaget and Bärbel Inhelder point out that: "From the rudimen- tary sensori-motor activity right up to abstract operations, the devel- opment of geometrical intuition is that of an activity. "(10) Piaget notes that all perceptual processes depend upon a 'centering', which makes the center of the field relatively more important than any other part. This centering relates closely to the visual technique of focusing, but it occurs (as Granit emphasizes) as well in the tactile and auditory spheres of sensation. The perceptual emphasis (which Piaget some- times describes as a 'distorting relativity') is subsequently altered by an integration of several different conterings into a general construct (in the 'correcting relativity' of conceptualization). The important consideration is, however, that the retrospective integrative process of concept-formation has to depend upon a series of active centerings.

Granit sums up a wealth of observations (after discussing the well- known experiments of George Stratton and of Wolfgang Köhler with inverting spectacles) that "the apparent plasticity of the psychological interpretation is an adaptation to the organism's needs. In this the conscious component follows and agrees with reflex motor perform- ance. The psychological datum which we try to trap in psychophysio- logical experiments is an organized response to a large number of cues. If experience proves them unreliable a new and better system of interpretation is elaborated" (emphasis added). (11) The notion presented is that vision is 'instructed' by motor activity: motor domi- nance is retained in what psychiatrists might call a 'reality-testing' in action.

When we understand something of the powerful influence of periph- eral muscular activity in relation to thinking, we can get a more significant view of the importance of the tiny muscles which control sensory organs from inside. The most significant experimental evi- dence available comes from work on the rapid-eye-movement-state (REMS) of paradoxical sleep in which dreams most probably occur. The clue which opened up this whole field was the chance observation of regular periods during sleep when the electromyographic evidence pointed to rapid movements of the eyes in conjoint fashion.

The tracing can be interpreted as indicating that the subject is 'looking', although he can 'see' only the backs of his eyelids (and he cannot in fact see them because they are too close). The interpretation given by Skinner is that these movements indicate 'the behavior of seeing', separated from the 'out-there' to which seeing is ordinarily oriented. (12)

In turn, we can assume that looking is subject to a separation of pattern from context such that after training the subject 'sees' by looking, even though he is not 'looking' at anything. To summon up "remembrance of things past" in "sessions of sweet, silent thought", it remains necessary to exhibit the minimum of the behavior of seeing. To see, even the dreamer has to look by converging. This impression is supported by the further observation that the behavior of the tensor tympani muscle associated with the eardrum gives the impression that the dreamer is listening. Further, the fact that the REM state is regularly associated in men with an erection of the penis indicates that even the unconscious experience of the dream has to involve at least minimal activity in the muscles intrinsic to sensory function in orientative, predictive behavior.

Not only is muscular activity essential in exploratory behavior related to the out-there, but it is equally essential in a different sense in relation to exploring in-here. The person trying to recall something or to think through a problem in a 'brown study' may be observed knitting his brows and gazing at a distant point, even though when asked what he is looking at he will often (sometimes with a start, doing what we call 'coming to himself') say, "Nothing."

Wittgenstein gives us an interesting description of his exploration of his own state of consciousness:

> When I ... turn my attention in a particular way on to my own consciousness, and, astonished, say to myself THIS is supposed to be produced by a process in the brain! - as it were clutching my forehead ... But what can it mean to speak of turning my attention to my own consciousness? This is surely the queerest thing there could be. It was a particular act of gazing that I called doing this. I stared fixedly in front of me - but not at any particular point or object. My eyes were wide open, the brows not contracted (as they mostly are when I am interested in a particular object). No such interest preceded this gazing. My gaze was vacant; or again like that of someone admiring the illumination of the sky and drinking in the light [emphasis added]. (13)

The religious person seeking inspiration or help from his deity gazes upward again focussing even though he is not looking at anything in particular. The psalmist says: "I will lift up mine eyes unto the hills, from whence cometh my help" (Psalm 121). Mystics using meditational techniques often begin with the assumption of a gazing stance, oriented toward an object - but specifically concerned with ignoring the objectivity of the object. The central theme that to concentrate perceptual process one must focus vision appears throughout. The apparently extraneous activity of the extraocular muscles is a crucially important part of the processes of perception and even of conceptualization.

Pursuing the idea further into the ways of describing mastery of a concept, we repeatedly encounter the notion of 'grasping'. The metaphorical use of this term suggests that possibly the technique of grasping has something to do with the internalization of knowledge. When we watch a baby first coming to terms with his world, we see him reaching out to touch, grasp, mouth, push - he exhibits a full range of manipulative behaviors which he associates with special sensory investigation of tasting, smelling, and seeing.

We find repeated evidence that the basic structure of knowing involves a dualism allowing a dialectical method in which opposition is first posed, then resolved. It becomes a difficult, even an impossible question, to wonder whether this universal structure follows the lead of a 'reality', which requires describing in this manner, or whether the series of descriptions structures the reality which we comprehend (note the derivation: we prehend, or grasp, together; for agreement, we have to resolve basic differences of opinion until we grasp the same thing).

In perception two separate lines of investigation are integrated into a single construct. In the usual case we can oversimplify by pointing to the importance of vision, on the one hand, and manipulation, on the other. For accuracy we must remember that the first category is actually that of the special senses, the familiar five. But abstract thinking in man is so predominantly a visually-based phenomenon that we can cover a great proportion of the field by looking mainly at the relation of vision and manipulation.

According to J. Z. Young, a demonstration of this kind of relation is apparent in as phylogenetically remote an animal as the octopus: "The octopus brain contains two anatomically distinct and localizable memory stores: one records the result of actions following visual events; the other the results of actions following the touching of objects by the suckers." (14) I would only suggest that it may well be more the grasping of objects than the simple touching of them.

In a series of studies relating to remote phylogenetic antecedents to the visual capacity of the human being, Richard Gregory points out that vision must always be informed or instructed by active exploratory movement. The retinal image, falling upon the two-dimensional retinal surface, can only give the impression of three-dimensionality by interpretation after the active participation of the limbs in exploration. Gregory states:

> Retinal images are symbols, like words in a language; however, like any symbols there must be a process of initial association to acquire significance, or the symbols are in a logical vacuum and cannot represent any reality. Furthermore, retinal images are but flat projections of a three-dimensional world and yet they give perceptions of three dimensions. There must be direct, non-visual, information of the third dimension. Other information comes from touch. It appears that any conceivable device for perceiving which relies upon two-dimensional images must use, at

some state, direct touch information if it is to interpret its images in terms of three dimensions of surrounding space. (15)

He goes on to describe two kinds of touch:

> ... which involve entirely different neural mechanisms. There are skin pattern touch and limb probe touch. Pattern touch involves the reception of patterns by contact with areas of skin, while probe touch is very different and requires exploratory movements of a limb. Pattern touch gives information only of structures lying on the two dimensional surface of the skin, while probe touch gives information in three dimensions, within the reach of the limb.

He comments upon the special function of the fore-limbs: "It is the fore-limbs, and especially their movements, which are available to vision but not pattern touch - which is hidden from the eye by (non-transparent) objects in contact with the skin. It is active rather than passive limb movement which gives visual learning."

When we compare and contrast the results of looking and grasping (including under grasping the notion of palpating or touching in an exploratory manner), we find that each approach modifies the other. In Marius von Senden's summation of the results of attaining visual competence in adult life, he notes that until the subject had an extensive experience of grasping round objects while looking at them, he could not see roundness; this ability is a derived and developed potentiality which has to be trained in action. (16)

Pursuing the notion further, Gordon Holmes reports from a study of brain-injured soldiers who had lost the capacity for spatial orientation: "It was only when they relied upon sight alone that they could not localize the positions of an object in space. If it touched any part of their own bodies they could always bring their hands to it immediately and correctly; touch gave them the necessary local knowledge that they failed to obtain from vision alone." (17)

Another British neurologist, Gordon Wright, comments: "The closer our physical relationships (this really means tactual relationships) with other people, whether by reason of kinship or by reason of our profession, the more intimate and thorough is our knowledge of them, and the more potent is the manual component of the images we have of them ... Manipulation is also of prime importance in constantly reaffirming the corporeality of ourselves and other people - in putting substance one might say into the body image." (18)

When we think of learning, we often use the rubric of the three R's - reading, writing, arithmetic - with the idea that some record of a mostly exteroceptive perceptual experience is stored in the brain. This model is implicitly supported in the notion of a classical Pavlovian conditioning as a basic process in learning. In many of the classical procedures of neurophysiology the procedures begin with anesthetizing the animal subject or with the ablation of all of the nervous system except that part in which the experimenter is interested.

Perhaps the most dramatic demonstration available in recent years
is that all of these procedures give an entirely erroneous notion of
the basic processes involved (Livingston). (19) Only when it becomes
possible to observe animals and human beings in effective action with
others of their own kind is it possible to get a clear look at learning,
as we know from many contemporary studies in ethology. The restriction is so great in any kind of simplification of animal life that
it is possible to find a very pronounced difference between the learning
porcesses of wild animals and those simplified by progressive dom-
estication. Lee Kavanau, for instance, has studied wild mice and
compared them with domesticated ones in a laboratory. (20) Wild
mice show a remarkably expanded capacity for learning, even in
situations requiring the simultaneous handling of several variables.
In contrast, domesticated mice are markedly limited. In a laboratory
environment the domesticated mice tend to be relatively placid, while
the wild mice explore incessantly, playing with any kind of apparatus
available to them in a continuous effort to get the better of the situation.

In a development of conditioning procedures derived from but
considerably extending the scope ot the Pavlovian variety, the Polish
investigator Jerzy Konorski gives an interesting account of the extension of varied behavioral learning in conditioning experiments
made possible when the exteroceptive stimulus used by Pavlov is
combined with proprioceptive patterns introduced by movement of
some part of the animal's body, whether that movement be passive,
a response to a reflex stimulation, or somehow actively induced. He
notes that the major difference of operant conditioning from the classical kind is that the former involves acitve participation of the experimental animal in the learning process. (21)

For example, if one trains a dog with a tone, he can be made to
salivate with either meat or acid, thus showing a similar reaction
to oppositely valued stimuli. With the type II conditioning procedure
the subject can be trained to show oppositely valued reactions to
oppositely valued stimuli - positive to pleasant, aversive to unpleasant. By varying the time of stimulation great differences in the
result could be obtained. Perhaps most importantly Konorski showed
that after appropriate intensive training, it was possible to remove
the afferent signals from the trained limb while leaving the reflex
movement possible. Since the deafferented limb was otherwise a
'flail' extremity, the fact that it could be directed to carry out the
appropriate action on exhibition of the conditional stimulus gives
evidence that the integration of movement with perception of the
exteroceptive stimulus makes fundamental differences in the way in
which the memory storage is effected in the nervous system.

Available evidence indicates not only that motor activity is essential
in learning, but that repetition of motor activity exhibited against consistent resistance is necessary for the maintenance of learned patterns.
Richard Held and Sanford Freedman reviewed studies showing that
unless the repetition of skilled actions takes place time after time in
the context of a predictable resistance, the schemata which control
those skilled actions are susceptible to deterioration. (22) This finding
suggests that not only is it extremely important to carry out training

in a situation which presents the appropriate resistance to the trainee, it is also necessary for subsequent exhibition of the skill to take place in the same context of resistance if the skill is to be maintained at a high level of competence. This result suggests that skills are stored in the form of schemata which are implicitly not so much <u>schemata of action</u> as <u>schemata of transaction.</u> The dialectical process is unavoidable even here. A properly performed skilled act represents a synthetic resolution of a conflict of thesis of action and antithesis of resistance. Neither can be ignored, although it seems possible, if we extrapolate from Konorski's finding, that in a highly skilled subject it may be possible to direct the performance of a skilled act without the immediate feedback of afferent information at the time.

These authors summarize their impressions, with special reference to the practical application of these findings in the space program:

> The maintenance and development of sensorily guided behavior depend in part upon bodily movement in the normal environment. Ordered information entailed in the motor-sensory feedback loop is responsible for the stable functioning of the plastic systems of coordination. It is found, from the results of experiments on vision and hearing, that the introduction of disorder into the motor-sensory loop changes the state of these systems and makes performance imprecise. In space, a freely moving astronaut will be exposed to a condition analogous to that of the subjects of these experiments. Consequently, he may lose his ability to perform certain tasks requiring precise sensori-motor control. (23)

Two further esoteric suggestions appear in material reported by introspective observers of great sensitivity. The first of these is a report by William James in the Principles of Psychology. There, reviewing the manner in which he finds imself, knowing himself, he says:

> ... this central part of the Self is <u>felt</u> ... It may be call that Transcendentalists say it is, and all the Empiricists say it is into the bargain, but at any rate it is no <u>mere ens rationis,</u> cognized only in an intellectual way, and no <u>mere</u> summation of memories or <u>mere</u> sound of a word in our cars. It is something with which we also have direct sensible acquaintance, and which is as fully present in any moment of consciousness in which it <u>is</u> present, as in a whole lifetime of such moments ... But when it is found, it is <u>felt</u>; just as the body is felt, the feeling of which is also an abstraction, because never is the body felt all alone, but always together with other things. (24)

He goes on to describe his own feeling of the "central active self":

> ... I am aware of a constant play of furtherances and hindrances in my thinking, of checks and releases, tendencies which run the other way ... when I ... grapple with particulars ... it <u>is</u> difficult for me to detect in the activity any purely spiritual element

at all. Whenever my introspective glance succeeds in turning around quickly enough to catch one of these manifestations of spontaneity in the act, all it can ever feel distinctly is some bodily process, for the most part taking place within the head ... the 'Self of selves' ... is found to consist mainly of the collection of peculiar notions in the head or between the head and throat ... it would follow that our entire feeling of spiritual activity, or what commonly passes by that name, is really a feeling of bodily activities whose exact nature is by most men overlooked.

A most interesting contrast to James' curiosity about how he knows himself can be found in a carefully reviewed experience by a Westerner learning a Zen Buddhist technique. (25) Herrigel spent a number of years in Japan, and while there he undertook a training process with a Zen master. The specific technique used was unusual, involving the learning of archery. Herrigel's fascinating report emphasizes throughout that the goal of his training is that of losing any feeling of an 'I' directing or controlling; rather he was indoctrinated with the ideal that he learned so to participate in the larger process that when the arrow was released, there was a feeling of 'it shooting'. Like the utterly disciplined ballet dancer, who seems to be moving effortlessly without trying, the Zen archer is undifferentiated from his task. The method is so efficient in transcending the usual limitations that, according to Herrigel, the master once demonstrated that it was possible to shoot an arrow in total darkness and have it land precisely in the bull's eye.

The significant word in descriptions of Zen, of Yoga, and of many others of the mystical religious pursuits is discipline. Not by chance the route to the complete discipline involves incessant repetitive activity, both of action and of the controlled inhibition of action. The meditator has to sit in a given position for long periods without allowing himself to fall asleep. The yogi prescribes to his disciples that they undertake a complicated set of breathing exercises, the adoption of the lotus position, of standing on one's head, and the like. Those who practice these esoteric forms of self-discipline report universally that the subject gains a marvellous sense of mastery - paradoxically by totally giving up the goal of mastering anything except the physical exercises involved in the training procedure. One has to learn a skill with implicit perfection, then forget the whole process in the exhibition of that skill or discipline for its own purpose. The subject could be said to learn how to enclose himself within a discipline having no purpose, no outcome except that of perfecting the discipline. Once this is accomplished, an enormous sense of liberation occurs: 'It' shoots!

To complete a review of a series of related ideas having to do with the participation of the muscular system and its related aspects in human mentation, studies of the rapid-eye-movement-state give further pertinent evidence. It was noted above that the muscles intrinsic to the special senses are active in the focussing process.

In diametrically opposite fashion, while these evidences of activity in tiny muscles related to orientation and preparation appear, there is an extensive relaxation of the large muscle masses of the periphery. The muscles which have the responsibility of taking action on the basis of the orientative preparation involved in sensory function are specifically relaxed. The internal state of the brain is of great activity, sharply contrasting to the inhibited state of the peripheral muscles. The contrast is so precise that it seems impossible that it should be without meaning.

A general characteristic of the activity of the brain is that its metabolism runs fast, no matter what it is going. The evidence from the REMS suggests that when the person apparently is sleeping, the brain may run fastest of all, while the great muscles are most relaxed.

The curious explanation that suggests itself for this internal physiological 'contradiction' is that in the eye movements we observe the ultimate degree of playing. Liberated from the dreary restrictions of ordinary everyday reality and the necessity for making a living or demonstrating one's worth in some public way, the dreamer indulges in 'ludic activity' (Piaget) with a maximal freeing of imagination. He evokes images at random and combines them with varying degrees of structure and meaning, putting impossible things together and separating the inseparable. In this ruminative play the main purpose is to give relief to the integrative function by allowing a comprehensive disintegration, with the dreamer protected from harm because he is incapable of action.

This idea, supported in depth by evidence from physiological studies, was suggested by Piaget from an entirely different line of reasoning, Piaget's basic description of behavior uses the unitary duality of accommodation, defined by him as a behavioral change imposed upon the organism by the environment, and assimilation, the structuring imposed upon the environment by the organism. Play is mostly assimilation because the playing child makes whatever he has be whatever he wants it to be. Imitation, an important method of learning in early life, is thus mostly accommodation.

Piaget comments about dreaming:

> Dreams are ... comparable to symbolic play, but play which, by lack of consciousness of the ego, is itself analogous to the lack of coordination between the visual and the motor, characteristic of the first year of life. The semi-consciousness of the dreamer is indeed comparable to the state of complete egocentrism characteristic of the baby's consciousness. In both cases there is a lack of differentiation between the ego and the external world, and the assimilation of objects to the activity of the subject ... The ego is unconscious of itself to the extent to which it incorporates external reality, since consciousness of the ego is relative to the resistance of objects and of other persons. (26)

When Piaget speaks of the lack of coordination of visual and motor components, we can remember that the REMS evidence indicates that even in the face of the loss of peripheral motor activity, the intrinsic muscular activity of the sense organs connot be dispensed with if the experience is to occur.

If we try to come to a general formulation having significance in light of all these disparate bodies of evidence, we can suggest that learning is specifically dependent upon acting, with the clear implication that only in the course of overt activity does learning occur. Then a major task of human education becomes the training of human learners to <u>minimize</u> overt activity while <u>retaining</u> the capacity to be alert and to process data. The function thus described is that of exerting and maintaining discipline. Discipline then has a function - to make learning efficient. When we learn to concentrate, to read silently, or to think 'in the head', we are learning a technique which bypasses much of the afferent input otherwise necessary. If we extrapolate from Konorski's finding, much of this would appear to be a matter of making intracerebral bypass connections, which, though dependent upon 'operant' processing in establishment, allow bypassing and economy in exhibiting the learning involved.

In the most efficient instances of this kind of learning, however, there remains a limit to human capacity. Most of those who think in abstract contexts have to externalize the thinking as they go along if they are to move progressively through a problem in complex subject matter. Francis Bacon said that "writing maketh an exact man", and I would propose that the act of writing provides the minimal but essential muscular participation. Mozart supposedly was able to 'hear' a complete symphony in his head before writing it down, but most people have to give themselves a great deal more help in working through to a solution or an artistic accomplishment.

As we study reports of experience of those who involve themselves in mystical, meditative, or contemplative disciplines, the notion emerges that the final state has a significant connection with the training. Discipline progressively improves predictability: the highly disciplined human being knows precisely what to expect of himself. I propose that when predictability reaches some ultimate point of perfection, the control of muscular activity allows the human being to transcend the dualism of perception that separates the <u>me</u>, <u>in-here</u>, from the <u>world, out-there</u>. The illuminated person loses both the objectivity of the resisting world and the subjectivity of the yearning self. He comes to feel an undifferentiated continuity with 'reality' or with 'god' or 'nature'. The feeling is reported as ecstatically satisfying. If we extrapolate to ultimate states, we find the oceanic, undifferentiated experience of the infant in one direction, the unconscious consciousness of the dream in another, and the ultimate loss of self in death in still a third.

The ultimately paradoxical character of human experience comes through loud and clear: if overt muscular activity of the peripheral musculature is necessary to thinking or to remembering, then what cannot be experienced in muscular movement cannot be either conscious or remembered. The states of bliss which we approach by attempting to achieve an ultimate disciplined control of muscular activity, or the ultimate loss of muscular activity in the total relaxation of the dream, are necessarily states of blissful ignorance. The analytic activity of differentiation, which is the correlate of planned

236

motor activity, is incompatible with intensity of feeling. Possibly we may all attain a new taste of the Garden of Eden from time to time in the REM state, but, as we are driven again from bliss upon re-attaining the condition in which we can know good from evil, we lose heaven without ever knowing we were there again.

When we awaken, we can sometimes report, in a procedure not too dissimilar from that of describing a receding seascape through a rapidly closing porthole, fragments of what we have been dreaming. But the limitation of this procedure is apparent to anyone who comes back to a record of such a report. What we remember is no longer the dream, but the report - I believe quite simply because we re-member not the view but the muscular participation of writing it down or saying it to someone else. The dream would appear quite unrememberable, except in the derived and grossly reduced frag-ments that one can quickly grasp in the specious present in which the reverberations linger.

The suggestion is clear that human experience is necessarily cir-cular in context after context. It involves a circulation of patterns out to the periphery, but equally importantly from the periphery back to the center; a circulation of patterns from the self to others and back and when we learn to internalize others (and a 'generalized other'), in a constant circular communication in the form of an inner speech system; and in the broadest terms a circulation from a state of un-differentiation in utero through a detailed process of differentiation in an 'object world' back to undifferentiation in dreaming and in the occasional but dramatic attainment of transcendental experience in mystic exaltation. Curiously enough, we only can understand this fact only after a long training in thinking abstractly, while the major purpose of the abstracting of patterns is to give human beings an entirely unjustified sense of spatial localization in a fallaciously mis-placed concreteness. We live in a process which has a specifically spiral character, always coming back to a place from which we be-gan, as Eliot put it, but knowing that place for the first time.

NOTES

(*) Reprinted from The Mental Health Field - A Critical Appraisal, ed. by Morton Levitt and Ben Rubenstein (1971), 331-352, by per-mission of the Wayne State University Press.
(1) (New York: Macmillan, 1953).
(2) Reflexes of the Brain (Cambridge, Mass.: M.I.T. Press, 1965).
(3) Nikolai Bernstein, The Co-ordination and Regulation of Movements (Oxford: Pergamon Press, 1967).
(4) Frederic Bartlett, Thinking: An Experimental Social Study (Lon-don: G. Allen, 1958).
(5) Alfred Whitehead, Science and the Modern World (New York: Mentor Books, 1960).
(6) Lev Vygotsky, Thought and Language (Cambridge, Mass.: M.I. T. Press, 1934).
(7) (New York: Cambridge University Press, 1954).

(8) Bernstein.
(9) Vision - Its Development in Infant and Child (New York: Paul B. Hoeber, 1950).
(10) The Child's Conception of Space (New York: W. W. Norton, 1967).
(11) Ragnar Granit, Receptors and Sensory Perception (New Haven: Yale University Press, 1955).
(12) "Behaviorism at 50", Science 139 (1963), 951-997.
(13) Wittgenstein.
(14) The Memory System of the Brain (Berkely: University of California Press. 1966).
(15) "Origin of Eyes and Brains", Nature 213 (1967), 369-372.
(16) Space and Sight (London: Methuen, 1960).
(17) "Disturbances of Visual Space Perception", British Medical Journal 2 (1919), 230.
(18) "The Names of the Parts of the Body", Brain 79 (1956), 188-210.
(19) Robert Livingston, "Some Brain Stem Mechanisms Relating to Psychosomatic Functions", Psychosomatic Medicine 17 (1955), 347-354.
(20) "Behavior, Confinement, Adaptation, and Compulsory Regimes in Laboratory Study", Science 143 (1964), 490; D. H. Brant and J. Lee Kavanau, " 'Unrewarded' Exploration and Learning of Complex Mazes by Wild and Domestic Mice", Nature 204 (1964), 267-269.
(21) "Changing Concept Concerning the Physical Mechanism of Animal Motor Behavior", Brain 85 (1962), 277-294.
(22) "Plasticity in Human Sensorimotor Control", Science 142 (1963), 455-464.
(23) Ibid.
(24) Principles of Psychology (New York: Dover, 1956). Originally published 1890.
(25) Eugen Herrigel, Zen and the Art of Archery (New York: McGraw-Hill, 1964).
(26) Play Dreams and Imitation in Childhood (New York: Norton, 1951).

XIII

PARADOXES OF CONSONANCE: A STRUCTURAL VIEW (*)

> It would follow that all reason is dialectical, which
> for my part I am prepared to concede, since dialec-
> tical reason seems to me like analytical reason in
> action.

> C. Lévi-Strauss (1)

To be invited to give a paper at a conference is always a compliment, and to argue with a compliment is often in bad taste. But when the invitational suggestion runs to some extent at least counter to a conviction, the problem becomes a delicate one of how to assert oneself without offending, a dilemma not uncommon to human beings.
In the present case, my invitation prescribed a title joining cognition and consonance, and the dilemma appears in my own conviction that these terms are often misleading. If I may, let me then suggest that the first term is better expanded into some such word as mentation, and the second is only half-relevant.

To elaborate: mentation is a complex function which includes the self-regulating methods of the human being imbedded, as he must be if he is to be human, in a culture. To differentiate cognitive functions as a separate class leads to the same kind of confusion introduced by the separation of 'unconscious' from 'conscious' mentation, that distinction which has been at the same time so valuable to the psychoanalytic tradition and so misleading when we try to understand human mentation in relation to animal mentation.

All animals show complex systems of self-regulation, as indeed do a large number of other kinds of systems, many of which are not 'alive' in the crucial sense of being self-replicating. Human systems of self-regulation are different from animal systems in the species-specific capacity to use language. What we find in language at the cognitive level is primarily the capacity to differentiate. The basic cognitive operation of definition is a way of separating the defined from its context, and it thus underlies the notion of an 'individual' or an 'object'. In this way we arrive at the half-word familiar in traditional Western thought.

In language, we think of the word as a 'unit' in a similar 'half' sense. But, in any verbal series the first requirement is that of opposition between any one word and its preceding and succeeding word (Saussure).(2) Thus, any word must oppose or be dissonant from its neighbors. To understand a sentence, we have to resolve the oppositions of all the words to each other by integrating or organizing the opposed terms into a single unitary 'meaning'. As in the highly refined language of mathematics we see a sequence of the differentiating and the integrating (cf. calculus).

Language displays a basic dialectical form. The initial relation demonstrated in the dialectic is dissonance; the ultimate relation is consonance. This fact is true of the words as well as of sentences or propositions. To any word as thesis, we oppose some other implicit term as antithesis. To understand 'cold', it is necessary at the same time to understand 'hot', 'up' to understand 'down'. Freud, (3) quoting an older source in the work of the philologist Abel, points out the 'antithetical meaning' of primal words - and we can easily find in our own present-day sophisticated language many such words. 'Sanction' is a good example. Certain kinds of behavior are 'sanctioned' in that they are specifically allowed or even blessed in cultural mores - but at the same time, the League of Nations found one of its severest problems in the question of whether to 'apply sanctions' to Mussolini's adventure in Ethiopia. In this second sense of 'sanction', we find the meaning of proscribed rather than prescribed, forbidden or punished rather than allowed or honored. Webster's Collegiate Dictionary gives as meaning (1.) 'confirmation' or 'approbation', and as meaning (2.b.) 'detriment, loss of reward, or other coercive intervention, annexed to a violation of the law as a means of enforcing the law'. To 'sanction' is the opposite, very nearly, of to 'apply sanctions'. The League of Nations implicitly sanctioned Mussolini's aggression by not applying sanctions.

Cognition is said to operate through concepts, but when we look closely, we find 'concept' as misleading a term as 'individual' or 'object'. A concept is what is formulated in a word; but, a word is useful only as related to a concept. To cite Saussure again, (4) a 'word' is a dual form in which the primary 'fact' is a relation of a signifying and a signified, a verbal form with its obverse, conceptual form.

Having once then noted the duality of signification, we can move immediately to the duality of formation. Many of the most important words we use are always to be differentiated primarily from the almost-twin. For example, hypoglycemia is always in contrast to hyperglycemia, afferent to efferent, process to product. The basic principle is that of opposition between close relatives. In this way we find in the linguistic universe a strong similarity to many of the inverse correlations of human brotherhood, as illustrated by the legend of the man in the iron mask, a man who was inherently treasonous because of his identity with his twin, the king.

When we say 'cognitive', we are making a differentiation which rests upon a deeper identity, since cognitive is only meaningful as artificially differentiated from affective, or even from that term that now sounds so obsolete, namely, 'conative'. Note here again that 'cognitive' and 'conative' are close morphemic neighbors. If one sees 'cognition' as mostly concerned with reducing 'dissonance', as in the well known theoretical statement by Festinger, (5) he ignores all of the evidence which indicates that the primary task of the scientist is, in Popper's terms, (6) to test hypotheses for the primary purpose of falsification. Falsification is the establishing of dissonance or of 'negation', in the terms Hegel was so fond of.

When we consider, on the other hand, cognitive function not as a separate entity (established, it may be noted, purely by definition) but as an aspect of a continuous spectrum of mentation, we find other aspects of that spectrum principally concerned with the discovery of novelty, which is to say the discovery of dissonance, the finding of what Kuhn (7) calls an 'anomaly'. Subsequently, the processing of this discovered discrepancy is oriented to the reduction of the encountered novelty. Here we find the dialectical system basic to Piaget's work, (8) in which we 'accomodate' to what is newly presented to us by the 'environment', then, after learning an appropriate schema through the process of accommodation, we find it possible to 'assimilate' a wide number of different phenomena to that schema. A trivial but interesting example of this dialectical process is that familiar to many 'dictionary freaks', who find that after looking up a totally strange word and learning a new definition, the previously 'non-existent' word becomes strikingly frequent, simply because of the new 'sensitivity' associated with the establishment of a new internal scheme. At a different level of self-regulation, we find a similar kind of sensitivity allowing or condemning the hay-fever sufferer (with his abnormal immunological schema) to 'find' pollen where others are totally unaware of it.

Every regulatory process is a continuously varying balance of negative and positive tendencies, of anabolism and catabolism, of input and output, inspiration and expiration - in the words of Solomon, regulation occurs in terms of "a time to live and a time to die", "a time to sow and a time to reap", "a time to make war and a time to give over making war". Whereas the spectrum of self-regulation spreads across the whole range of living organisms, the difference we find in man is that of the development of an abstractive method which allows man to assume that single events occur, or that individuals exist, or that a word may have some meaning in and of itself.

Self-regulatory processes, otherwise described, are naturally organized along an analog scale, with the range from more to less and less to more, in a continuously spiral form when the more-or-less is seen to be in movement through time (as a wave form). In self-regulation and in description we find the continuous alternation of the moving and the stable. Time considered as process is differentiated from time considered as successive slices (present moments) in the customary temporal 'calculus'. In structural linguistics the temporal distinction is between the 'diachronic' and the 'synchronic'.

When we move to the question of description of these continuous self-regulatory processes, however, we find another duality, since description necessarily uses linguistic-symbolic methods closer by far to the digital than to the analog. When we begin to formulate in terms of digital method, we use the dual system of zero and one, (0, 1). In such a system we see duality in its simplest form - each term has meaning only with reference to the other. When we learn implicitly how to think digitally, we find the curious possibility of thinking of the one without the other term consciously present. Thus we can talk about a one without reminding ourselves overtly that one is only meaningful in relation to zero, or 'cognitive' without its relatives, or even of 'consonance' without consciously dealing with the necessarily negative implication of dissonance.

When we realize the implications of these limitations, we find the basic identity of 'analytic logic' and 'dialectical logic' is obscured in the same way that we differentiate physiological from mental self-regulation, behavior from 'affect', and the like. In his comment on the opposition between himself and Sartre as regards dialectical reason and analytical reason, Lévi-Strauss says, (9)

> The term dialectical reason ... covers the perpetual efforts analytical reason must make to reform itself if it aspires to account for language, society and thought; and the distinction between the two forms of reason in my view rests only on the temporary gap separating analytical reason from the understanding of life. Sartre calls analytical reason reason in repose; I call the same reason dialectical when it is roused to action, tensed by its efforts to transcend itself.

Pursuing the theme of dualism, in the two words cognition and consonance, we find a different kind of connotation which deserves scrutiny. Note that both terms (or indeed, all three if we include connotation as well) begin with the prefix, co-. Etymologically, we know that all such terms derive from the Latin cum, meaning 'with'. Combining the prefix, we find the meanings of 'knowing with', 'sounding with', and 'noting with'. In each case, the clear implication is that some social process is involved. Through a variety of other studies, it has become increasingly clear that we must always take language into account when we talk about human thinking - and the use of a language necessarily implies a group, at least a group of two.

The context of consonance, cognition, or connotation is a social one. The implication is that of togetherness, and the more we delve into the problem, the more we find the unavoidable nature of relatedness. To know, we must not only have something to know, 'out there', we must know it with someone, and together with that someone we know whatever is 'in here' in some kind of knowing system. Not only is this true, we have at the same time to realize that the words we use to 'grasp' any idea can never have any meaning except in context, as for example in a sentence, a paragraph or book. Each word in any verbal series can be considered in some sense an 'individual', but as soon as we begin to understand verbal process, we have to conclude that it is the series, the organization, in which meaning is implicit. If we then consider a series of words as a 'small group', we see that words, like human beings, live in 'social systems' in which the importance is always that of membership.

A 'message' on a tape produced by recording technique is a function of a series of magnetic patterns established by the conjoint activity of a mechanism and a medium. Within the medium, in this case a tape, we find that each pattern is significant by virtue of its relation to prior and subsequent patterns, and these serially opposed patterns must have a basic relation of membership within a system for them to be jointly susceptible to the recording technique. Only recordable patterns are recorded, and we find again a 'social system' of recordable patterns.

Everything of which we can in any way become cognizant has to be understood as the emergent consequence of some kind of oppositional problem in resolution. Sophisticated cognition emerges in the kind of human social system which allows the development of the capacity to 'talk to oneself' in some very real sense. Internal cognitive data-processing requires an organization in which 'I' can speak to 'me', and then, in a rapid about-face, the 'I' that was 'me' speaks to the 'me' that was just now 'I'. Such internal discussions take place at a nearly implicit level in the expert case, and the shifting centrality of the points of view expressed may be entirely without the awareness of the 'conscious' notational system available. One of the most interesting of the activities of the psychotherapist, to cite a specific example of the problem, is that he says to his colleague, the 'patient', "Did you notice that you just presented an argument between 'you' and 'yourself'?" By emphasizing the internal contradictions emerging in the flow of 'material', the therapist in some important sense 'introduces the patient to himself' or highlights the oppositional relation between statement A and statement B or between point-of-view A and point-of-view B.

Pursuing the problem further at a meta-level, we can see that the usual scientific formulations in terms of rationality and objectivity are themselves dissonant not only with easily replicable observations but also with the basic principles of physics since the turn of the century. As far as we can tell, the structure of nature is dissonant from the structure of language. This problem can again be illustrated with reference to the psychotherapeutic-psychoanalytic situation. There we find the formulation that the 'patient' develops a 'transference' relation to the 'therapist' while the therapist is developing a 'counter-transference' relation to the patient. This is quite similar to saying that Cain developed a murdering relation to Abel while Abel was developing a 'being murdered' relation to Cain.

We then find a remarkably paradoxical fact, namely, that the illusion created by linguistic practice in the above two examples is that of the separation of two inseparable aspects when the 'fact' is necessarily a whole. Cain murdered Abel at one and the same time that Abel was murdered by Cain. To separate two kinds of transference is obviously as fallacious as to separate murderer and murderee from the action through which the two attain reciprocal status. In an important sense, 'murder' is nearly instantaneous and it is an act of participation (though usually involuntary). Not only is this true, but to separate the act from the actor, the murder from the murderer, is a falsification imposed by the syntagmatic structure of language.

Language thus fragments and separates in a falsification of wholeness, but paradoxically it is only through the mediation of language that simultaneity or instantaneousness can be imagined - and can be imagined only by ignoring the medium in which it is formulated. To illustrate, it is only necessary to note that the ultimate transformation in the religious context is predicted to take place 'in the twinkling of an eye' - but one only has to measure how long it takes to say 'in the twinkling of an eye' to realize that that comment requires a period in which a large number of eye-twinklings could occur.

The self-contradictory conclusion that can be reached then is that the mediation of language is that factor in the intellectual grasp of experience which falsifies in two directions. First, it spreads out the participation by breaking down an event into two actors each with his own action. Second, and conversely, through the 'collapsing' of process into formulation, it allows the illusions of simultaneity and instantaneousness. Einstein's basic epistemological insight is to be found in his becoming aware of the necessity of mediation for description, (10) and the requirement that we understand how these illusions are implicit in linguistic or mathematical mediation. A subsequent development of this insight is to be found in the 'oper-rationalism' of Bridgeman, (11) a recognition of the equivalence of the statement that an "object is three feet long" with the statement that "to measure this object, one can apply a one foot rule in three successive steps". In other words, Bridgeman points out that any 'measurement' is in fact a 'measuring process' necessarily extended in time no matter how much one can imagine that 'three feet long' is an instantaneous relation.

By taking objectification to its logical rxtreme, scientific method in the traditional sense introduced the kind of stabilization in data-processing which allows the illusion of a comprehensive grasp of 'reality' - while the self-same stabilization falsifies everything we know about the basic structure of nature as a moving, ever-changing complexity. Piaget (12) recognizes the paradox in using an internally contradictory metaphor, the 'mobile equilibrium'. It is easy to see that an equilibrium is never moving, while a mobile system cannot be in equilibrium. What Piaget refers to can be said more precisely in the notion of a balance, an 'asymptote' toward which a system moves never to arrive. It is only through the mediation of language that we arrive at such similarly contradictory notions as the 'uncaused cause' or the 'irresistible force' or the 'immovable object' or 'perpetual motion'.

From this point it is easy to move far back in history to Zeno's paradoxes to find there that the hare that never catches the tortoise or the arrow that never reaches its target are simply illustrations of the lack of fit between the natural fact and the linguistic description. The idea that some day with appropriate symbolic or mathematical techniques one can reach an 'ultimate reality' behind and beyond the grasp of the fallible senses (as restated as recently as the work of Max Planck) (13) becomes then the ultimate illusion. The 'fact' if fact is an applicable term in this context, is that the fit is in principle and forever impossible. There can never be an equilibrium, 'mobile' or 'stable'. We realize that falsification is inevitable, and that therefore the basic relation of description and reality is that of dissonance.

The practice of psychotherapy - and to a lesser extent, the practice of clinical medicine - is a study in tolerating the ambiguity imposed by the incorrigibly dualistic forms upon our descriptive processes by the exigencies of linguistic formulation. We exit then with the double paradox that to expect consonance between 'nature' and theory formulated in linguistic-symbolic method must necessarily be re-petitively dissonant from experience, while to expect dissonance will prove consonant!

NOTES

(*) Reprinted by special permission: in: Annals of the New York Academy of Sciences 193 (1972), 194-199.
(1) Claude Lévi-Strauss, The Savage Mind (Chicago, Illinois: University of Chicago Press, 1966).
(2) F. de Saussure, Course in General Linguistics (New York: McGraw-Hill, 1966).
(3) Sigmund Freud, "The Antithetical Meaning of Primal Words", Standard Edition of the Complete Psychological Works of Sigmund Freud, Vol. XI (London: Hogarth, 1957).
(4) Saussure, 1966.
(5) Leon Festinger, A Theory of Cognitive Dissonance (Stanford: Stanford University Press, 1962).
(6) Karl R. Popper, The Logic of Scientific Discovery (London: Jutchinson, 1959).
(7) Thomas Kuhn, The Structure of Scientific Revolutions (Chicago: University of Chicago Press, 1962).
(8) J. Piaget, Play, Dreams and Imitation in Childhood (New York: Norton, 1951).
(9) Lévi-Strauss, The Savage Mind, p. 246.
(10) Albert Einstein, in Paul Schilpp (ed.), Albert Einstein, Philo-sopher Scientist (New York: Harper Torch Books, 1959).
(11) P. W. Bridgeman, "Quo Vadis?", Daedalus 87 (1958), 85-93.
(12) J. Piaget, Six Psychological Studies, edited by David Elkind (New York: Random House, 1967).
(13) Max Planck, Scientific Autobiography and Other Papers, trans-lated by F. Gaynor (New York: Philosophical Library, 1949).

PART SIX

APPENDIX: PAPERS OF HISTORICAL INTEREST

XIV

THE RELATIONSHIP OF CERTAIN ASPECTS OF PERSONALITY DEVELOPMENT TO LANGUAGE FORMS

This paper was written, according to a date on the manuscript, in March of 1951. Much of the material was later abstracted in a theoretical paper, but in this one, the outlines of much of the later developments noted above can be seen. Of special interest, looking back, is the distinction made here between the three categories of form, meaning, and movement. The notion of form or shape became the central theme of a book, The War with Words, and the notion of meaning is the principal theme of a book now in preparation entitled Meaning and Madness, with a subtitle, The Reality of Communication in the Communication of Reality, The discussion of the impossibility of treating form and movement at the same time is closely related to the impossibility, in modern physical theory, of determining position and velocity of a particle simultaneously - it thus forms the nucleus of a psychiatric theory of 'indeterminism' that parallels the ideas discussed by Heisenberg.

The historical interest of this unpublished paper is that of indicating how far linguistic theory had begun to penetrate into psychiatry even at the beginning of the nineteen fifties.

In a case history and a paper dealing with general emotional reactions observed, we have previously reported in part upon our experiences with a group of patients with various sorts of malignant disease. In this place, we propose to outline certain aspects of this experience as it may be related to quite general considerations dealing with some theoretical aspects of the problem of the development of the personality, especially with reference to the manner in which the forms of the language used by the patient in his thinking and his efforts to communicate with others influence his reactions to the environmental situation in a state of stressful adaptation to a very severe illness.

We began this project with a background of psychoanalytic theory but without any very specific plan of procedure in mind. As we proceeded, a number of concepts slowly emerged in the context of listening to these patients and wondering about what was going on inside them as they reported certain aspects of their inner experience. This process was so slow and halting that certain of the ideas which seem at the moment most illuminating to us emerged only after the project was completed, in the attempt to write down a summary of the material in some sort of frame of reference. For this reason, no statement of explanation or hypothesis is presented as in any way proved; if it were possible to begin again at the beginning, it seems likely that some of the framework could be put on much firmer grounds.

In reporting our interviews with these patients, it has appeared to us that the material is best analyzed into three categories for presentation. Upon reviewing much material gathered in interviews with psychoneurotic patients, it has appeared that the same categories are appropriate. We propose then to outline a frame of reference about these categories and to present material from both types of source to illustrate and to buttress the hypothetical structure presented. The hypothesis is not brought forward as in any sense a very original one; most of the ideas have been borrowed from theoretical material available in a variety of writings.

The three categories are those of form, meaning, and movement. Whatever perceptions are dealt with consciously in symbolic or verbal terms must first be delineated or defined, i.e., they must be given form; secondly, these forms are understood as bearing a certain relationship which gives meaning to the form; and, thirdly, the relationship is never static but is always in process, moving in one direction or another. The human organism is so remarkably efficient an apparatus for dealing with symbolic material that the three categories may be separated out only by stopping the movement in some way and analyzing the whole in various steps which are, however, never separable except in this way.

Before any object or 'thing' can be referred to by means of a symbol, most importantly by means of a verbal symbol, it must be separated in some way from the rest of the world by definition. There is a great variation in the degree of separability of perceptual object from the world, or, to use another type of referent words, the figure from the ground. Certain perceptual experiences occur as highly discrete ones which naturally lend themselves to this type of relation, e.g., the usual solid objects which surround us; others, however, especially those derived from within one's own body, are extremely difficult to define in universally acceptable terms. All states of disease and of emotion fall into the latter indistinct grouping. As soon as a form can be distinguished in any way among a mass of data presented to the individual by the activity of his senses, he attempts to recognize the form by means of analogy, i.e., he assumes that this form is in the same class as a similar form previously encountered by him.

There is a very close relationship between form and the meaning. We may define the meaning as the relationship of the form of the perceptual experience to the individual. Where the configuration is understood to have a very distant relation to the individual, he remains rather indifferent to it; where it is very close, his reaction tends to be intense. An individual learns and retains a vast number of forms and of reactions to these forms in his passage through time, and there is a tendency for the processes concerned to become automatic as the individual learns. More and more of the transactions of living pass from the center of the stage to an unconscious level; as they recede from consciousness the processes become stereotyped. Forms are given meaning by the automatic reaction of the individual, and only the more important forms which pose a problem to the individual are eventually present to any great degree in consciousness. On the other hand, the reaction inside the individual is given form and

definition only as it is expressed and viewed in its entirety retrospectively after the expression. It is a very common experience for an
individual to be surprised by the character or intensity of a feeling
as he looks back at it after it has occurred. This fact is basic to any
type of psychotherapy.

In the third category, movement, we understand movement both in
time and in space. Both of these may be reduced to movement in time
for many purposes, since an object in the near distance may be considered an object in the near future as one goes toward it. Movement
occurs in all different relationships: between figure and ground, between object and individual, and from one to another stage of development in the same individual. In the latter case, we are particularly
interested in the material cited below to note the instances of movement in regression and progression in the individuals observed under
stress. It has been pointed out many times how unbearable stress dis-
turbs the adaptive steady state of the individual and is followed by the
resumption of an earlier type of adaptation which may be appropriate
to the degree of disorganization in the individual but is not at all appropriate to the current situation.

1. Form

The problem of cancer - indeed, of any illness in the body - emphasizes the difficulty and the primacy of the isolation and definition of
the configuration of inner experience. The object in question is an
elusive one in many ways. In the first place, it is inside (except in
skin cancer) and thus is inaccessible to investigation. The lesion is
frequently initially painless, and the symptoms referable to the lesion
are general and inconclusive: the amount of concrete information
which is available about the object is small. At the same time, especially with the wide publicity given to the problem in recent years,
a vague persistent lesion or group of symptoms is well calculated
to arouse the suspicion of cancer and the anxiety attendant upon the
suspicion. The two groups of factors combine into a situation in
which it is imperative to make a judgment upon which to base planned
action and expectation, but the major object of concern is vague and
shapeless. In this condition, we find patients establishing configurations and treating the lesion in categories which have been useful
in the past in times of stress. In our discussion, we should like to
take up first a general discussion of the forms which the patients
treat as analogous to the cancer inside; second, a discussion of the
manner in which the relationship of the form to the individual shifts
at times of stress; and third, a brief review of the material collected
in this series as it reflects the shifting background of preoccupation
with varying degree of illness, and the manner in which the patient
selects from the environment those aspects of it which are appropriate
for the expression of the emotional state.

In the situation which confronts any patient with an uncomfortable
group of sensations which have no clear relationship to an agent in
the external world, it is obvious that these signals refer to something
which is awry, but in very many instances it is impossible to deter-

mine what with any accuracy. The signals obviously refer to an alien condition existing inside. In the resulting search for some answer as to the definition of this 'something', there is a general form into which the resultant conception is prone to be cast. This form is well known in psychoanalytic literature as the 'bad internal object'. The human tendency to search for an explanation immediately leads the individual on to an effort to determine in some way how this object got there, but for the moment, we may direct our attention primarily to some of the alternative forms into which this general concept emerges into (conscious and preconscious) fantasy.

This idea, if it may properly be called an idea in its first emergences, is so primitive that it must be inferred rather than observed; i. e. , it seldom becomes conscious in any concrete way, except in the preoccupations of a patient with hypochondriasis or schizophrenia. In our patients, it appears in a form far removed from the presumptive original form, as in the case of a woman who attributed her lesion to her "alienation from the Divine Intelligence", i. e. , in this . instance she saw herself as a 'bad' person punished by an all-encompassing God, of which she was an alien part; on the other hand, another patient explained her lesion as a transformation of all the hatred inside herself. In these two instances, we see the same form of 'bad internal object' with an opposite relationship to the individual: in the one case the patient identifies herself as the bad internal object within God; in the other the patient identifies herself as the locus within which the bad object exists. We acknowledge here a considerable debt to Mrs. Klein for clarifying this particular idea.

There is a direct bridge from this material to language problems; this insight is derived from a paper of Freud's in which he reviews some ideas of Abel's about primitive words. In primitive languages, the same word applies frequently to antithetical ideas, such for instnace as wet and dry. The paradox is resolved by the idea that the word refers to the system, wet-dry, since either word has meaning only as seen in relation to the other, and in this sense either word is 'inside' the other (as context) when it is used.

From the Gestalt psychologists, we borrow the concept of figure and ground, as mentioned above. In this context, the figure of the group of sensations is perceived upon the ground of the body image as a whole. Because of the character of this relationship between perceptual object and background, a change in one leads to a change in both, so that not only is there a preoccupation with the group of sensations as a focus of attention, but there is a preoccupation with the consequences of the relationship; it is at this point that the individual begins to deal with the meaning of the form in terms of its current and (here enters movement) future relationship to the whole.

The idea of the bad internal object implies a 'container-contained' relationship. As we follow out the course of the ideation of any human being we find many exemplifications of this general trend. For our purposes, we note particularly the manifestation of this concept in the somewhat less general one of 'protrusion-hole'. It must be pointed out here and later that the selection of one of these as figure and the other as ground depends entirely upon the situation at hand; and the relationship of the self to the figure in the attention at the moment similarly is determined by the situation. Simply, a child sucking his thumb for solace is apparently concentrating on the sucking as a figure comprehended upon the background of the thumb as object; however, if he pokes his finger into an interesting receptacle in an exploring way, the finger is the figure, the receptable the ground. There is an illuminating discussion of this process in Goldstein's book on language.

It will be immediately apparent to any psychoanalytically trained observer how the general conceptualization tendency here described naturally finds expression in the preoccupations of the oral, anal, and genital epochs of the developmental history of the individual. We would like to cite some very interesting examples of this fact in the material derived from a patient seen in psychotherapy over a period of several years. The intense concern with the 'control' of the internal object so clearly stated in this patient's remarks is a consistent part of the effort to deal with the danger inside in patients with cancers and those with other types of emotional problems.

The patient was an obese woman with an 'operation habit'; there were a number of references to her fear of cancer. She went to a funeral of a young woman friend who had died of cancer, and there had a severe anxiety attack with a fantasy that under the cold impassive exterior of the corpse there was a violent rending process still going on. In talking about her hated father, she remembered with intense emotion her reaction when he urinated leaving the door of the bathroom open: she felt insulted and wished to repay him by tearing him to bits. She described her stomach as a domineering organ which made her eat and remain fat; she said again and again that she had no appetite but felt compelled to humor the implacable demands of her stomach. Other associations dealt with her feeling that there was something black and monstrous within her in control of her; this resembled a tapeworm. She talked about her husband's swarthy skin, the opposite of her own fairness; she felt especial repugnance to his penis because of its blackness. She had anxiety dreams, especially at the time of her marriage, in which she felt smothered. When her baby, a brunette, was born, she said when they brought her in: "Take her away; she's not mine" (my baby is a bonde like me). In awakening from a nose operation at the beginning of her symptoms, she looked at herself in the mirror and screamed in horror: "They have cut my nose off. " This whole complicated series of associations is resolvable into manifestations of the tendency to react to the malignant thing which protrudes and penetrates on the one hand, and the hole and surrounding body into which it penetrates on the other. The penis of her father, envied on the outside, comes to be the hateful internal object which is destroying her in talion fashion on the inside, and the long series of operations a vain attempt to remove the offending member at an inappropriate level of action.

Examples of the way in which these tendencies achieve concrete manifestation are frequent in any deep psychotherapy; because of the primitive nature of this kind of thinking, dreams are a common medium for expression. The internal object may be identified with the whole body image of the patient or with any part of it. Two dreams in this connection may be briefly cited. A girl with atopic dermatitis whose main problem was her uncontrollable tendency to scratch herself reported that her illness began when her mother had a menopausal depression, and that the mother was currently greatly disturbed when the patient scratched herself. In the dream the patient saw the back of her mother's neck very much bruised and scratched and felt in the dream that she was responsible for this, although it was not clear to her in what way this was so. The other patient was a man with a cancerphobia. In his dream, he saw himself with a young boy who was run over and badly smashed by a truck; he awoke with a seminal emission which he thought of a few minutes later as a fecal discharge. The association to the mutilated boy in the dream was of a fetal monster which had been responsible for the death of the mother. It seems clear from the situation that the expression of relief in the seminal discharge was associated with the idea of the externalization and removal of the patient's own destructive infantile ways of behaving. Melanie Klein has reported very similar material from the analysis of a patient with cancerphobia.

It has been of particular interest to us in the course of this investigation to note the way in which the bad internal object which is an introjected hated person finds concrete expression in a fear of cancer inside, while in patients with actual cancers, the preoccupations frequently demonstrate the reverse, i. e., the actual malignant lesion inside is reported as an internal or internalized person.

Mrs. K. (cancer of the cervix) in a conversation with a social worker, suddenly asked the worker if she had heard the good news: Dr. X had told the patient that her lesion was not a cancer but was rather the deformed incomplete twin of her eight-year old son. The patient went on to remark what a relief this was after having suffered so long under the impression she had a cancer. Around the same time, the patient told the interviewer that she had wanted an operation very much, since before the operation she had been able to feel something growing, becoming harder, and pressing down in her abdomen.

Mrs. M. was preoccupied with impressions of something dropping or falling out when she began to get around again after an extensive operation: at times she had bearing-down sensations which reminded her of labor pains, and once she asked the nurse to examine her clothes to make sure she had not had a bowel movement (although she knew she had a colostomy). In the terminal stage of her illness, she asked her husband as he came in one day if he had heard that she had had a baby.

Suggestions that somewhat the same process was involved were found in other patients: Mrs. W. described in identical terms her reactions of despair in relation to finding she had a cancer and in relation to a psychopathic son over whom she had no control; Mrs. G., who referred to her 40-year old husband as a 'boy', described the same emotional reaction to his alcoholism and to a pain in her chest which she correctly suspected to be a sign of recurrence.

Mrs. Z. described her idea of a cancer as a sort of mushroom shaped object which swelled and swelled; when it finally burst, it sent bits of itself throughout the body as metastases. It is probably unnecessary to add that his patient had a number of hysterical conversion symptoms.

Another woman with a cancer of the cervix had a nephrostomy. A day or so later she had a dream in which she saw a Negro man being injected with all sorts of needles. She made a comment to herself in the dream that he was getting as many needles and as much attention as whilte people do. The Negro man began to swell, getting bigger and bigger until he suddenly burst like a balloon, and the patient awoke in a fright. About a week later, the patient had a blood transfusion and an injection of adrenalin; while the transfusion was still in progress she dozed off and had a dream in which the doctor was injecting her with a huge needle and syringe. The injected material seemd to be destroying her will power and the doctor kept demanding money and other items of value from her. She felt unable to resist. In the same dream there was a baby being injected by a doctor with the same material. In association to the dream, she was reminded of the recent birth of a grandchild, and of her strong feelings of disapproval of tobacco, whiskey, etc. She remarked how important it was to her to be clear-headed at all times and that she was very reluctant to take anything harmful into her body, although she had always attempted to avoid influencing others by her attitudes.

Mrs. G., in the terminal phases of a breast lesion with metastases, had two pathetic dreams a couple of weeks apart. She had a strong narcissistic need for perfection, and the loss of her breast and the succeeding procedures of oophorectomy and X-ray therapy had been extremely traumatic to her. She had a very strong identification with a younger brother who had been severely injured in the war; she herself was a veteran. One day she reported reminding her husband of the childhood story of a man who married a woman only to find on the wedding night that the bride removed a wig, false teeth, an artificial leg, a glass eye, and so on, asking the husband if he felt he had been cheated in their marriage. Several days later she had a dream in which she and an older brother walked along the street and met a man who carried a sign: "Be kind to a bullet-ridden veteran"; the man insisted on stopping them and demonstrating his artificial leg. The second dream occurred at a time when she had marked feelings of unreality and noticed a progressive loss of interest in the world and a strange blank absence of desire of any type. In the dream she and her husband had just bought a house (one of their greatest wishes). They moved into the house but were distressed to find it too small for them; they had to sell. Just after the final papers had been passed, she noticed a door in the house that she had previously overlooked and upon opening the door found, too late, two large rooms that would have served admirably. The rooms were in fact large enough for the new owner to store his boat there. The patient was too sick to pursue associations, but she remarked spontaneously how much she loved the ocean and how long it had been since she had been able to be out on it. It is perhaps significant that the patient had two small children that she had finally admitted to herself that she would have to relinquish to the care of her sister.

2. Meaning

It cannot be too much emphasized in this discussion that our description of these processes does violence to them in that it is impossible to convey adequately a complete picture except as isolated
fragments which bear only a very remote and abstract idea of the
dynamic mivement observed. Any such description is hopelessly inadequate as a representation of reality in that by the time a single
fragment has been isolated, it has changed, and the individual has
moved on. Movement is always implicit in meaning, and we are referring only to single 'frames' out of a very complicated and integrated 'cinema'.

In certain patients, it has been interesting to see how understanding
a situation in static terms alters the response. Two examples of this
may be cited: In one case, the patient was disturbed and irritated
because the radiologist expressed doubt that the chest film actually
showed the recurrence that she had been told was there; she asked
anxiously if there was real doubt, and her attitude and words conveyed
clearly that the implication of the possible absence of recurrence
was not immediately peasant; she was distressed by the disagreement
among her medical advisers. In the other instance, the patient, a
woman with a cancerphobia of many years' duration, who had been
rejected by many doctors as a tiresome neurotic woman reported a
distinct feeling of vindication and triumph when it was finally demonstrated that she was right after all, and she did have a cancer.
She later became depressed, but the immediate reaction was one of
relief.

In the material which we have collected, it has been apparent that
in certain instances the meaning of the illness is very different in
different situations depending upon the relationship of the patient to
other significant figures in the environment. The patient's behavior
has been quite different at successive periods depending upon his
orientation to the whole environmental situation. It has appeared to
us that this depended to a very considerable extent upon what could
be inferred from the patient's behavior to be the estimate of the locus
of 'control' on the situation. There is a peculiarly logical explanation
of these findings in the consideration that in any given situation, the
locus of control is the same as the source of the significant initiative.
There is a very strong tendency to confuse the control of perception
with the control of the external situation; perhaps the simplest example
of this process is the fairly frequent remark made by the patients
that, although they resented and feared hearing cancer discussed at
the time of concern with the problem, nevertheless in the same period
they remembered a very great interest in any printed material dealing
with the same facts. It seems likely that it is the lifelessness of the
printed word which gives the patient an illusion of greater security,
and, conversely, it is the unpredictable nature of any other human
being's behavior which makes the patient fear what the neighbor, relative, or physician will do with the word. We may remind ourselves
here of the material described by Frazer, in which he demonstrates
the primitive idea that the possession of the name of another person

gives control of the individual to the possessor.

Magic thinking of this type could be inferred from the actions of a woman with a cancer of the cervix. In the hospital, she avoided any mention of cancer, saying she was glad "they hadn't found anything". On her return home, she went to the Red Cross chapter and told them she was incurably ill with cancer; she immediately became the object of a general community sympathy and concern. She returned to the hospital for X-ray treatments and told both the interviewer and the social worker she was glad "they had gotten it all out" and that "they didn't find any of what they found before". Throughout both admissions she displayed an unusually marked aversion to any conversation about her illness. It is our impression that his woman had a strong unconscious feeling that the doctor was 'in control' of the cancer, and that he could injure her if she allowed him to know she knew anything about it. On her own grounds, herself in control, she used 'cancer' for her own ends as an offensive weapon to demand narcissistic gratification from her community.

A striking example was found in a woman who had perhaps the most violent reaction we have seen when she first heard the word 'cancer', even though she had previously stated to herself that there were many indications that she was incurably ill. She used the word aggressively to the interviewer in the first statement she made in the initial interview she reported that for months after her first experiences, she felt wounded whenever she saw even the word 'cancelled' because of the identity of first syliable. She defended herself by using the word herself; it was then 'under control'. Her need for control was also demonstrated by her feeling that the rectal suppositories she had used had resulted in the cancer; a few minutes later she remarked that she had encouraged her brother for years to use the same suppositories.

In cases where the relative intensity of the stimulus situation is far too great for the assimilatory mechanisms of the individual there are two reactions which we have observed which seem to have the function of immobilizing the process until the patient can recover enough to be able to take the information in. In the first type, we have observed reactions which seem to us to represent chaotic disorganization of the ego with widespread paralysis of function; these reactions were most clearly seen where a patient suddenly received the news that a cancer was present. The second type we have called reactions of fragmentation, since may be observed in the period of recovery following a surgical procedure, where the basic physiological mechanisms are in a state of severe impairment.

Both of these reactions fall under the general class of depersonalization reactions. It may be seen that in both cases the meaning of the situation is greatly altered by an alteration in the concept of the self. In the first case, the self is disorganized by the information and ceases to exist for a few moments; in the second instance, the self is not experienced as a whole, but rather as separate pieces which are not seen in relation to each other. It is our conjecture that it is probable that this is the way in which experience is first apprehended by the very young infant.

a. 'Chaos' Reactions

In the immediate reaction of chaotic disintegration, the patients remembered feeling confused, disoriented, paralyzed, and speechless.
The immediately subsequent reaction was frequently one of 'numbness'
with severe feelings of depersonalization.

Mrs. M., for instance, a woman with a cancer of the breast, went
to a surgeon, described her lesion, and in response to his request,
bared her breast to show him the spot. The lesion happened to have
the characteristic orange-peel appearance, and the doctor, without
further ado, said that the lesion was a cancer and would have to be
removed at once. The patient immediately felt numb all over; she
felt as though she had been struck a heavy blow over the head, and
for a few minutes was unable to move. She noted then in a detached
way that she was able to get up and leave the office, feeling very
dazed. On the street she allowed several street cars to pass before
she was able to pull herself together and get on one. At home she
went through her household tasks with a feeling of being an automaton.
In the evening she went to a neighbor's house, poured out her story
with a flood of tears, and began to feel like herself.

Miss B., upon finally getting confirmation of her fear that she had
a cancer, walked out of the doctor's office, saw one of the signs of
the cancer drive across the street, burst into loud hysterical laughter
which she could not stop; when she got home sat bolt upright all night
in her living room with the lights blazing, quivering with fear the
entire time.

A similar reaction was reported by a young woman with cancerphobia as she related the abrupt communication to her by the physician
that her mother had a cancer. She felt paralyzed and speechless for
several moments. This patient reported in another interview that she
had had an identical reaction when suddenly and callously rejected by
her fiancé after an unsatisfactory sexual experience (a musician, he
dismissed her with the remark that he was going to use the money he
had saved to buy a new instrument instead of getting married).

b. Fragmentation Reactions

We have found in two patients immediately following operations evidence of experience which appears to represent regression to very
early forms of conceptualization. In these reactions, the patients
reported feelings of fragmentation. In addition to these experiences,
we can also note a variation in the report of a patient in psychotherapy; he had a very difficult relationship with a violent mother
whose behavior was always unpredictable. When she suddenly began
a tirade, he remembers (at three or four, he thinks) feeling 'shat-
tered' and paralyzed; there was no memory of an affective experience.
At this sort of level of fragmentation of experience, and again as
illustrated below by the convalescent experiences, the apprehension
of the self as separate pieces prevents the comprehension of the
meaning of the situation (cf. the 'fragmented ego' of Mrs. Rank).

In the recovery from the anesthetic following a nephrostomy, Mrs. D. said her thoughts appeared to come in bits and pieces; she was at first unable to bring them together. When she forcibly attempted to understand, she broke out into a cold sweat; it was a great effort to focus on any one thing. She felt she was "struggling up to the surface", as she became aware enough to recognize people dimly, she was conscious of severe pain which made her "let go" and "sink down again", losing at the same time both the ability to recognize the faces and the feeling of pain. Throughout the whole series of patients, parenthetically, it has been notable that the dissolution of the unitary sense of oneself is accompanied by a marked diminution in the suffering experienced by the patient.

Mrs. M. had an 'exenteration' operation in which the uterus, ovaries, and bladder were removed in an effort to eradicate an extensive cervical cancer. For several days after the operation she was out of contact, avoiding any notice of the interviewer and not speaking at all. When she began to be able to speak again she described a feeling that her body was "in pieces". When her wound was dressed, she averted her eyes, fearing that if she looked she would find "nothing there". A day or so later, she described a generalized reaction of hyperalgesia, everything was painful, she wanted nothing to come in contact with her body, the light hurt her eyes, and she wanted only to sleep. As she recovered, she described "having to learn to walk all over again, almost as though I were a baby learning to walk".

3. Movement

In the context of this paper, movement is a concept which includes the developments in a personality from any one stage of adaptation to any other. We have been particularly concerned with movement in the direction of regression and of progression in complexity of the individual's relation to the world. More specifically, we have collected material dealing with the processes of dissolution of the ego under the influence of unbearable stress, and of restitution of the ego to one or another stage of adaptation under the influence of the compensatory mechanisms of the body. The material is not precise enough to draw conclusions which are other than very suggestive, i.e. none of our assertions can be considered as proven, but in the main our hypotheses support the suggestion of Clothier which might be paraphrased to state that restitution of the ego recapitulates the ontogeny of the personality. In the section just preceding we have described the reactions of dissolution occurring with acute stress.

It is of considerable interest to us that apparently the stress of the information that this lesion is a cancer produces a disorganization which is almost as profound as that following very severe operative trauma; however, it is clear that the restitution process which occupies a matter of minutes or hours in the former case requires weeks or months in the latter. From two quite different sources, Anna Freud and Proust, there is a suggestion that as an individual emerges from the dissolution of the ego experienced in deep sleep, he goes through the various developmental stages in very rapid succession; this process is so rapid, however, that it is quite impossible to see what is happening except in very unusual circumstances. Similar observations on a neurological level have been described in the awakening from hypoglycemic coma in the course of insulin shock treatment. It appears from our experience with these patients that the period of convalescence following a surgical operation offers unusual opportunity to investigate this problem. The observations presented here are suggestive enough to provide a basis for certain hypotheses. The movement in a group of patients with cancer is of especial interest in that it occurs in both directions. As patients recover from the operative trauma while the general health is maintained, the restitution process is apparent; whereas as they go downhill over a long period of time in states of metastatic disease, there is opportunity to observe chronic progressive regression. Parenthetically here we may point out that we have encountered many opinions that it is rather cruel to use patients in such severe distress as objects of observation; it is quite clear from our experience, however, that patients in this distressed state experience enough gratification from the continued interest of a willing listener so that they feel much less like guinea pigs than many patients in psychotherapy.

A most interesting series of dreams occurred in the case of a woman who was being treated with massive doses of stilbestrol in an attempt to control the spread of a breast lesion. In the course of the treatment, the patient developed a severe reaction which led to her being put on the danger list; her life was in jeopardy for several days. As she came out of this reaction over a couple of weeks she had three dreams which she remembered after the illness. (1) The first dream was that she was an infant and had been thrown out in the garbage heap at the back of a hospital. (2) The second dream, some days later, was that she was a child who was sleeping in the "head doctor's" bed; she wet the bed. (3) The third dream, still some days later, was a repetition of a delivery experience. Upon waking from this dream, she was confused, grasped the hand of a nurse in the room and asked if the baby had been born yet. Some days later, when her husband informed her, according to a pact made previously between them, that she had a cancer, she replied with great vigor to him that this was obviously a lie told by the doctor to cover up the fact that his medicine had almost killed her.

Frankly paranoid fantasies and statements have occurred in these patients to a degree which was very surprising to us. It may well be that this tendency is exaggerated by the personality structure of those patients seen.

Mrs. M., previously cited, displayed a number of paranoid reactions. She experienced panic with each change in attendant nurses or doctors, saying that "You can't trust strangers - you never know what they are going to feel like doing." During a back rub by a rough nurse, she was terrified, feeling that the nurse was "going all the way down to the bone", she "clung to the bed for dear life". When the nurse returned later on another errand, the patient "went limp all over". She said the food in the hospital tasted like poison, and

she singled out with special disgust frankfurters, beans, and the
hard lumps of hamburger she was given. After a second operation,
a colostomy, in her convalescent period she developed a systematized
delusion which she presented with great persuasiveness to the effect
that her husband was having an affair with a friend of ther daughter's.
This persisted for about two weeks, then faded, and the patient wondered how she could have had such a ridiculous idea.

Mrs. G. described herself as a suspicious person; in the service
she wondered if the government life insurance was a trick to get
money from the servicemen; she always had felt salespeople were
trying to take advantage of her. In the terminal phase of her illness,
when she was in a state of advanced disintegration and pain, she told
the interviewer that a nurse who had just left the room was crazy;
another day she complained first that she was not being given enough
medication to soothe the pain, and a moment later said she knew she
was being doped.

In the course of restitution of the ego at more advanced levels, it
may be observed that the patient frequently reacts to the situation
by a method of identification with whole objects. It may be pointed
out here parenthetically that his method, which has the advantage
of supplying the patient with a whole set of expectations at a very
economical price in terms of the construction of predictions for the
estimate of his own future, has the disadvantage of leading the patient
to expect that the course of the illness in themselves will be just the
same as in the model with whom they identify.

a. Resolution of the Situation by Identification

In a situation where the identification was at a relatively mature
level, a woman, after pouring out her troubles in an effective cath-
artic experience with a neighbor, identified with an acquaintance who
had died one year after the diagnosis of a cancer; the identification
led to a very unhappy year since she firmly expected to die at the
same time.

This sort of thing is so familiar as to need only the briefest illustration: Several patients reported that they knew it was of no use to
go to a doctor when they discovered the lesion, since a parent of
friend had had cancer and all lesions of this type were incurable.

A young woman with a lymphoma related the abrupt reversing of
a relationship with a younger sister after learning of her illness.
She had been a mother-surrogate to the sister for years, but when
after a biopsy, the family was informed of the diagnosis, the sister
forthwith took care of her in exactly the same way that she had previously been cared for; the patient remarked when she began to relate this that she had never understood how it was that she had suddenly become the younger sister.

A reciprocal relationship which similarly reversed its direction
was seen in three women; all three were aggressive and domineering, with strong masculine identifications. They had married rather
passive men and had for years made all the major decisions in the

family. All three husbands by chance had alcoholic tendencies, although none of them was a confirmed chronic alcoholic. Under the stress of the knowledge of the disease, these women all immediately assumed for the first time in years an attitude of great dependence, delivering the directing role immediately to the husband. Two of them, for instance, found it impossible to make the decision to visit a physician but they complained in bitter tones to the interviewer that they had not been taken to the physician by the husband. In all of them, the difficulties encountered in mobilizing the husband led to severe anxiety and feelings of hopelessness. In brief encounters between members of our project and the husbands, there was a distinct impression of great confusion on the part of the husbands, since the new definition of the situation experienced by the wife only puzzled them. One husband formed a strong psychotherapeutic relationship to the social worker and had a series of regular interviews with her. In this context, he became much more effective and began to make decisions about the children, etc. The wife displayed a remarkable sense of satisfaction in witnessing this process and spoke glowingly of her pride in him.

b. A Specific Type of Identification with the Physician

Our patients frequently demonstrated examples of the 'doctor-game'. One patient in particular did this so expertly as to enlist a remarkably strong sympathetic reaction from the physician in charge. She described how in the very long interval between first finding she had a cancer and the eventual recurrence, she had studied everything she could find about the disease. She said it had become her whole life. In a remarkable display of rationalization, she told all the physicians how much they had her sympathy since she could lie at ease in bed while they had to work for her and the other patients.

Another woman felt very greatly pleased with her doctor when her cervical cancer disappeared for some years after a course of X-ray therapy. She would aggressively stop anyone she heard saying that cancer was incurable and announce that it was not, she had been cured. When the cancer recurred, she became depressed and changed physicians.

The patient we saw most intensively in psychotherapeutic interviews became ward psychotherapist when she entered the hospital. She was especially proud of persuading, by encouraging catharsis of her fears, a young woman to allow herself to be placed in traction for treatment of arthritis. In undergoing X-ray therapy, she was at first very anxious and reluctant, but after a pleasant talk with the roentgenologist, changed her attitude and began to speak of her interest in roentgenology, the long and difficult training for it, and the intellectual prowess of anyone who could comprehend all the mathematics involved.

c. Restitution by Sublimation

In a relatively small number of patients we have seen examples of
the realistic and successful restitution of the self-concept in the
face of the enormous threat by means of a process of sublimation.
This feat is one of extraordinary difficulty and one which evokes a
reaction of intense admiration in even a hardened psychotherapist.
The means by which this is accomplished in the cases we have seen
is that of transferring a very large part of the narcissistic cathexis
of the self to others. The patient accomplishes a mourning reaction
to relation to the self and directs his efforts then to the assistance
of the adaptation of his intimates to his own death. This is most often
a reaction directed toward the family; one patient, however, hopelessly ill with cancer of the breast, exerted a tremendous influence in
the clinic by her calm and reassuring discussion of the problem with
the other patients in the waiting room. She allayed many anxiety reactions simply by offering herself as a really good model for identification.

DISCUSSION

The problems with which we are concerned are all obscure details
of the way in which experience is organized into the functioning unit
we know as a personality, and all of our explanations are of necessity
somewhat conjectural. It is possible on the basis of the material detailed above, however, to state some hypotheses of possible heuristic
value.
    In the first place we are concerned with the mechanisms by means
of which the world is passed across the ego boundary into the personality. The two processes by means of which the world is apprehended
are perception and memory, in a circular relation. A perception is
obviously necessary as the unit which leaves a trace in the memory,
but every perception is modified by the residual left from previous
perceptions in the same series, so that in fact one never sees the
same object twice, even though for practical purposes this fact is
unimportant in most instances.
    We conceive then of experience as the integrated mass of percep-
tions and the residues deposited in the nervous system in the process
of perception. It is evident that in the perception of a whole situation,
an extremely important part of the experience is the automatic response of the body to the stimulus; the perception of the response
feeds back into the experience of the whole and alters it retrospectively. (1)
    There is then a unit of perception which may be expressed in tem-
poral terms as the instantaneous situation in the present moment; it
seems likely from neuro-physiological evidence that this is a quantum, of the nature of approximately a tenth of a second. In the complicated world of the adult there are units of experience which combine many of these neuronally limited instants. In any case, we
understand the world by means of successive instantaneous percep-

tual experiences.

The process of development and of learning is in large measure the process of the integration of these instantaneous perceptions into series. For the very young infant it is probable that the situation at hand is the only reality and the instantaneous experience is understood as the whole of experience. It appears to us that at a very much more complex level, this same situation applies in the case of the woman quoted above who felt triumphant when she was finally proven to have a cancer. In this case, the patient's reaction is clearly logical in view of her need to be right and the instantaneous situation in which she was proven correct, to (in her view) the total defeat of all the doctors who had rejected her as neurotic. Her awareness of doom in the next few seconds was not integrated into the whole picture in the momentary flash of triumph. We may state this another way by saying that she was attentive for the moment only to the changed position of herself relative to doctors.

In the instantaneous perception of the situation at hand, it is essential that the problem be defined for the individual. The definition is reached by the construction of the appropriate form in the individual's awareness. We say construction because there is a variety of evidence which indicates that the process of perception is not in any way a passive one, but rather one in which the individual is actively concerned. This is clearest in the studies of visual perception, especially the studies which demonstrate that a blind individual gaining his sight at an adult age is quite unable to perceive form without an extensive training.

In the instantaneous perception the situation is resolved into figure and ground. This is a complicated process in which the situation in focus can be anything at all. The original situation, as many psychoanalysts have indicated (especially Bertram Lewin in his recent book), is that of nursing; it seems to us probable that the world for the moment to the infant is resolved into the nipple and the sucking sensations in the mouth, presumably with the oral component as figure upon the ground of the nipple and breast (the 'dream screen'). It is clear further that any tendency once formed influences any further action in the same individual; from a variety of evidence we can further postulate that the two forms thus differentiated in a very vague way tend to become generalized and to influence by an analogical mechanism the entire further development of the individual. The generalized form under which these original forms are subsumed can be stated in adult terms as the forms 'hole' and 'protrusion'. In the successive stages of the libidinal development of the child, these forms find concrete manifestation in the figure-ground pairs of breast-mouth, food-mouth, feces-anus, penis-vagina, and baby-womb.

As Freud has pointed out in the paper referred to above, when a particular aspect of the environment is presented to an individual as a problem, he develops (or constructs) for purposes of understanding a universal which is in fact a range of variation between two extremes, but which is at first apprehended as a two-part system of antithetical ideas. Freud quotes Abel, from whom these ideas derive: "The essential relativity of all knowledge, thought, or consciousness cannot

but show itself in language. If everything that we know is viewed as
a transition from something else, every experience must have two
sides; and every name must have a double meaning, or else for every
meaning there must be two names. "

In order to make this idea a bit more concrete, we may point out
from everyday psychiatric experience the commonnesss of this type
of thinking: the idea which at once comes to mind is that of the good
mother-bad mother antithesis, expressed in fairy-tale terms in the
fairy godmother and the witch. From other points of view, there is
the mother-child combination, as well as such things as weakness-
strength, inside-outside, etc., in various contexts and at various
levels of abstraction.

In addition to this general tendency, there is a particular manifestation which is of especial importance in human beings, by virtue
of the specifically social, interpersonal nature of the environment.
It may be pointed out parenthetically here again that this is an essential aspect of the problem of language, since a language is a medium of communication which implies the existence of another, similar, being with whom one communicates by means of mutually agreed-
upon symbols. The manifestation referred to is the tendency to form,
in addition to the static figure-ground differentiation previously described, a judgment of relationship of the particular aspect of the
environment to the self; specifically, in addition to the bifurcation of
a particular experience, e.g., nursing, into figure and ground, i.e.,
into mother and infant, the individual further bifurcates the experience
into a mine-not mine system and decides which of the two forms has
a close relationship to him. (2)

It may be observed very early in the course of human development
that the young child begins to be able to identify himself with either
of the two parts of the situation, or, to express the development more
nearly as it probably occurs, he begins to differentiate the ambiguous
situation into self and other with a great deal of confusion between
the two and a frequent shifting in his view of where he belongs. A
particular case in point here is the way in which 'atypical' children
display a great deal of confusion in the use of pronouns, referring
to themselves as "he" or as "you", at a time when the use of the
pronoun 'I' is well established in the normal child.

This tendency is a very important part of the fantasy life of the
child, in that he pretends to be someone else a great deal of the time,
and the assumed identity is very frequently that of the other member
in a two-membered system (a 'diadic' relationship).

A symbol is of such a general nature as to be readily displaceable
from the object ot a part or a representation of the object; in everyday life we find innumerable examples: I say: "I am writing", but it
is evident that "I" am also occupied in sitting, breathing, digesting,
and so on. Only the task in focus at the moment is consciously associated with the symbol, although the symbol covers the whole of
one's self-experience. Further in observing a play, the experience
is very much that "I" am undergoing the adventures displayed.

In the young child it is very common to find him completely losing
himself in a role in playing; the importance and frequency of the

'doctor-game' is familiar. In this instance, usually after an experience in the passive role of patient, he displaces the symbol 'I' from the passive to the active role in an effort to 'control' the situation. This displacement has the great advantage in fantasy that as the individual in control, the possibilities of attack in the relationship are felt to be much diminished.

In our patients we have cited many examples of this process as it persists into adult life, where for many important situations the identity of the other is no longer assumed consciously but rather by the unconscious method of acting in a way previously experienced as behavior of another person. Such instances are those of the woman who suddenly changed roles with her younger sister, and the several examples of the patients who identified with the doctor, playing an adult version of the 'doctor-game'.

It is obvious that this tendency has a great survival value to the individual in that it is one of the most important methods of learning. On the other hand, it is also obvious that it is a tendency which leads the individual easily into pathological or deviant forms of behavior in that he may assume the role of another person who is an inappropriate model, as in the case of a child who identifies too closely with the parent of the opposite sex.

We may digress from the main path of this discussion long enough to point out how the mental mechanisms of the human being fall into two classes on the basis of the processes described above. In the first place, the mechanism of projection is one by means of which the individual assigns experience to the 'not mine' area of his experience when in fact it belongs to the 'mine', and the process of introjection is the reverse, although in this latter instance the introjected experience actually changes category in the process. The defense mechanisms fall into this scheme, in that repression and denial are methods of refusing to accept the fact that a certain experience is 'mine'; displacement and disassociation are somewhat more advanced methods of accomplishing the same end; and the mechanisms of reversal, reaction formation, and identification with the aggressor are methods of maintaining the situation relatively stable while identifying with the originally alien member of the system.

We have mentioned previously our conclusion that the apprehension of movement in the organism-environment complex and its integration into the scheme of things appears to be a relatively late and complicated development of the human being; we may state the same conclusion in another way by saying that for the apprehension of an event as one which has become a present reality from an earlier manifestation and is in the process of becoming a future event, it is necessary to have in mind at the same time a perception, a memory, and an anticipation of the situation. In the process of learning to deal with motion, the individual differentiates his black-white system of constructs into various shades of gray and alters the static system into a dynamic one.

In the aspects of movement displayed by the material from the patients as described in the preceding material, it may be seen that there is a correlation between the severity of the illness and the stage

of development which is most clearly demonstrated in the patient's
report of his preoccupation. In a general way, the more severe the
overall disturbance, the more primitive the material. The degree
of primitiveness of the material is to be estimated in this context
most clearly by the comprehensiveness of the world-view which may
be seen in the patient. Where the disturbance is maximal, the individual is aware only of fragments; as the patient emerging from
anesthesia reported on looking back at the experience, her thoughts
appeared to come in bits and pieces. Beyond this, the patient is
aware largely of his distress as the whole of experience; then he
slowly begins to include other people in his frame of reference as
individuals to whom he wishes to respond, e.g., the wan smile of a
patient several days after a tremendous operation was the first sign
that she was in any way able to deal with the interviewer as anything
other than an interruption. In the first stages of recognition of the
outside world, it seems to occur as a very menacing and hostile affair; the patient dying of metastasis reported that the nurse was crazy,
and that 'they' were doping her; another patient reported that a nurse
who had given her a vigorous back rub was digging her fingers all the
way down to the bone, and when the nurse reentered the room, she
said she got limp all over.

As the patient becomes more nearly in contact with the world there
is a tendency to operate as though there were no other people in it
besides patient and doctor, and in this exclusive relationship, any
slightest remark or behavior on the part of the doctor is loaded with
enormous significance to the patient.

Patients who are less sick tend to adapt to the world in terms of the
incorporated whole experience of another person, as in the instances
where the suspicion of the diagnosis cancer leads to the construction
of the future by means of a prediction that the patient will experience
the disease in precisely the same way as that witnessed in the case of
a relative or neighbor. A more mature version of the relationship
with the doctor in patients at this stage is the identification en masse
with the doctor and the consequent tendency to regard oneself and
others from the more remote and less intensely affective therapeutic
viewpoint, most clearly demonstrated in the patient who remarked
how sorry she felt for the poor doctors, they had to get up early and
work hard while she could remain at her ease in bed.

The highest level development may be seen in those few patients
who were able to sublimate their distress into a effort to make life
more tolerable for their families. It seems to us that this is best
expressed as an ability on the part of the patient to retain at a time
of great stress a view of the world in which the related persons are
seen as more important than the individual himself, a real and quite
extraordinary triumph over the natural narcissistic view of the self
as the center of the universe.

We may in conclusion attempt to state the hypothesis which has
emerged for us from this material. Human beings apprehend the
world as successive instantaneous perceptions; at the moment of perception in the naive individual it appears that the perceived situation
is the whole of reality, and it is only with a good deal of learning that

he is able to expand the idea of reality to include the past in memory and the future in anticipation. This process appears to us to be analogous to the construction of a sort of calculus of experience wherein all of the successive instants are understood as serial manifestations of one event, the self. In the process of perception, there is a differentiation of the field into figure and background; where the events in question are apprehended in symbolic terms, the figure in focus is understood against the ground of its antithesis. In interpersonal situations, the two antitheses are roles. In relating the situation to the self, the individual identifies with one or the other (e.g., 'I' am 'child' in this 'mother-child' situation) in behavioral terms by claiming the perquisites of the particular manifestation or by acting in the manner appropriate to it. In many situations, the opposite member of the pair has the more gratifying role, and the individual selects the inappropriate role in fantasy or in acting out as a means of solving the problem presented by the situation.

Where the ego boundary is poorly understood, i.e., where the process of differentiation of self from world is incomplete, it is possible to understand the self as combining both aspects in the familiar problems of bisexuality. One dream produced by a patient apparently to order for this paper illustrates this point. The child in the dream is the son of an acquaintance with whom she can converse only when the child translates, since the mother speaks no English. In the dream, the bilingual boy is sitting on a couch which reminds the patient of the one in the therapist's office. His penis is visible; it is bleeding, and he is mopping up the blood with a sanitary napkin.

Throughout the development of the personality it may be seen that there is a progressive ability to deal with wholes as they exist in reality rather than as they appear to the naive perceiving individual. In a sense the entire development may be expressed as the individual's battle with language, in the course of which he becomes able to subjugate the forms previously constructed in the history of the culture to a point where he is liberated rather than bound by them, It is only with the greatest difficulty that anyone is able to force the static fragments of experience reflected in language forms to yield meaningful relationships of wholes bound to each other as aspects of one constantly changing and shifting universe.

NOTES

(1) It is possible to conjecture, on the basis of a variety of evidence, that the intellectual functions, which are most closely related to the distance receptors, are responsible for the acquisition of primarily qualitative information for the purposes of the organism; on the other hand, it appears that the kinesthetic, postural mechanisms, operating automatically, are responsible more largely for quantitative information. Thus, for instance, a sudden pain or feeling of insecurity leads to an urgent sense of the intensity of the situation, but the individual must examine the situation consciously with the more discriminating senses to find out what it is that is wrong. It is a truism that

an observer from outside has a much clearer view of the meaning of
almost any situation than the individual viewing it from the inside. In
a very speculative way, one can assume that the visual and auditory
senses, operating upon a primarily neuronal basis, convey primarily
'digital' information to the self, whereas the kinesthetic mechanisms,
depending upon continuous lengthening and shortening reactions in the
muscular apparatus which are combined and integrated much more
at successive stages in their passage toward conscious appreciation,
convey primarily 'analogical' information to the self, to express the
problem in 'cybernetic' terms.

(2) Whitehead had described in his characteristic manner the problems with which we are concerned here, as seen from a philosophical
point of view. We quote a small section: "It is important to discrimi-
nate the bodily pattern, which endures, from the bodily event, which
is pervaded by the enduring pattern, and from the parts of the bodily
event. The parts of the bodily event are themselves pervaded by their
own enduring patterns, which form elements in the bodily pattern.
The parts of the body are really portions of the environment of the
total bodily event, but so related that their mutual aspects, each in
the other, are particularly effective in modifying the pattern of either.
This arises from the intimate character of the relation of whole to
part. Thus the body is a portion of the environment for the part, and
the part is a portion of the environment for the body; only they are
peculiarly sensitive, each to modifications of the other. This sensi-
tiveness is so arranged that the part adjusts itself to preserve the
stability of the body. It is a particular example of the favorable environment shielding the organism. The relation of part to whole has
the special reciprocity associated with the notion of organism, in
which the part is for the whole; but this relation reigns through nature
and does not start with the special case of the higher organisms. "

XV

AVOIDANCE OF THE PARTICULAR AS A DEFENSE MECHANISM

Intellectualization is both a 'defense mechanism' and a most important part of the process of learning. Intellectual activity is largely
concerned with abstracting patterns from series of particular events.
The more familiar the events, the more easily may the whole pattern
be evoked by a sign or cue: an experienced clinician can make a whole
diagnosis from a single pathognomonic sign, the 'myxedema reflex',
for example.

The defensive function of intellectualization lies in its tendency to
stabilize sets of patterns: the 'old dog' who cannot learn 'new tricks'
is the dog whose patterns of behavior have become too firmly fixed
to adapt to new problems. The adaptive effort in a novel situation
goes along with anxiety of an unpleasant degree, and the old dog who
persistently tries old tricks attempts to deny his helplessness and
allay anxiety. The crystallization of a whole pattern may thus allow
an individual to avoid anxiety completely until the strain of novelty
becomes too great; in such an individual then the whole interlocking
structure may collapse at once.

Emotional reactions on the other hand are associated with particular activities carried on with particular people in reality and in
fantasy. This fact is evident in psychotherapeutic techniques: the
therapist learns early to insist on particular references, and he
knows that a statement about 'a friend' will carry much less feeling
than the same statement about Bill Green or Sam Smith.

Clinical work with a very intelligent patient in a highly specialized
occupation has demonstrated certain aspects of this problem in an
interesting way. For a long period in therapy this patient's intellectual defense was invulnerable, and the perfection of this lesion
aroused a sort of admiration in the frustrated therapist; perhaps an
accurate analogy is the surgeon describing a "beautiful tumor".
Defensive tactics of this sort are not uncommon, but in this patient
the consistency of the strategy was remarkable.

The productive function of intellectualization is the possibility of
making predictions on the basis of general patterns. Every scientific
law is a general statement, covering a number of past instances,
which allows an extrapolation into the future. Intellectual processes
are then characteristically oriented toward the future. In this particular patient, the illness occurred at the time of achieving a very
considerable success. As the psychotherapeutic work progressed,
it appeared that the breakdown was the result of a loss of the system
of expectation in which he had lived: like Alexander the Great, he
was dismayed by completely achieving his goal.

This patient falls into Freud's category of those spoiled by success. His breakdown we understand as dependent upon (1) the loss of goal implied in attaining the goal, and, (2) the loss of a transference relationship to a 'boss' which is the inevitable result of assuming the 'boss' role oneself. In this particular patient, his overriding need for independence made it impossible for him to deal consciously with his dependent wishes in the transference situation.

After assuming the position which represented the goal of a long apprenticeship, this patient first broke down with severe anxiety which responded to hospitalization; it was suggested that he seek further treatment, but he did not. A second attack brought him into outpatient treatment. The usual rules were discussed, as to bills, making no major decisions, and so on. Shortly thereafter, when the therapist was away for a long weekend the patient suddenly quit work. A week or so later, the therapist called the patient to change an appointment and identified himself by his given name - thereupon the patient used the given name exclusively for a brief period, but he refused to admit that this might have any significance. A few weeks later the therapist left town again for several days. The patient did not appear for several weeks thereafter - then came with a story of not having known the therapist was back in town.

In the several months subsequent to this, the defense of generalization was impervious. The patient never addressed the therapist directly at all. He spoke of general matters, of patterns he observed, and of the future. No trace of a reference to a particular person appeared. During this period he continued to have anxiety, but it no longer was severe enough to interfere with his carrying out his usual activities. The patient remarked a number of times during the next several months that he was aware of a good deal of improvement, but he was quite certain that the improvement had no relation to the therapy other than an accidental one of occurring at the same time.

To a remarkable degree, this patient refrained from referring to any other person by name, except, as mentioned, for the period of time during which he insistently addressed the therapist by his first name. In his position, his most pressing feelings were those of sole responsibility. When any disturbance occurred in his department, he feared a reprimand from the authorities (never more precisely defined) - but in reviewing the mistake he found good reason not to reprimand any subordinate.

He went to a meeting of department heads; there the executive in charge of the meeting reported in general terms indication of ominous conflict with various competing organizations. The patient became very anxious; he wondered what he might do to avoid the disaster. When it was suggested that his feelings about the executive might be an important aspect of his disturbance, he denied it, even though he remembered a fantasy of asking this man for details in seeking to allay his anxiety. He was further unable to see that his wish to discuss this problem in the therapeutic session had anything to do with the transference relationship.

The formula upon which these interpretations is based can be stated: "<u>They</u> will blame me, and <u>I</u> must avoid being blamed". He consciously prevented himself from blaming those inferior to him - they are weak and obviously not responsible, and the possibility of conscious rebellion against higher-ups has apparently never occurred to him.

He manipulated his observations in such a way that in his entire world he is the only identified person. 'They' on top are balanced by 'them' below; 'they' have assigned responsibility to him but he is unable to delegate it to 'them'. In a crisis, he is inevitably alone at the controls. In a prophetic fantasy, he remembers as an outstanding preoccupation of his childhood an intense interest in Mowgli, the human child growing up in a wolf family - the only identified human being in the whole jungle. Like Mowgli, the patient has some facility in talking to other beings, but he has little feeling of belonging in the same category.

The patient was the only child of rather obsessional parents, members of a strongly puritan group. He was aware from earliest childhood of much antagonism between his parents, but he very early developed a compulsion to make no choice between them. He rather adopted the position of disinterested judge and peacemaker, again prophetically placing himself in a position of sole responsibility, above and outside the human frailties exhibited by the parents.

A character structure of this type is of interest to us in relation to the therapeutic problem, and further, it highlights certain epistemological problems. Both of these aspects center around the development and function of emotions.

Prior to the onset of his illness, this patient functioned well in an important subsidiary position. He was given a promotion which involved moving to a distant place and assuming sole responsibility in an isolated way - and immediately broke down with severe anxiety. To understand this occurrence in the context of the present discussion we may refer to this patient's inability to deal with individual persons. In his previous position, he was oriented by role in relation to a role occupant, 'the boss'. But the superior is identified as important only as a role occupant, and the patient is unable to feel any sense of personal loss in accepting the promotion. Like his parents, the boss was not the object of conscious affection or dependent feelings but rather the focal point in a system. The curious lesion which we may see here is the loss of an orientation point, a sort of pole star: by the assumption of the role of boss the patient loses a boss in becoming the boss. In the transference situation we see the process in another aspect in the way in which the patient notes improvement with no awareness of the transference effect nor of the identity of the therapist. Even in the phase of intense feeling characterized by the recurrent use of the therapist's given name, the patient insisted that this had no special significance. The first transference comment made by the patient was, "It feels good to lie down", with no awareness that relaxing in one setting rather than another made any difference.

The therapeutic problem can be seen as closely related: for the patient to avoid anxiety he requires a boss, but for the preservation of his habitual concept of the world he is unable to assign responsibility to any named individual. In therapy, he came with regularity but said he could not see that it did him any good. But when it was suggested that he might be dissatisfied, he said that the therapist was by definition an expert, and he could not then be dissatisfied: the doctor must know his job. The therapist has no name; he is identified as a doctor. In spite of this comment, following the brief period in which he called the therapist by his first name he never once addressed the therapist by name or title. The therapeutic problem involves assisting the patient to become aware of the therapist as a human being, with a name and personal characteristics - but the system upon which the patient's character stands demands that others be identified only by the role occupied in the social structure.

From the epistemological side, we may point to two comments. The first, by Piaget, in his book The Psychology of Intelligence, concerns the difference between affective and intellectual functions: he notes that affective functions deal with persons, intellectual with things. In this patient we find a remarkable intellectual development so that he handles instruments and ideas with great facility; but he cannot describe consciously any relation to persons. In the illness, the patient was aware of only two states of feeling: (1) anxiety and (2) little or no anxiety. Pleasure became unknown to him except upon occasion when he met some friend of long before and enjoyed reminiscing - but again he attributed his pleasure to the situation and not to the personal relation.

The second comment is made by Dewey and Bentley in their book, Knowing and the Known. They state that knowing in human terms is equivalent to naming: the named is the known. The patient demonstrates the essence of narcissism in his refusal to use proper names. The only identified person in his world is himself. Like the egocentric baby, he ignores others when they satisfy him, but is racked with terrible anxiety 'for no reason' when he finds himself alone. When overwhelmed by his distress he reaches out for an intimate relation by denying the formality of the therapeutic relation; but when he cannot force the situation into an intimate relation, he refuses to allow the therapist any identity at all.

The epistemological implications of defense mechanisms deserve a more formal and comprehensive study. This brief note is presented in the hope of calling to the attention of readers certain bridges to disciplines which may be more closely related to clinical problems than has generally been emphasized.

XVI

LANGUAGE AND PSYCHOTHERAPY

The most interesting aspect of the world to any of us is initially himself; we learn with difficulty to restrain this interest as we find it conflicting painfully with the same tendency in our fellow. We learn to
shift interest from the individual to the group. This shift leads us to
a generalization in the object of the self-regarding function from a
single person to mankind as a whole, and men have spent many life-
times trying to answer the question, "What is Man?"
    The outstanding distinguishing characteristic of man is language
and the various closely related aspects of human living which go along
with the language function. These include, in our reckoning, culture,
an awareness of time, and a susceptibility to neurosis. All appear
convincingly based upon group living and depend upon consensus.
    Human beings live in a universe different from that of other species:
to a remarkable degree we live in time rather than in space. As Shelley
says, "We look before and after, and pine for what is not". For each
of us the temporal series of which the self is comprised in the core
of living. The Freudian distinction between the pleasure principle and
the reality principle is a temporal one; the two might be more precisely
termed the principle of immediate action and the principle of action in
relation to the historical series. Ortega y Gasset has stated with emphasis in this respect that human beings have a history rather than a
nature.
    But the perceptual mechanisms which man shares with other animals
are oriented to the immediate situation. We cannot sense anything except at the immediate moment; what has been and what will be have to
be understood with the help of preserved sensation. In a manner similar in some ways to the technique of the pathologist, we must find
means of fixing observables for repeated examination. The essential
tool of human beings in this respect is that of the linguistic forms by
means of which we refer to experience and re-present it to ourselves
and to others. Edward Sapir, who may with considerable justification
be considered the father of modern linguistic science, has said:

    Language ... does not as a matter of actual behavior, stand apart
    from or run parallel to direct experience but completely inter-
    penetrates with it ... [It is] as though the primary world of re-
    ality were a verbal one and as though one could not get close to
    nature unless one first mastered the terminology which somehow
    magically expresses it ... Language may not only refer to ex-
    perience or even mold, interpret and discover experience, but
    ... it also substitutes for it in the sense that in those sequences

of interpersonal behavior which form the greater part of our daily lives, speech and action supplement each other and do each other's work in a web of unbroken pattern.

As soon as one begins to look critically at many of the problems involved in using language, it becomes difficult to understand why this central function of human beings has not been more in focus previously. It appears that we are accustomed to use language as a means of looking through a situation towards its meaning. In this way metaphorically we may compare language to a pair of spectacles. Spectacles are an essential adjunct to many people in order to get a clear view of the world, but once having put on the spectacles the fact of their involvement in the process tends to become ignored. We look through rather than at our customary lenses. In many instances, the glasses may become outmoded or defective long before the individual understands that his view of the world has imperceptibly changed to a deviant or pathological form. I should like to spend some time discussing some of the ways in which human beings are essentially dependent upon the processes of communication and how, in fact, personality development may be seen as an adventure in learning the use of the language forms current in one's own time and place.

The series of events to which the person has been a party in the past persists into the present in two forms: 1) in conscious, describable memories; and 2) in a system of expectations embodied in habitual postures and attitudes. A pathological history is demonstrable repeatedly in attitudes and in behavior which reveal a pathological system of expectations. The patient tends to be helpless to change his expectations because he cannot change his history, but the psychotherapist begins with the assumption that histories change when the point of view is changed. Psychotherapy may then be regarded as a review, re-interpretation and reconstruction of the patient's history. The eventual goal of psychotherapy can be put as that of rendering the individual the master of his history rather than its victim.

We infer in observing repetitive patterns of behavior in man or animal that the individual has some prior knowledge of the sort of situation in which he finds himself. His behavior gives us definite indications of the category into which he classifies the situation: for example, he attacks or retreats or salivates or demonstrates sexual excitement. At an entirely different level of the transfer of information we hear or read descriptions in verbal form which preserve and interpret something to us. In the former situation we are dependent upon the direct observation of the skillful behavior of an actor, but observations transmitted by means of verbal symbols achieve an endurance and autonomy which makes them independent of their source. This fundamental distinction between direct and indirect cues we indicate by using the terms sign and symbol. Skillful behavior is a sign of familiarity in somewhat the same way that thunder is a sign of lightening. Symbols, on the other hand, are arbitrarily selected forms such as words or mathematical notations which have only a conventional relation to the object. In this respect, the primary goal of insight psychotherapy is to help the patient substitute understanding for action. As he can use symbols instead of signs as primary cues, he can achieve independence of the spatial context by learning to describe his experience in a conscious way.

The past may be reconstituted, as Bartlett has pointed out, by recognizing and by remembering. In recognizing, one uses a sign, that is a part of a situation, as a node around which to crystallize the whole. In remembering, the situation may be reconstructed on the basis of symbols having only an arbitrary learned relation to the natural phenomena.

The process of dawning recognition gradually becoming remembering was seen in an interesting way in a schizophrenic woman in electric shock therapy. A series of experimental interviews was being carried out with this patient in a room filled with gadgets which frightened her. She was obviously reluctant to go to the experimental room on the occasions when an interview was to be carried out and indicated many times that she would prefer not to be a subject, although she did not directly refuse. After a period of time in this set-up electric shock therapy was instituted, and after several shock treatments she was brought back to the experimental room. On the way back she displayed no memory of the room nor any memory of the purpose for which she was being taken there. In the room, however, after a few minutes she began to reconstruct the situation and as portions of her experience there came back to her, she was able to say that the room had been painted a different color in the meanwhile and that the arrangement of the furniture was quite different. Both these observations were accurate ones. Here we see the result of a disturbance which makes it impossible for the patient to remember the room, but the disturbance is limited enough in extent so that within the situation she is able to recognize and reconstruct parts of her experience and to be able at this point to describe them.

This change in the patient's relation to the situation may be put into more familiar terms by saying that the experimental situation had become unconscious to her in the course of her shock treatment or that she had developed an amnesia for it. Perhaps it would also be accurate to say that the patient had repressed the disagreeable situation in a comprehensive way. The recovery of the past depends upon finding herself back again in the same situation, and the process which we see taking place can be expressed in many ways. We may say, for instance, that the unconscious becomes conscious, that what has been Id is now Ego, that a repression has been lifted, or that the patient's relation to the situation is changed so that she can now describe an aspect of her past experience which she could not describe a few minutes ago.

In the therapeutic situation in psychoanalytic therapy, somewhat the same process may be observed. Here, however, the relationship to the therapist - the transference neurosis - becomes the present context in which unconscious tendencies are manifested. The patient acts in habitual ways, the therapist observes and interprets to him. By means of participating in this description, the patient is enabled to see himself as the other sees him; this is a more indirect relation, one in which the patient learns to objectify himself. The construction of a self follows the same processes as the construction of objects, with the important qualification that a self is an incredibly complicated object of which it is difficult to get a total apprehension.

The case of Marcel Proust is of interest here. You will remember that Proust was a severe asthmatic and that he spent the last decade or so of his life completely isolated in a soundproof, darkened over-heated room furiously creating a world of his own in his great novel, The Remembrance of Things Past. It is essential, however, to notice that Proust created a world rather than a self. The only reality in which he could exist was this private one of his own; it is easy to con-jecture that this enormous work of art is a controlled facsimile of a psychosis. Proust's facility in the use of language in the construction of this world is abundantly clear; but his dependence upon more primi-tive methods of communicating with his own past may be seen in both his symptoms and the discovery around which the book is written.

In respect to his symptoms, modern psychosomatic theory equates the asthmatic attack with the reconstruction of an unsolved relation with the mother; the asthmatic attack is the past made present at the level of the unconscious behavior in the autonomic nervous system. In the discovery of a method of re-evoking the past Proust describes his dependence upon a sign, i.e., a direct sensory cue by means of which to establish a relationship with the past event. The taste of the little cake dipped in tea, the sound of a spoon on a plate or the shifting of a cobblestone under his foot each brought back to him poign-ant memories otherwise unavailable.

In the therapeutic situation we speak of two roles, actor or patient and observer or therapist. But it is important to point out a subdivision in the role of the observer in human affairs: he is both reporter and critic. To make this distinction clearly, especially with reference to one's own actions, is a task of great complexity. The independent or emotionally mature person acts as his own observer and critic, where-as the dependent person continues to rely upon the descriptions of other persons for the establishment of the values of his own actions.

The development here is a complex one, however, since for the individual to become an independent observer, describer, and evalu-ator of his own actions his system must have a reasonably large co-incidence with that of the consensus. It is of crucial importance that the individual attain independence, but this independence must take place within his culture, and this can be accomplished only by the acceptance of at least a minimum number of the standards of the culture.

The process of the internalization or incorporation of these standards is again a fascinating one. In an arresting metaphorical language, Freud described the superego as the heir to the Oedipus complex. The child gives up his individualistic rebellion in the interest of being initiated into the privileges shared by the group bound together by ritual forms. From the standpoint of the mechanism by means of which this is accomplished, the sociologist, George Herbert Mead, has described the process in more abstract terms. The individual, Mead says, becomes a subject to himself by first becoming an object to himself. In other words, he achieves an identity and an individuality by describing himself, but this description can only take place from the point of view of another person. In these terms then the child becomes conscious of himself by accepting the parents' description. He identifies with the parent and looks at himself.

This conception of Mead's clarifies in a significant way some of the problems which we routinely encounter in dealing with emotional illness. It is paradoxical but regularly observable that the degree of emotional illness may be most accurately estimated by two factors: (1) the punitiveness of the superego, and (2) the tenacity with which this punitive position is maintained in the face of evidence to the contrary. For example, a severely depressed person describes himself over and over again as a worm, beneath contempt, and totally reprehensible. Any effort to convince him otherwise, however, is met with an impregnable arrogance. The depressed person can be described as an arrogant worm. He is a person who cannot be told anything. Both the punitiveness and the arrogance, however, become quite clear when one realizes that the series of statements made by the patient represents half of a dialogue between an angry parent and a terribly frightened child. The patient has paradoxically both saved himself and destroyed himself by the assumption of the role of the angry parent. In the adult this process is made much more difficult to understand by the generalization of the role of the parent; so that the patient speaks the part of the generalized other, and it is only with great difficulty that he can be persuaded to look for the specific model from whom these destructive sentiments originally emanated.

With specific reference to the problems of psychotherapy we may say that it is not until the patient has been able to form a close relationship to the therapist that he can externalize the punitive role of the parent and assign it to the therapist. As the patient demonstrates his archaic expectation system and describes it with the help of the therapist, he becomes able to resolve the internal contradictions which are the essence of conflict.

T. S. Eliot has said, "In our end is our beginning". this process of the acquisition of knowledge by means of a dialogue is reminiscent of the Socratic method of acquiring self-knowledge. It is of interest to pick out one of the perceptual aspects of this problem. The self observer operates primarily in terms of sensory modalities which are strictly limited in their synthetic powers and in the comprehensiveness of their command over the field of observation. They are intensive and emotional rather than extensive and intellectual. The outside observer, on the other hand, operates primarily by means of the distance receptors, especially that of vision. In the process of self knowledge then the self observer must borrow another person's eyes for a very long training period. Many of the tragedies of human life can be traced to the fact that the borrowed eyes are themselves grossly distorted.

The dialogue taking place between therapist and patient goes on constantly at two levels. The more conscious part takes place by the medium of symbolic representation in verbal forms, the more unconscious in significant postures, tones, gestures, and so on. A very considerable part of the therapist's function is to point out and interpret to the patient the significance of the unconscious concomitants of the verbal flow. There are two descriptive distinctions which we can make here that are of considerable importance. The first is the familiar one that the words are primarily denotative, the arrangement of the words and the postural and gestural concominants are primarily connotative. Another distinction is that the words falling in sequence one after the other represent a communication in discursive terms, whereas the set and attitudes of the patient as represented in the gestural and postural components convey information to the therapist presentationally.

If we may, like Mr. Eliot, come back to our beginning in our end, we should like finally to point out the object of therapy in these perhaps unfamiliar terms. So long as a human being is related to his immediate environment in an essential way, he remains dependent. If the environment upon which he is dependent is disrupted, he becomes ill. He gets well either by finding an environment which is a reasonable facsimile of the lost one or by rendering himself independent of any particular environment.

The method by means of which a person is enabled to become independent of particular environments is that of orienting himself along a temporal rather than a spatial frame. Specifically this is accomplished by changing his focus from that of his relative position amongst his fellows to that of his position in relation to previous versions of himself. A standard of comparison becomes not this or that other person whom he sees but rather himself and his own realization of his potentialities in terms of the accidental events which have occurred to him.

In order to compare oneself with previous selves, it is necessary to have the previous selves clearly in mind at a conscious level, and this can only be accomplished by a reasonably accurate description in verbal terms. The change in axis from a horizontal spatial presentational axis to a longitudinal temporal discursive axis is the specific human achievement. A construction, a history which is composed of impalpable images, becomes more real, more significant than the immediate material and tangible contemporary environment. Meaning achieves a victory over matter; this appears to be both the goal of human life in general and of psychotherapy in particular.